THE GOOD FIGHT CONTINUES

THE GOOD FIGHT CONTINUES

World War II Letters from the Abraham Lincoln Brigade

EDITED BY

Peter N. Carroll, Michael Nash, and Melvin Small

NEW YORK UNIVERSITY PRESS

New York *and* London

NEW YORK UNIVERSITY PRESS
New York and London
www.nyupress.org

Frontis: Poster by José Bardasano, 1937. Courtesy Abraham Lincoln Brigade Archive, Tamiment Library, NYU.

Library of Congress Cataloging-in-Publication Data
The good fight continues : World War II letters from the Abraham Lincoln Brigade / edited by Peter N. Carroll, Michael Nash, and Melvin Small.
p. cm.
Letters selected from the Abraham Lincoln Brigade Archives collection at
New York University's Tamiment Library.
Includes bibliographical references and index.
ISBN–13: 978–0–8147–1659–5 (cloth : alk. paper)
ISBN–10: 0–8147–1659–8 (cloth : alk. paper)
ISBN–13: 978–0–8147–1660–1 (pbk. : alk. paper)
ISBN–10: 0–8147–1660–1 (pbk. : alk. paper)
1. World War, 1939–1945—Public opinion.   2. World War, 1939–1945—United States.
3. World War, 1939–1945—Personal narratives, American.   4. World War, 1939–1945—
Participation, African American.   5. Anti-fascist movements—United States—History—
20th century.   6. United States—Foreign relations—1933–1945.   7. Soldiers—United
States—Correspondence.   8. Spain. Ejército Popular de la República. Abraham Lincoln
Battalion.   9. Spain—History—Civil War, 1936–1939—Veterans—Correspondence.
I. Carroll, Peter N.   II. Nash, Michael, 1946–   III. Small, Melvin.   IV. Abraham
Lincoln Brigade Archives.   V. Title: World War 2 letters from the Abraham Lincoln
Brigade.   VI. Title: World War Two letters from the Abraham Lincoln Brigade.
D810.P85U535   2006
940.54'8173—dc22   2006012451

This book is dedicated to the memory of twenty-four veterans of the
Abraham Lincoln Brigade who were killed in World War II:

David Altman

Herman Bottcher

John Delehanty (Merchant Marine)

Mike Feller

Ben Gardner

Joe Gordon (Merchant Marine)

Joseph Hecht

Dr. Julius Hene

John Kozar (Merchant Marine)

Ernest Kozlowski

Sidney Kurtz

Frank Kustera

Lawrence Lustgarten

Andrew Militiadov

Ignatz Moscowitz

Pedro Penino

Tom Rissane (Merchant Marine)

Sidney Rosenblatt

Venerio Rossetto

Joseph D. Sacal

Conrade Silverman

Abe Susnov

Joseph D. Truy

Gerald Weinberg

CONTENTS

ILLUSTRATIONS

PREFACE

Europe had been at war for twenty-seven months before the Japanese attacked Pearl Harbor on December 7, 1941, drawing the United States into World War II. But except for what the public could glimpse through newspapers, newsreels, and radio, few Americans had faced the horror of modern warfare: the use of airplanes to terrify and destroy civilian populations or the coordinated air and ground attacks that the Germans called *blitzkrieg* (lightning warfare). There was, however, one group of Americans who had already confronted the fascist enemy on the battlefield and had first-hand experience of the political stakes. These were the U.S. veterans of the Abraham Lincoln Brigade,[1] a volunteer army of about twenty-eight hundred men and women who sailed to Europe to fight against fascism in the Spanish Civil War (1936–1939).

The men and women who formed the Lincoln Brigade in Spain had gone to war in violation of U.S. neutrality laws that were intended to isolate Americans from foreign conflicts. American political leaders, including President Franklin D. Roosevelt, hoped to avoid the entanglements that had drawn the United States into World War I by prohibiting military aid to warring countries and forbidding civilians from exposing themselves to hostilities that might inflame public opinion. After General Francisco Franco staged a military rebellion against the elected Spanish republic in July 1936, the State Department barred civilians from traveling to that embattled country. Although the major European powers accepted similar principles of nonintervention in the Spanish conflict, it soon became apparent that Hitler's Germany and Mussolini's Italy were providing vital military assistance to the fascist rebels. The Soviet Union and the Communist International then moved to assist the legal government and called for volunteers to aid the republic. In the end, some thirty-five thousand volunteers from fifty countries joined the International Brigades to fight for Spanish democracy.

In responding to these pleas, the Lincolns perceived Spain as a place where they had an opportunity to stop further fascist aggression. Viewing

Spain as one domino on the fascist road to world conquest, they believed that the defeat of Franco and his allies would avert a larger world war. "Here finally the oppressed of the Earth are united," wrote a young New Yorker, Gene Wolman, shortly before he was killed at Brunete in 1937. "Here finally we have weapons, here we can fight back. Here, even if we lose, which possibility we will not admit, in the fight itself, in the weakening of Fascism we will have won." Such attitudes may explain the high proportion of Jewish volunteers in the International Brigades, many of whom were refugees from fascist countries.

After nearly three years of bitter, cruel warfare, Franco's armies defeated the republic in March 1939. President Roosevelt acknowledged that U.S. neutrality in Spain had been a great mistake. Six months later, the same German air forces that bombed the Basque village of Guernica in 1937 were flying over Poland, launching the world war that the Lincolns thought could have been prevented. By then, the Spanish Civil War veterans were angry at the failure of the United States and the Western Allies to save the republic or to assist the hundreds of thousands of Spanish refugees who suffered in French concentration camps. (After the German defeat of France in 1940, the French government transferred many of these refugees to German jurisdiction, and many were sent to the Nazi death camps.) Moreover, most Lincoln veterans had ties to the Communist party and sympathized with Soviet Russia's efforts to protect its borders by signing a nonaggression pact with Nazi Germany. When World War II began in September 1939, the Veterans of the Abraham Lincoln Brigade (VALB) opposed U.S. intervention in the war.

Twenty-seven months later, their opinions had changed again. The advance of Nazi armies in Europe—the fall of France in 1940, especially the invasion of the Soviet Union in June 1941—had drastically altered the political context. While many noninterventionists continued to oppose U.S. involvement, the Communist party and the VALB were pleading for American entry into the war. Pearl Harbor ended the debate. Some Lincoln veterans had already entered the armed services; now they enlisted in droves, eager to participate in the destruction of their old enemies. Indeed, nearly all believed that the defeat of Germany and Italy would accelerate the removal of General Franco's dictatorship from Spain.

Enthusiasm for a second chance to achieve victory over fascism dominates the letters written by veterans of the Spanish Civil War. Even when U.S. military authorities, who were concerned about the veterans' ties to the Communist party, attempted to thwart their ambitions by blocking officers' commissions and overseas combat assignments, the Lincolns remained doggedly loyal to the struggle. African American volunteers, who after serving in the integrated Lincoln brigade were forced into second-class duties in the segregated U.S. army, maintained their commitments to destroy the fascist beast; and when finally given the chance to fight, they proved to be exceptional soldiers. Wherever they served, individual Lincoln veterans won innumerable medals for bravery and sacrifice.

Despite their heroism in their second war against fascism, the Lincolns never overcame the stigma of having been "premature antifascists." By going to Spain in violation of U.S. law, they marked themselves as radicals whose loyalty to the government was suspect. The discriminatory treatment they received from the military during the war foreshadowed their reception by political leaders after the war ended. As their writings clearly demonstrate, the veterans of the Abraham Lincoln Brigade were among the earliest victims of the postwar Red Scare.

The letters in this volume were selected from thousands more that may be found in the Abraham Lincoln Brigade Archives (ALBA) collection in New York University's Tamiment Library. Most of them were originally part of the office records of the Veterans of the Abraham Lincoln Brigade. Others came from the personal collections of individual veterans and their families that are also part of the ALBA collection. In addition, we have included a few other primary sources to illuminate related issues and contextualize the letters. Unless otherwise indicated in the footnotes, the documents come from these sources. We have also drawn on a few letters held by the Bancroft Library of the University of California at Berkeley; the National Archives and Records Administration; the Princeton University Library; the Walter P. Reuther Library of Labor and Urban Affairs at Wayne State University, Detroit; and the Special Collections Library at University of Illinois at Urbana-Champaign. Unless otherwise noted, all illustrations are from the ALBA collection.

The letters are here published as they were written, except for ellipses placed in brackets that indicate editorial excision of material deemed unimportant to the ordinary reader; nonbracketed ellipses were written in the original letters. Although they provide a glimpse into the personal lives of the authors of the letters, we have often omitted material in the opening and closing paragraphs that related to family members, discussions of previous correspondence, and subscriptions to *The Volunteer*, the Brigade journal. In cases of obvious typographical errors, we have silently corrected spellings, but spelling and grammar were not corrected when in our judgment they reflect the voice of the letter writer. This means that some letters contain misspellings and awkward constructions. However, we were surprised to find that most of the letters, the majority of which were composed by people in foxholes or otherwise on the move who had not been to college, were well written and often followed the most arcane rules of grammar and punctuation. We have also deleted accompanying military addresses when they do not directly indicate the whereabouts of the writers. Information about the correspondents may be found in the biographical index that follows the text; the brevity of some items indicates the absence of additional information.

The first chapter introduces Lincoln brigaders writing about their experiences in the 1930s, confronting the Depression, reacting to the rise of fascism, and participating in the Spanish Civil War. Chapter 2 deals with the many unsuccessful attempts by Lincoln veterans to serve in the military and, especially, to see combat after U.S. entry into World War II. Chapter 3 examines the problems encountered by African American veterans and the general conditions of service in the segregated military. Devoted to letters from Lincolns in all the combat theaters, chapter 4 offers a wide variety of perspectives on the nature of the war, comparisons with experiences in Spain, and commentaries on politics in the United States and the shape of the postwar world. In the concluding chapter, the Lincolns write about the discrimination and even persecution they confronted as "premature antifascists" associated with the international Communist movement during the Cold War.

NOTE

1. The first volunteers named themselves the "Abraham Lincoln Battalion," part of the Fifteenth International Brigade. Later units were named the George Washington battalion, the MacKenzie-Papineau battalion (including Canadians), the John Brown Artillery group, Regiment de Tren (transport), the American Medical Bureau, and others. On the U.S. home front, U.S. volunteers were known collectively as the Abraham Lincoln Brigade.

ACKNOWLEDGMENTS

In preparing this book, we have benefited from the support of many people who contributed advice, time, and material aid, among them many members of the Board of Governors of the Abraham Lincoln Brigade Archives (ALBA). The following people donated letters written by members of their families or friends: Hon Brown, Allene Carter, Dan Czitrom, John Fisher, Wendy Fisher, Helen Rucker, Abe and Rose Smorodin, Helene Susman, Lise Vogel, Nancy Wallach, Susan Wallis, Dan Lynn Watt, and Mollie Lynn Watt. Others generously transcribed letters and assisted in proofreading files: Lotti Berenson, Libby Bouvier, Natasha Carroll-Ferrary, Burton Cohen, Joan Cohen, Henry Foner, Peter Glazer, Anne Gordon, Shirley Mangini, Sue Susman, Anne Taibleson, Lise Vogel, and Fredda Weiss.

For critical financial assistance, we thank Tom Knight, Ronald Perrone, Irving and Miriam Barr, Norman Eisner, Judith and Frank Greenberg, and Don and Doris Shaffer. For helping to solve various historical puzzles, we are grateful to Chris Brooks, Dan Bertwell, Sylvia Thompson, Julia Newman, Fraser Ottanelli, and Jessica Weglein. We appreciate the assistance of Madeline Gibson and Gene Rinkel of the Special Collections Library, University of Illinois in Urbana-Champaign. Natasha Whitney, a student intern, proved to be an excellent editor. Closer to the home front, Jeannette Ferrary, Sarajane Miller-Small, and Jeanne Ross encouraged the work all the way.

PETER N. CARROLL
MICHAEL NASH
MELVIN SMALL

CHAPTER ONE

BEFORE PEARL HARBOR

The Lincoln Brigade volunteers were for the most part members of the generation that came of age during the Great Depression. Born in the years before World War I, these men and women grew up in the 1920s, the so-called decade of prosperity. During the 1930s they became involved in the labor movement and radical politics through the industrial union movement, civil rights activities, efforts to organize the unemployed, and participation in hunger marches that were often led by the Communist party. These were idealists whose radicalism was formed by hard times and class struggle. Many years later, veteran Milton Felsen, who grew up in New York City's Bedford Stuyvesant neighborhood, remembered, "I graduated from high school in 1930. I bummed around the country a great deal, trying to find a job. There were about 500,000 young people on the road in those days, and you'd sleep along the railroad sidings. I was pretty sure the system was not working politically. I was ready to do something to change and make things better."[1]

For the young men and women who would join the Lincoln Brigade, making things better often meant joining the Communist party. As the U.S. economic system was breaking down and becoming increasingly chaotic, many radicals saw the Soviet Union's model of scientific socialism as a blueprint for the future—a utopian society based on principles of rational organization and egalitarianism. Joe Dallet, a Dartmouth College graduate and labor union organizer who became a political leader in Spain, compared his vision of the Soviet Union with the reality of Depression-era America. "In the Soviet Union, the more machinery they have, the more products are available for the masses, the higher the wages, the shorter the hours of work. In the U.S., the more machinery, the more unemployment, the more intensification of labor, the smaller the buying power of the workers, the larger the profits of the corporations."[2]

The vast majority of the Lincoln Brigade volunteers came from working-class families. Of the twenty-eight hundred volunteers who went to Spain,

at least 1,250 were Jewish (mostly from the New York City area), around
three hundred were Italian, over eighty were African Americans, and fifty-
four were women. Most of the Lincolns were children of immigrants from
urban areas. As many as 70 percent were members of the Communist
party or one of its affiliated organizations, such as the Young Communist
League; but there were also significant numbers of Socialists, anarchists,
and adventurous antifascists who volunteered.[3]

At a time when most radicals supported the Popular Front against Hitler
and Mussolini, many saw the connection between the domestic movement
for social change and opposition to fascism abroad. Most men and women
on the Left knew that if fascism triumphed, the labor and progressive
movements would be destroyed. Communists and many Jews and African
Americans were certain that they would be the first victims. As historian
Robin Kelley has shown for African Americans, the fight against fascism
had an immediate urgency in the aftermath of Mussolini's imperial
adventure in Ethiopia; for them, the Spanish Civil War was an extension of
the Italian-Ethiopian conflict, not just a "white man's war." According to
Langston Hughes, who spent six months in Spain as a journalist, "by
fighting against Franco," the African American volunteers believed "they
were opposing Mussolini."[4] James Yates, a sharecropper's son who helped
organize the Dining Car Waiters Union, explained this connection in his
autobiography: "I had been more than ready to go to Ethiopia, but that was
different. Ethiopia a Black nation was part of me. I was just beginning to
learn about the reality of Spain and Europe, but I knew what was at
stake. . . . Spain was the perfect example of the world I dreamed of."[5]
Yates, like many other African American volunteers, made the connection
between the fight against fascism abroad and racism at home. For some,
this commitment to racial equality became a reality on the battlefields of
Spain. A decade before President Harry Truman ordered the desegregation of the U.S. armed forces, blacks and whites fought side by side in the
Lincoln Brigade. Oliver Law, who rose to leadership in the unemployed
demonstrations in Chicago during the early 1930s, became in Spain the
first African American to command white troops when he was appointed
commander of the Lincoln battalion in May 1937.

The volunteers saw the war in Spain as both the front lines of the class
war and an attempt to halt the spread of fascism and Nazism. This
"ideology of commitment" is what drove these young Americans to go off

to war on a foreign battlefield and in defiance of their own government.[6] Many were convinced that they would change the world by fighting fascism in Spain. As volunteer Bill Susman remembered, "The decision was not even a decision. I was absolutely certain. The only question that I had was how soon would I be permitted to go. I was absolutely convinced that there was a possibility of beating the fascist axis."[7] For many Lincolns, the Spanish Civil War would become the most important experience of their lives, the place where they truly came of age and confirmed a lifetime commitment to the struggle for progressive social change.

Coming home in defeat was a searing experience and many were consumed by a sense of tragedy for the rest of their lives. "So much blood had been spilled, so much suffering endured, so much heroism displayed, so much sacrifice cheerfully accepted," wrote Alvah Bessie, "that [the] final defeat was totally unacceptable to the mind."[8] The victory of Franco's dictatorship deepened the sense of loss and grief. Many of the Lincolns were convinced that the arms embargo by the United States and the Western allies was responsible for the defeat of the Republican govern- ment. They were particularly angry with the French for preventing the volunteers from crossing the Pyrenees to fight in Spain and arresting those whom they caught trying to enter Spain. This sense of betrayal and outrage increased when after the war the French began incarcerating Spanish refugees in detention camps in Europe and North Africa, where they languished under extremely harsh conditions. By early 1939 it had become clear that more than two million Spaniards who had fought for the Republican government were in Spanish prisons while the democracies remained silent. This convinced many veterans that the United States, Britain, and France would never join the struggle against fascism.

This feeling of loss and betrayal shaped the lives and politics of the volunteers for years to come. Maury Colow remembered that upon returning to the United States he went back to work in the fur shops in New York City. "By that time, Spain had fallen; there was great sadness. People wanted to go back again. People felt guilty of not being there, of being alive I suppose." For Colow, it was this feeling of guilt and sadness that drew him to the "trade union movement organizing among leather workers." Making the connection between this work and the unfinished business of the antifascist struggle, Colow remembered that he "got involved in that struggle in a heavy way" in order to carry through on this "commitment."[9]

These emotionally wrenching experiences encouraged the volunteers to seek the comradeship of fellow veterans. In 1937, the first returning volunteers organized the Veterans of the Abraham Lincoln Brigade (VALB), whose main mission was to raise money for the wounded and to function as a support group. VALB was also a political organization, which for the most part supported the programs and tactics of the Communist party, but with a particular emphasis on Spain, the antifascist struggle, and the ongoing problem of Spanish refugees. This connection with the Communist party became evident after the signing of the Nazi-Soviet Pact of 1939 and VALB's immediate and enthusiastic support for the "The Yanks Are Not Coming!" campaign that militantly opposed American involvement in World War II and all aid to Britain and France.[10]

For young men and women whose self-identity was intertwined with the fight against fascism, this anti-interventionist position forced them to reexamine their political commitments and loyalties. A few veterans broke with VALB on this issue and began working with the faction of the Trotskyist Socialist Workers party that opposed the Nazi-Soviet Pact.[11] Others, like Jack Shafran and Harry Schoenberg, remained in the Communist party, but enlisted in the army. Syd Levine followed his own course and left the party, but continued to maintain his membership in VALB.[12] However, these dissenters formed a distinct minority. For most, loyalty to the Communist party remained strong. This commitment was reinforced by the ongoing issue of international brigade veterans held in French detention camps, and the conviction that the struggle against fascism continued to be betrayed by the Western democracies. During the period of the so-called phony war, after the invasion of Poland in September 1939, most of the Lincoln Brigade veterans uncritically accepted the Communist position: that the Nazi-Soviet Pact was essential for the defense of the Soviet Union and that those who objected were looking to provoke a German attack that would lead to the collapse of the socialist state.

There were also other arguments to support the peace program. African American Lincoln veterans and many other civil rights activists thought the struggle for racial equality at home was far more important than the war in Europe. They often pointed to the fact that America was a Jim Crow society and that blacks were unable to get work in the defense industries. Furthermore, Britain and France were colonial powers that were keeping Africa in chains at a time when Pan Africanism was becoming an increasingly visible movement.

Despite these justifications, most Americans interpreted the Communist party's uncompromising support for strict neutrality as an unprincipled adherence to Soviet foreign policy. This view encouraged renewed attacks from the government and charges that the Party and its allies, including the Lincoln veterans, were agents of a foreign government. As its ties to the Communist party became increasingly evident, the Lincolns found themselves targets for the Justice Department's subversive activity investigations. As part of a wide-ranging investigation into fascist, Nazi, and Communist subversive activities, Attorney General Frank Murphy began to make inquiries about the Lincolns' recruiting practices. Murphy also accused the brigade of executing deserters and prisoners in Spain. FBI interrogations and an investigation by the House Committee on Un-American Activities pursued these questions. During this period federal and local law enforcement authorities closely monitored the activities of the Lincoln Brigade veterans. Several, including Commander Milton Wolff, were arrested and spent time in jail when police broke up their demonstrations against the Spanish fascist government and the French incarceration of Spanish refugees.

The Lincolns' unequivocal opposition to supporting the Allied cause began to erode during the spring of 1941. Several months before the German invasion of the Soviet Union, a number of veterans had begun to raise questions about the "Yanks Are Not Coming" campaign. John Gates remembered considerable discussion within the YCL about the fact that the "unjust character of the war was changing." Germany's brutality in suppressing the Yugoslavian uprising of April 1941 appears to have been a pivotal turning point for many of the veterans who were once again becoming increasingly nervous about "the potentially anti-Soviet orientation of Hitler."[13] Sometime in early 1941, as the phony war was turning into real combat, William Donovan, a prominent Republican lawyer who was serving as a troubleshooter for President Franklin Roosevelt and assisting British intelligence, contacted Milton Wolff to discuss the possibility of Lincoln veterans working with him on a secret mission. Unfortunately, the precise date of this contact is unclear. Wolff remembered it being in the spring of 1941, several months before the invasion of the Soviet Union. Other Lincoln veterans who participated in the project (Milton Felsen, Irving Goff, and Vincent Lossowski) recalled that they were not informed until August.

The mission, underway by the early fall of 1941, involved establishing contacts with former members of the international brigades—Italians, Greeks, and Yugoslavs who were working with the partisan resistance against the German occupation of their countries. This underground work also involved guerrilla warfare and sabotage of German installations. Donovan believed that the Lincoln Brigade veterans were ideal for this assignment. They could capitalize on their contacts with the Communist underground and they also had experience handling firearms and engaging in what was called "irregular warfare." According to Irving Goff, in late 1941 Donovan abruptly changed direction and instead of working with British intelligence decided to establish his own special operations group that was secretly trained in the Maryland mountains on a site that was later named Camp David.[14] Wolff, Felsen, Goff, Lossowski, and William Aalto immediately joined these special forces.

A number of other veterans were also involved in counterintelligence and counterespionage. When Mexico opened its doors to former members of the international brigades, Robert Colodny and a small group of volunteers moved there temporarily, and according to Milton Wolff, in late 1940 and 1941 worked with British intelligence, recruiting sympa-thizers in an effort to counter German subversion in Latin America.[15] It is unclear whether these veterans were working as individuals or whether their actions were endorsed by VALB and/or the Communist party.

Eugene Dennis, the CPUSA's representative to the Comintern, played an important role in recruiting veterans for undercover work in Eastern Europe.[16] A May 19, 1941, memorandum titled "Notes on Some of the American Veterans of the International Brigade" appears to have been written in order to convince the leadership of the U.S. Communist party to support the project. It is, however, unclear whether these discussions took place before or after the invasion of the Soviet Union. What is certain, however, is that there was considerable opposition within the Communist hierarchy to this project, as many were concerned that working on under-cover missions with British and American intelligence would expose the Party to infiltration by government agents that would compromise the security of secret operations. On his end, Donovan also had to defend himself from people like Martin Dies (D-Tex.), chairman of the House Committee on Un-American Activities, who charged that he was using known Communists for top-secret missions. Donovan conceded that he was working with Lincoln Brigade veterans because of their unique qualifications for underground warfare, but he denied that any of his recruits were Communist party members. The Lincolns working for the Office of Strategic Services, he said, "clearly evidenced loyalty to this country and the principles for which this country is fighting."[17]

The bombing of Pearl Harbor on December 7, 1941, changed everything. The war became America's national mission and the United States and the Soviet Union were now allies. The Communist party and the Lincoln Brigade veterans became enthusiastic advocates for the war effort and for opening a second front in Europe. Robert Colodny soon left Mexico to enlist in the army. Identified as a security threat because of his politics and Lincoln Brigade connection, he was assigned to a remote outpost in the Aleutian Islands, where he found himself attached to a cryptanalysis unit with the famed mystery writer Dashiell Hammett and other suspected radicals. Hammett and Colodny established a base newspaper, *The Adakian*, which was probably the only armed forces newspaper that covered the partisan armies and told the story of their participation in the war effort.[18] Milton Wolff remained with the OSS until June 1942, when he volunteered for the infantry. Other veterans whom Wolff had recruited continued working with Donovan's special forces until the end of the war. They served in North Africa, Eastern Europe, and Italy with antifascist partisan groups, including Spaniards who had fled the Franco state during the period when the Allies were preparing for the invasion of Europe.

By early 1942, Lincoln Brigade veterans were enlisting in the U.S. Army with great enthusiasm. It was almost as if a great weight had been lifted off their shoulders, freeing them to return to the war against fascism. However, the Nazi-Soviet Pact and the Lincolns' willingness to change their position on the antifascist struggle in order to conform to Soviet policy would forever cast a shadow on their legacy, as it would with the other elements of the Communist Left.

The letters in chapter 1 illustrate the ways in which the Lincoln Brigade volunteers were shaped by the Great Depression and the left-wing politics of the 1930s. As radicals fighting for progressive social change, they were among the first to see the threat presented by the rise of Hitler and Mussolini. They went to Spain both to halt the march of totalitarianism and to support the Spanish people in their fight for democracy. The first letter was written on November 19, 1929, by Joe Dallet to his family and his young wife Kitty. It shows that for Dallet and many of his comrades the road to Spain began with the fight for industrial unionism in America's mass production industries. Joe Dallet died on the Aragon front and Kitty later married the physicist J. Robert Oppenheimer. For the Lincolns who came home, however, the Spanish Civil War was but the first chapter in a nearly decade-long struggle against fascism.

From Joe Dallet

November 19, 1929

Dear Family,

[. . .] There is not very much news—except that continued search for work reveals the situation as being even worse than I had thot it. Was in Gary [Indiana] today and at every mill they told of men laid off by the thousands and that those that were working were only working two, three and four days a week. One plant alone, the Illinois Steel (U.S. Steel subsidiary) has laid off no less than 5000 men within the last couple of weeks. (This they admitted at the employment office). Imagine what the figures really are.

You ask me, mother to give Hoover credit and to "cooperate" with him. I don't want to argue with you. I have explained my position often. Once again I will try, in the hopes that sooner or later you will understand.

[. . .] I will not cooperate because it would be cooperating in a further attempt to keep workers down, to keep their wages low, to keep their hours long, etc. I would be cooperating to perpetuate a system that is basically rotten and that must go. Until capitalism is overthrown there can be nothing but temporary improvement (if that). I will not work for merely temporary improvement. I will not lend my efforts to make the workers think that this system is not so bad that it is all right. I will not help to perpetuate a system of private capital [. . .] .

You see, the Wall Street crash was not an accident. It was what we have been heading for due to over expansion [. . .] . [Henry] Ford is right when he says the buying power must be raised. But he himself, with all his talk, is as bad as almost any others. Think I told you that he's laid off 30,000, and many more who were getting $6 a day he's fired and replaced them with men at $5. Many of his plants have been down for weeks now. U.S. Steel has had its biggest year since the war, yet the steel plants are running on about a 60% basis—that is, about 20% of the workers definitely laid off, fired, and the rest working only a few days a week. Are the dividends cut? No, the dividends are continued—paid for out of the pockets of the workers. Of course the system is headed for complete disaster. They are made by economic forces. The system of private capital is crumbling. To bolster it up the workers are laid off, speeded up, hours lengthened, etc. But even these measures cannot hold the rotten system together indefinitely. It must go. It will crash of its own rottenness. What we do is to point these things out in advance, establishing ourselves among the rest of the workers as leaders, winning over the masses to see what is happening and why, and to accept our leadership, and when the time comes we will clear away the wreckage and start to build—not for parasites, not for coupon clippers—but for ourselves, the workers, those that produce that make the wheels go and build the wheels too.

We do not pledge, as did the yellow AF of L fakers, that we will not ask for increased wages. We will demand, and strike for them. We will demand unemployment insurance—paid for out of the profits of industry. We will demand a shorter workday so that more workers will be employed. And whenever possible we will strike for these things. Strikes make for misery—yes, but misery is only comparative. There is much misery without them, and there would be far more misery today had there not been strikes. There will be bigger strikes, better strikes, bigger and stronger and more militant organizations of workers, until we are so well organized that we can take over the fields, the factories, the mills, the railroads and run them for the benefit of the only ones who are entitled to benefit from them, the people who work on and in them [. . .] .

You know that I am fond of my father, and that as long as the system prevails, I hope he profits from it as anyone else (that isn't really true), I feel ashamed of it his profiting—(but I mean that I want him, and you, to have the things you want). What does he add to the world—aside from his personality, etc? Does he produce anything? Does he make oil cheaper, more obtainable, for the masses? He does not. He produces no oil. He, if he could he would make oil scarcer so that prices would go up and his profits with them. What does he add in wealth (real wealth, not money) to the world? Nothing. What does he get for his participation in commerce and industry of the world? Enough to keep you all and anywhere from 20 to 40 other families who are today either starving or on the verge of starvation. He is a nice guy, and kindly, and generous according to his lights. But he adds nothing to the wealth (again, real wealth) of the world, and he takes (or gets) thousands. This is not meant to be an attack upon him. He was chosen as an example. Most of your friends produce nothing. They live on the production of others. You say, "Well, if they can do it why not? If they are cleverer, etc., why shouldn't they profit from their cleverness?" You see the result of their profiting. You see the army of unemployed. You see the millions of child laborers. You see the thousands of workers children with T.B. You see (all of these things I mean you would see if you looked, or if you read or studied) the thousands of workers' families living on what is way below what the U.S. government's statisticians themselves have set as the minimum amount for the maintenance of cleanliness, health, and decency. And you will see these things, under Hoover, under capitalism, not getting better, but getting worse. You will see things getting so bad that they can't get any worse. The worm will turn, and there will be a workers and farmers government.

You see the babel about peace. Even you, mother, think there is something in the idea that there can't be such peace if they talk so much about war. There will be a great war, a tremendous war, soon—within the next ten years surely. It will make the last war seem like a snow-ball fight. It will be followed by revolution after revolution. The starving workers of one country will refuse to shoot down the starving workers of another country. Oh, I know, the jingoist will fool many of them, for a while, but not for long. You will see mutinies in the trenches as you saw in every army toward the close of the last war. The last war led to the overthrow of the Czar, by the establishment of a workers and farmers government in Russia, by deposing the Kaiser, the temporary setting up of a workers government in Germany, and then the betrayal of the German workers by the Socialists (the Ramsay McDonald's,[19] and the Norman Thomases[20] etc. of Germany) and the counterrevolution and the setting up of the "republic" over there [. . .] .

[. . .] But the next war will be different. Today we are better prepared.

Love and good luck

Joe

Nice newsy letters from Peg, Kitty, and Dad. Hope that this weekend has been a big success, Kitty.

FROM JOHN TISA[21]

214 Benson Street
Camden, N.J.
July 13, 1936

John W. Martindale
Brookwood Labor College
Katonah, N.Y.

Dear John:

[. . .] The strike of the radio workers is keeping me busy. The police and courts are working openly with the corporation to break the strike. The strike is on its last legs; the spine has been broken. The best the strikers can hope for is a poll to determine the majority union between the "company union" and the legitimate outside union.

The strikers face murderous attacks of the press of the A.F. of L officials and the "liberal" city administration. Arrests are made wholesale on the slightest provocation. Deliberate frame-ups are common.

I was calmly working around the plant with two friends of mine when a newly hired special officer of the RCA, who stood about 6 feet 11 inches tall and weighing over 200 pounds violently seized me by the coat and pulled me into the office of the RCA company where I was put under arrest. In court he testified that I had made a pass at him and tried to take his gun away. He produced a witness another guard, who assured the court that he saw me tangle up the special officer. Oddly enough this witness was in the office when I was dragged in, so he could not have seen me on the outside. My two witnesses bore no weight in a court that preferred to believe the words of gangsters, brutal professional strike breakers, and lying police. I have since discovered that the arrest was secretly ordered by the Campbell Soup Company. The charge was to have been more serious. Their plot didn't work out. If this strike is defeated it will mean that all efforts to reorganize the soup workers will be futile, for many months to come.

You have stated the truth when you said in your letter that once you have done volunteer work for a group, they get used to taking it for granted that sort of work will be continued and never think of offering a regular job. It isn't that I mind doing volunteer work; its just that one can't possibly exist doing that, especially with me, since I am in business. A business man has to keep his hands washed of all activities in the labor movement if he wants to keep his business. And you know that I can never do that. Separating myself from the labor movement I can make plenty of money if I stick to barbering. But money means nothing to me, except as a medium of exchange, in its real sense. I want to devote my entire time and life to labor.

I am glad you have spoken to Tucker [Smith],[22] I had meant to talk with him at the State Workers Education Conference in Long Branch. I was prevented because there were too many people around. I'll write him a letter.

Your remarks about the tour of the Southern Chautauqua Troupe sounds interesting and I should like to hear the exact details of the trip.

Would I be crowding if I came to Brookwood and stayed a couple of days? I know that summer school is being conducted and all sleeping quarters possibly occupied. What are the weekend rates at this time of the year? If you should happen to come in this section, make sure to stop in to see me.

Workers education in New Jersey seems to be taking hold. The last conference in Long Branch, in my opinion, was encouraging. I had expected to see you there, but was told you were on your vacation.

Do you think that if I wrote to John L. Lewis[23] asking to assist as an organizer in his steel drive, he would consider me? I could ask because I am not out of the A.F. of L. I am secretary-treasurer of the Cannery Workers Union Local 20124 which has a Federal Labor charter.

Can you suggest names of individuals that I could write or see?

Comradely yours,

John

FROM WALTER DICKS

April 1937

To FALB [Friends of the Abraham Lincoln Brigade] Office

The world has for some time known of the heroic fight for democracy of the Spanish people with the aid of the International Brigade. The world still waits to hear of the reception of the Negro soldiers in the International Brigade by the Spanish people. The advent of Negroes from all parts of the world fighting in the International Brigades marks an epoch in the history of European invasions. The keen appreciation and warm sympathy shown by the Negro volunteer in this relation won the heart of the Spanish nation.

As we enter towns, the people, old and young, would cheer us, get around the Negroes of whom many had never seen in their life, and they would start guessing among themselves who we were. The life of the Negro with the Spanish soldiers were not any different for nothing was too good for him to have. The Spanish people behind the lines as they worked their fields by day, would ask them to their homes at night although many of them didn't have electric lights, they had only a can of oil and they made you welcome. Other places where things were better, that welcome was there also.

In many of the towns I was not able to be on the streets alone for the children would go along with me. I was taken to their social affairs by the male and female. Even the children would write their names and addresses and ask me to have the Negro boys and girls write them on my return home. In the barber shops, the movies, the cafes, and all other places I walked in as one of them. The only differences was that some of them would look at me because they had not seen a Negro before.

One could see the earnestness within them while they talked and asked questions such as: You are an American, why are you not the same color as many of the white comrades? Even this didn't have in any way of lessening their care. Some Negroes while walking in the streets of Madrid were taken to their homes where they stayed for three days.

There was a professor who had a daughter. It was his wish that she married a Negro. Why all this that is so much different than at home? The Spanish people know nothing of discrimination but at home we have all of the germs of fascism as discrimination, jim-crow, and lynching.

This is one of the many reasons that the Negroes have found joy in the fight of the Spanish Peoples. Not that he in any way runs from the fight at home against these damnable things, for you will find these Negroes on the front lines in the fight against them. We with the Spanish people know of the victory where they are united, and it is this kind of unity that the Spanish nation is asking of the world those that care for democracy for the independence of all nations.

Walter Dicks

Age 36

Cleveland, Ohio
April, 37
Sonidad (first Negro front liner)
(Bru—Ebro).

From Harold Smith

Somewhere in Spain
May 16, 1937

Dear Jeanette,

Have just made myself comfortable and settled down to write a letter to you. I should also write a letter to Clara, Phil, the Union, and other people—but we shall see.

First:—We still are in training and being held in reserve. As I have said in every other previous letter our marching orders may come at any time. But now we realize why we have been trained so long and intensively and I know that I speak for most of the fellows when I say that we are damned glad of the training we are getting. We, that is, the I.B. [International Brigades] boys as well as the thousands of fresh Spanish troops—have a big job ahead of us.

The first major phase of the war is over—the Fascists have been stopped by sheer guts and self-sacrifice. They were stopped by troops and sometimes, you couldn't call them troops—but groups of men and women—who weren't afraid to die for something bigger than themselves—

I've fought at Valencia road. They had no time to train, Jeanette. They had no time to learn the things we are learning—how to take cover under machine gun fire—how to dig in while lying on your stomach when the automatic rifles let go across an open field. They had no time to learn these things and let me tell you, Jeanette, the best way to learn the importance of these defensive measures is to go out and handle that delicate little toy called an automatic rifle or light machine gun. You lay on your stomach and sight for a half-moment and then BRRRRRRP BRRRRRROP 100 meters away a target the size of a man's head is torn to pieces. D— for example, can do this—3 bursts of 3—. After my first experience handling this baby, I conceived a very healthy respect for our modern weapons of warfare. And since then in practice manouevers our instructors (incidently the most competent military, dyed in the wool anti-fascists all are acting as our instructors) [I] can find no fault with the speed with which I take cover. But as I've said before most of those who went before us, Spaniards as well as International Volunteers, had no time to learn these things. The Fascists were driving against Madrid and they had to [be] stopped. . . . Well they're stopped. . . .

But stopping isn't enough. They've got to get out of Spain and they'll need more or less gentle urging to convince them that perhaps its easier to fight against they're own bosses than against a people determined to keep their freedom.

So, there you have it, we're building a People's Army here second to none. A trained army. . . . A unified army. . . . Able to coordinate every branch of service . . . and an army able to lose an offensive and keep it going. In my opinion, when we got into action . . . the big push will be on . . . and once we crack the Fascist lines the reverberations will be felt in Berlin and Rome as well as Seville and Granada. . . . Jesus Christ. . . . [Joseph] Goebbels will have a hell of a time explaining that away to the German people. And I got an idea the sweat will be down the crack of his can when he does. I don't think I would want to be in [the] Fascist's officer's pants when we come thru. . . . I think he would be safer as our prisoner than with his own men.

But I'd better pull myself in. I'm jumping way ahead. But the thing in Spain is the main link today. Wallop the hell out of Fascism here and we'll see a World's People Front that opens up possibilities that makes me thankful that I can play some little part in bringing it about.

It is now 9:05 P.M. and taps are blown at 9:30 P.M. That's right . . . you want our daily schedule O.K. . . . Reveille at 5:30, and roll mattresses, drink coffee and swallow a few churros or bread and butter, clean up quarters, fall in at 6:50 A.M. maneuvers until 11:30 A.M., lunch and siesta till 2:30. Instructions till 5:30, dinner at 6 p.m., free time till 9:30 and usually we are quite ready to go to sleep. Today, for example, we started from scratch and laid our complete trench system for a complete company. Machine gunposts, rifle pits, communication trenches. Right now, I'm trying to nurse a honey of a blister on my left hand, write a letter to you, watch a double pinochle game and carry on a conversation with two guys all at the same time.

How swell the guys are, how we kid around and every once in a while when you're marching or sitting in the barracks or lying in little hole in the woods during practice waiting for the word to advance, you get the warm feeling of companionship even if you're not saying anything. Or you begin thinking of home and how [?] is doing and the Union. We'll have a lot of fun talking about these things, Jeanette but I'm so tired now I can't keep my eyes open.

So Long,
Harold

From Eugene Wolman[24]

June 22, 1937

Dear Brother and Sister, Mother and Dad:

Yesterday I received letters mailed on the 4th & 5th by Milty & Miki. As usual I was more than pleased to get news from home. The "Costume Party" given for the brave boys "fighting" tickled us all. Danny is in the same Battalion but a different company and I had to show it to him. Al Warren was one of the truck drivers who conveyed us to within 6 kilometers of where we are now. Although all of us are far from heroes, Westchester [N.Y.] can so far be proud of its candidates. Al is looked upon as one of the most responsible drivers and has a rank corresponding to Corporal with increased pay. Danny is group leader with a warrant which means increased pay and I am now a group leader, and if I keep the job when we go further into combat I will get increased pay too. The pay means little, but the honor and responsibility entrusted to us means much. Theoretically, our army is divided up as follows: A group equals twelve men including its leader and moves as the smallest basic unit. Three groups make a section and are led by a section leader. Three sections equal one company and three companies equal one battalion. In combat it is the group leader who is in the same line as his men, forming the peak of the triangle in advances, falls back a little when they are set so as to direct their fire. The section leaders are further so he can direct his three group leaders thru runners and vocal commands, and the company commander is still further back so as to see the whole line of combat and direct the section leaders through runners and signal men.

Today I heard the most disquieting news since I have been in Spain. *Mundo Obrero*[25] says Fascist troops are in the streets of Bilboa. If Bilboa falls it will be even worse than the fall of Malaga. All we can do is to fight back harder. Miki, you should have no feeling of helplessness because Almeria[26] was bombed in the brazen manner of the Nazi. For the first time in history, for the first time since Fascism began systematically throttling and rending all we hold dear—we are getting the opportunity to fight back—to make a determined struggle against Fascism. Mussolini rode unopposed in a Cooks Lit[27] to Rome. Hitler boasts that he took power without bloodshed. The Austrian workers were bombed into defeat in their beautiful Karl Marx Hof[28] for which the Fascist Catholic Government now cynically thanks them. In little Asturias the miners made a brave, but unsuccessful stand against the combined reactionaries of Spain. In Ethiopia the Fascist machine was again able to work its will without any unified opposition. Even in Democratic America the majority have had to undergo every sort of oppression without being able to fight back. I have had to sit in my roadster near a lettuce field while a cop struck me with his gloved fist full in the face, while the blood burned in my veins unable to strike back. From our June 10th Daily [Worker] I see what is happening now to workers in my Union. Here finally the oppressed of the Earth are united, here finally we have weapons, here we can fight back. Here, even if we lose, which is a possibility we will not admit, in the fight itself, in the weakening of Fascism we will have won.

Well enough of this. I am corporal of the guard tonight and as such must see that none of the boys are shooting any of our own men.

Much love.

Gene

FROM CANUTE FRANKSON

Albacete, Spain
July 6, 1937

My Dear Friend:

I'm sure that by this time you are still waiting for a detailed explanation of what has this international struggle to do with my being here. Since this is a war between whites who for centuries have held us in slavery, and have heaped every kind of insult and abuse upon us, segregated and jim-crowed us; why I, a Negro, who have fought through these years for the rights of my people am here in Spain today.

Because we are no longer an isolated minority group fighting hopelessly against an immense giant, because, my dear, we have joined with, and become an active part of, a great progressive force, on whose shoulders rests the responsibility of saving human civilization from the planned destruction of a small group of degenerates gone mad in their lust for power. Because if we crush Fascism here, we'll save our people in America, and in other parts of the world, from the vicious prosecution, wholesale imprisonment, and slaughter which the Jewish people suffered and are suffering under Hitler's Fascist heels.

All we have to do is to think of the lynching of our people. We can but look back at the pages of American history stained with the blood of Negroes, stink with the burning bodies of our people hanging from trees; bitter with the groans of our tortured loved ones from whose living bodies, ears, fingers, toes, have been cut for souvenirs—living bodies into which red-hot pokers have been thrust. All because of a hate created in the minds of men and women by their masters who keep us all under their heels while they suck our blood, while they live in their bed of ease by exploiting us.

But these people who howl like hungry wolves for our blood, must we hate them? Must we keep the flame which these masters kindled

constantly fed? Are these men and women responsible for the programs
of their masters, and the conditions which force them to such degraded
depths? I think not. They are tools in the hands of unscrupulous masters.
These same people are as hungry as we are. They live in dives and wear
rags the same as we do. They too are robbed by the masters, and their faces
kept down in the filth of a decayed system. They are our fellowmen. Soon
and very soon they and we will understand. Soon many Angelo Herndons[29]
will rise from among them, and from among us, and will lead us both
against those who live by the stench of our burnt flesh. We will crush them.
We will build us a new society—a society of peace and plenty. There will be
no color line, no jim-crow trains, no lynching. That is why, my dear, I'm
here in Spain.

On the battlefields of Spain we fight for the preservation of democracy.
Here, we're laying the foundation for world peace, and for the liberation of
my people, and of the human race. Here, where we're engaged in one of
the most bitter struggles of human history, there is no color line, no
discrimination, no race hatred. There's only one hate, and that is the hate
for fascism. We know who our enemies are. The Spanish people are very
sympathetic towards us. They are lovely people. I'll tell you about them
later.

I promised not to preach, but by all indications this seems more like
a sermon than a letter to an old friend. But how can I help it, being
face to face with such trying circumstances? I'm quite conscious of the
clumsiness of my effort to write you an intimate letter, but your knowledge
of my earnestness and sincerity, with your intelligence and patience will
enable you to understand and be tolerant. Later, after I've overcome this
strain, I'm sure I'll be able to write more intimately. The consciousness of
my responsibility for my actions has kept me under terrific strain.
Because I think it has caused you a lot of unpleasantness.

Don't think for one moment that the strain of this terrible war or the
many miles between us has changed my feelings towards you. Our
friendship has meant a great deal to me, and still means much to me. I
appreciate it because it has always been a friendship of devoted mutual
interest. And I'll do whatever is within my power to maintain it.

I, a soldier in active service, must know far less about how far or how
close is death. But as long as I hold out I'll keep you in touch with events.
Sometimes when I go to the front the shells drop pretty close. Then I think

it is only a matter of minutes. After I return here to the base I seem to see life from a new angle. Somehow it seems to be more beautiful. I'd think of you, home and all my friends, then get to working more feverishly than ever. Each of us must give all we have if this Fascist beast is to be destroyed.

After this is over I hope to share my happiness with you. It will be a happiness which could not have been achieved in any other way than having served in a cause so worthy. I hope that the apparent wrong which I committed may be compensated for by the service I'm giving here for the cause of democracy. I hope that you're well, and that you will, or have, forgiven me. My sincere desire is that you are happy, and when this is over that we meet again. But if a Fascist bullet stops me don't worry about it. If I am conscious before I die I don't think I'll be afraid. Of one thing I'm certain: I'll be satisfied that I've done my part.

So long. Until some future date. One never knows when there'll be time to write.

There's so much to do, and so little time in which to do it. Love.

Salude.

Canute

FROM VINCENT LOSSOWSKI

Garcassone,[30] France

July 27, 1937

Dearest Mother & Wanda:

I am staying in the little town of Garcasssone [sic] for a few days before I go further on to eventually arrive at my ultimate objective. Please don't feel bad about me leaving the way I did mother but after all you will understand if you but realize that I am not doing this thing out of the desire so foolishly as romantic adventure, but with a sound determination to do my little bit that working people may live like human beings instead of like slaves under the rule of fascism. Nobody influenced me Mother it was my own desire to come across. The duty that I will perform will be entirely free from all danger. I will but act in the capacity of instructor. This section of France is very beautiful and picturesque being the champagne section of the country. In the town is a castle hundreds of

years old that brings to me memories of stories I used to read of knight-
hood and adventure when a boy. It is very stately looking situated on
top of a hill commanding a view of the whole town. It is full of halls
passage-ways and dungeons where enemies of the Duke of the period
were kept for safe keeping. I am staying with some French people here
in the town who are very kind and considerate of my wants. They have
certain customs that to us Americans seem strange, for example they only
eat twice a day, but when you sit down to a meal it takes you a couple of
hours to store it away. . . . I suppose you are in the YCL [Young Communist
League] by now aren't you sis, I know you could do some good work within
that organization. Will write more later. With love & kisses I remain

    Your loving son & brother

    Vince

From Hyman Katz

November 25, 1937

Dear Ma,

    It's quite difficult for me to write this letter, but it must be done; Claire
writes me that you know I'm in Spain.

    Of course, you know that the reason I didn't tell you where I was is that I
didn't want to hurt you. I realize that I was foolish for not understanding
that you would have to find out.

    I came to Spain because I felt I had to. Look at the world situation. We
didn't worry when Mussolini came to power in Italy. We felt bad when
Hitler became Chancellor of Germany, but what could we do? We felt—
though we tried to help and sympathize—that was their problem and it
wouldn't effect us. Then the fascist governments sent out agents and
began to gain power in other countries. Remember the anti-Semitic
troubles in Austria only about a year ago. Look at what is happening in
Poland; and see how the fascists are increasing their power in the
Balkans—and Greece—and how the Italians are trying to play up to the
Arab leaders.

    Seeing all these things—how fascism is grasping power in many
countries (including the U.S. where there are many Nazi organizations
and Nazi agents and spies)—can't you see that fascism is our own problem

t may come to us as it came to other countries? And don't you
e that Jews will be the first to suffer if fascism comes?

t if we didn't see clearly the hand of Mussolini and Hitler in all these
ntries, in Spain we can't help seeing it. Together with their agent,
anco, they are trying to set up the same anti-progressive, anti-Semitic
egime in Spain as they have in Italy and Germany. If we sit by and let
them grow stronger by taking Spain, they will move on to France and will
not stop there; and it won't be long before they get to America. Realizing
this, can I sit by and wait until the beasts get to my very door—until it is too
late, and there is no one I can call on for help? And would I even deserve
help from others when the trouble comes upon me, if I were to refuse to
help those who need it today? If I permitted such a time to come—and as a
Jew and a progressive, I would be among the first to fall under the axe of
the fascists—all I could do then would be to curse myself and say, "Why
didn't I wake up when the alarm-clock rang?"

But then it would be too late—just as it was too late for the Jews in
Germany to find out in 1933 that they were wrong in believing Hitler
would never rule Germany.

I know you are worried about me; but how often is the operation which
worries most, is most necessary to save us? Many mothers here, in places
not close to the battle front would not let their children go to fight, until
the fascist bombing planes came along, and then it was too late. Many
mothers here have been crippled or killed, or their husbands and children
maimed or killed; yet some of these mothers did not want to send their
sons and husbands to the war, until the fascist bombs taught them in such
a horrible manner—what common sense could not teach them.

Yes, Ma, this is a case where sons must go against their mothers' wishes
for the sake of their mothers themselves. So I took up arms against the
persecutors of my people—the Jews—and my class—the Oppressed. I am
fighting against those who would establish an inquisition like that of their
ideological ancestors several centuries ago, in Spain. Are these traits
which you admire so much in a Prophet Jeremiah or a Judas Maccabbeus[31]
bad when your son exhibits them? Of course, I am not Jeremiah or a
Judas; but I'm trying with my own meager capabilities, to do what they did
with their great capabilities, in the struggle for Liberty, Well-being and
Peace.

Now for a little news. I am a good soldier and I have held several offices in the few months that I've been in Spain. I am now convalescing from a wound on my thigh, received October 13. I'm feeling swell now; I got such good treatment in the hospital that I've gained an awful lot of weight. Now, I'm at a seaside resort which was once inhabited by Franco and other swanks. In New York, when it got cold we used to hear about people going to Florida, but who would ever have thought that I, too, would someday celebrate Thanksgiving (and Armistice day) by swimming and playing volley-ball dressed only in tights.

I'd better stop writing or I'll have nothing to say next time. I've been writing to you regularly thru the Paris address, which did not turn out to be very reliable. I only received one letter from you, which Claire typed the first week in September. Now all this will be changed; you can write me direct:

H Katz

    Lovingly,

    Chaim

FROM DONALD HENRY[32]

Socorro Rozono. 270
D.E. [Donald] Henry
Plaza de Altazano
Albacete, SPAIN
July 4, 1937

Dr. E.R. Henry[33]
2300 Sedgwick
University Heights
New York, N.Y.

Dear Ed:

I have joined the International Brigade Company three of the MacKenzie Papineau Battalion. It is a Canadian Battalion but over half of the force is composed of U.S. citizens. When training is over I expect to be moved—along with the other Americans—into the newly formed Patrick Henry Battalion or the George Washington or Abraham Lincoln.

About the proposed trip to France and tour of all Europe. I can only say it was a hoax for the delicate position of comrades headed for Spain made it necessary to conceal all information about our actual destination. Also, for the same reason I cannot say how exactly we came to be here or where exactly we are in Spain but the address heading on this letter will be my future mailing address. We have been some 3 weeks now making this journey and have undergone some severe hardships already to join in this fight against Fascism.

The group I traveled with and am stationed with is composed of students. I have five or six particularly good friends here among whom is a man from Harvard and from Cornell, one from Columbia, one from Michigan, Graeber from K.U., and a Professor of Physics at Washington U,—ph.d. Harvard, Cornell, Johns Hopkins—and others, ranging from seamen to plumbers. At our first stop inside of Spain there was an excess of 500 men with 21 races represented. The Americans are most numerous with the Poles and Canadians running a close second. In order to get around one should know how to speak French, Spanish, German, Polish, and English, least of all it seems.

At this stage in the Spanish War both sides are marking time while they build up their fighting equipment. By the time of the next offensive the loyalists will outnumber the fascist forces by some 100,000 it is generally believed, but the fascist equipment is certainly more abundant and most likely better for the simple reason that the fascist army [had] practically no difficulty at all running the blockades and procuring the equipment. They outnumber us with planes and guns but there is practically no doubt that we have the superior forces. One thing we are sure of is that Hell is bound to split side open before much longer.

The people here are a real treat to a radical's eyes. Everywhere is the clenched fist salute of the Popular front government and every man's name is comrade. The Spanish people go on about their affairs calmly and efficiently as though no danger at all awaited them. In Valencia and all along the East Coast from Catalonia on there are practically no signs of the war excepting the speeding govt. cars and packed trains of troops headed for the front. Ambulances, trucks, and military cars of all kinds are on the roads headed all directions. On the train we passed car after car of wounded comrades headed for the hospitals in the rear. In the streets, at the railway stations, and everywhere is posters and pictures all describing the horrors of the front. Most appalling of all is the parade of one armed and one legged comrades in every station. It seems that the civilian bombardment is the worst ever known to man with complete cities practically demolished in the central part of Spain [. . .] .

All of us here are perfectly aware of the dangers involved in this war yet we are positive that this method of fighting fascism is the correct method and we intend to give our lives if necessary to maintain the independence of Spain. Another fascist gain in the world would mean another invitation to world war and gangster government. The political situation here is not much different than the political situation of the U.S. in 1776 when the French people helped the U.S. throw off the British monarch because the masses believed in a democratic govt. Now U.S. citizens close their eyes to an assault on a democratic people and in doing that are actually aiding the spreading of fascism. You may say that we are suffering from the same decisions that the world war veterans suffered in 1918 but the political line up is entirely different with a threat not to bourgeois government but to a genuine proletariat mass movement.

Salud,

D.E. H.

FROM ELLIS BEALE

April 26, 1938

Dear Mike [Simms],

I am not going to ask you to write any more. I got used to the idea of not receiving mail so if you don't get any more mail you know why.

The last operation which you no doubt know about from all the press I would merely say the following. The fighting was bitter. The enemy used all it had against us. All day long the Italian fascists and the Germans bombed us and streifed us mercilessly. There we were hopeless and helpless against these monsters of the German and Italian war machines. The non-intervention has saved Franco, but that is not all. . . . You can speak of the great artillery concentration by the Germans as the world war, with out doubt it surprised even us with its brutality, for we did not have any means to counteract it. Its clear men can stand just so much and no more—some weaker ones could not stand it no more when 30-40 taurets[34] of Italian make came up. We our side did not have nothing even to match for days we did not see a single one of our planes, surely when 6 enemy bombers are accompanied with 100 chasing planes, it is useless to send our arrow out, the fellows knew it but—worst of all is when the arrows streife and then suddenly dive out of the sky lowering to 50-60 meters you can see the aviators laugh at you, while throwing hand grenades and endless machine gunning. So was the victory of the fascists up until this moment.

I recall in Madrid, when I accompanied the English parliamentary delegation with a single rifle, we met Brigades counting to relieve those on the lines without a single rifle. Those leaving the lines gave their rifles to those taking their place. . . . In the early days it was possible to stop the enemy with the rifle and self sacrifice, but to-day we are faced with a mechanized army—they can only be stopped by the same mechanized army as that of the enemy force. France is strangling itself to death. England is cutting its own throat in the Mediterranean. Dr. Negrin[35] in his last speech said the fate of France will be decided on the Aragon front.

Hitler and Mussolini even if they shall be successful, they can capture troops & pillage fields—they can take all the soil—but they can never nor will ever trounce the spirit of the people of Spain. Those who with sticks and rocks halted the fascists at the very gates of Madrid—to-day, the Spanish people are much more determined and willing to sacrifice no pasionaria[36] is written all over, in every heart there is this no pasionaria determination.

To-day the enemy has been stopped but Hitler and Mussolini are still determined, more arms, more troops will come. We need all the troops and arms—we are sure we will not be deserted by the people of France and England, and the USA with this confidence we are sure of victory.

I hope mom is ok, give my regards to all Hy, Louise, Ruby, and the rest of them.

Good luck,
Eli

SALARIA KEE *A Negro Nurse in Republican Spain*[37]

What have Negroes to do with Spain? What has Spain for us? What about Ethiopia? Why should Negro men be fighting in Spain? What do we expect out of it? These are questions Negroes are continuously asking. It is their immediate response to any appeal for Spain. Quite apart from the broad question of humanitarianism the answers are simple.

Fascist Italy invaded and overpowered Ethiopia. This was a terrible blow to Negroes throughout the world. Ethiopia represented the last outpost of Negro authority, of Negro self-government. Hundreds of Negroes in this country attempted to join the Ethiopian forces. But Ethiopia at that time was so remote that few succeeded. I say 'at that time' advisedly. Since then the rapid move of world events has brought Europe and the Orient much closer to local thinking and knowledge.

Even at that time thousands of dollars were collected from people in all the liberty loving countries of the world. Sweden and Denmark sent ambulances and medical supplies. Negroes from New York sent a 75-bed field hospital and 2 tons of medical supplies. They sent two delegations to Emperor Haile Selassie. They brought two Ethiopian delegations to this country to win support for Ethiopia. A young white physician from Evanston, Illinois was the first foreign casualty. He was killed in an Italian-fascist airplane raid on the Ethiopian field hospitals. Germany and Italy and Japan conspicuously sent nothing except poison gas with which to slaughter the Ethiopians.

Italy moved on from the invasion of Ethiopia. She advanced her troops into Spain. Here was a second small nation, feudal and underdeveloped. Bitter resentment against Italy still rankled. The hundreds of Negro boys who had been prevented from going to Ethiopia understood the issues more clearly now. To them Spain was now the battlefield on which Italian fascism might be defeated. And perhaps Italy defeated in Spain would be forced to withdraw from Ethiopia. Ethiopia's only hope for recovery lies in Italy's defeat. The place to defeat Italy now is in Spain.

The lynching of Negroes in America, discrimination in education and on jobs, lack of hospital facilities for Negroes in most cities and very poor ones in others, all this appeared to them as part of the picture of fascism; of a dominant group impoverishing and degrading a less powerful group. The open pronouncements of Germany and Italy against all non-Aryans is convincing evidence. Thinking thus, hundreds of Negro men went to Spain. Here in the international Brigade of Volunteers they found other Negroes.

From Djibouti,[38] Emperor Haile Selassie's chief mechanic came to strike a blow for free Ethiopia. From South Africa, from Cuba, from French Senegal, from Haiti, from the Cameroon's, Negroes came, stayed and fought. Negro physicians came to man hospitals and serve the wounded. Negro ambulance drivers and stretchers. And one young Negro nurse.

FROM MILTON WOLFF[39]

1602 West 6th Street
Brooklyn. N.Y.
March 30, 1939

Officer in Charge of Reserve Affairs
Headquarters, Second Corps. Area
Governors Island, N.Y.

Dear Sir:

With reference to applying for a reserve commission in the United States Army, I should like to arrange an appointment with you. I had discussed this with Colonel Stephen Fuqua, Military Attache in Spain and he suggested this appointment.

I am twenty four years old and have had a high school education. Previous to going to Spain, I had no military training. However, during the twenty three months that I was there (March 1937–December 1938) I was continuously in front service, and held the following ranks:

Sergeant, in command of a machine gun platoon
Lieutenant in command of a machine gun company
Captain, Brigade Staff
Major, in command of American Battalion

I went to Spain sincerely believing that in fighting for Spanish Democracy I was helping preserve American Democracy. In view of recent world events and the growing threat to America, I am anxious to volunteer my experience and myself for the United States Army.

Respectfully yours,
Milton Wolff

LA ESPAÑA DE BURGOS

Los reputados malabaristas « Adolfo and Benito » en un peligroso juego de equilibrio con la paz del mundo.

Los Nacionales

MINISTERIO DE PROPAGANDA

Spanish Civil War Posters

To Milton Wolff

HEADQUARTERS SECOND CORPS AREA
OFFICE OF THE CORPS AREA COMMANDER
GOVERNORS ISLAND, N.Y.

June 19, 1939

Mr. Milton Wolff[40]
1602 West Sixth Street
Brooklyn, N.Y.

Dear Sir:

The Commanding General has directed me to acknowledge receipt of your application for appointment in the Officers Reserve Corps.

The War Department has informed this headquarters that in view of the fact that you rendered service in the Spanish Army, which service was undertaken in violation of the policy of the United Sates as announced by the State Department, it is impractical to take favorable action on your request for appointment in the Officers' Reserve Corps.

Very truly yours,

G.H. Baird,

Colonel, Cavalry,

Acting Assistant Adjutant General

From Alvah Bessie

Wednesday night
[September 1939]

Dear Ed [Rolfe][41]

I'm sorry I'm a false prophet and I'm quite definitely going out of business so far as you're concerned. But what the hell; you have two facts to console you: 1—you deserved it more than anyone who will get it: 2—Bennett Cerf[42] loves you and has already announced that your are writing a book for Quondam House.[43] Salud!

On my wall is a magnificent poster that says HOY MAS QUE NUNCA—VICTORIA [TODAY MORE THAN EVER VICTORY]. One year ago tonight I was still riding in a box-car on my way to the front and Batea.[44] Tonight I'm thinking of

Aaron, that lovely ugly bastard, and I'm low as hell. Tonight Hitler is sleeping in the great castle of something or other at Prague and Mr. Chamberlain deeply regrets what is going on.

May your book be more successful than my own.

May your tribe increase and wax and grow powerful in the land.

May your wife increase and wax too. (See above)

Call me again, and so on. Yesterday I soared over Flatbush on stiff wings, riding behind 85 horse-power and avoiding two Douglas Army twin-motored bombers that were also using the field to practice take-offs and landings. I was alone and felt like a God for the half-hour.

Go thou and do likewise. And when Master Bates shows, let me know,

ALB

"THE YANKS ARE NOT COMING."

David McKelvy White
The Main Report of the Veterans of the Abraham Lincoln Brigade's National Executive Committee, by David White, to the VALB Convention, December 23, 1939, in New York[45]

Three years ago, aboard the "Normandie," the first group of American volunteers sailed from New York for France, on the way to join the International Brigades in Spain. They knew well, as did the some 2800 of us who followed them, that they were embarking on a mission which was in every sense truly American. They were offering their lives in a desperate struggle for peace and freedom and democracy.

They saw that victory for the Spanish Republic and the Spanish people would greatly strengthen the cause of peace, for it would turn the tide of international lawlessness and fascist aggression. They saw that it would greatly strengthen democracy, not only in Latin America, where nations and peoples look to Spain as their mother country, but throughout the whole world, because it would reassert the principles on which our country was built, the right of the people to determine their own government, and because it would strengthen everywhere those organizations of labor and of the people which are, more and more clearly every day, the indices of democracy and guarantors of freedom [. . .] .

In Spain we read our President's brave words about "quarantining the aggressor" and we saw the joy and hope they evoked in the Spanish people. But we remembered our State department officials, with their suspicion and hostility; we remembered the U.S. Consular agents at Le Havre and their "tender concern for our safety"; we remembered the American press, its slander against the Spanish people and their leaders, its pious and indignant denial of German and Italian intervention, its praise of Franco, the Christian gentleman, and the eagerness with which it repeatedly captured Madrid for him. We wondered whether these brave words from the White House were not also hollow, as indeed they proved to be, for our Government continued systematically to strangle democracy in Spain [. . .] .

Today, in our own country and in different circumstances, we face the same enemies. When the governments that stabbed Spain in the back claim they are fighting for democracy, we have good reason to call them hypocrites and liars. We denounce the present war as we do the War of 1914–1918, as a war not for freedom, but for profits. We take our position now, as always, in determined opposition to America's aid and to our participation in such a war, which can bring only suffering, misery and death to the common people in whose name and for whose welfare we fought in Spain.

There are mighty forces in America now working day and night to stir up war—hysteria. The powerful propaganda machine that, for fear of mythical "involvement," crushed all attempts to lift the arms embargo on Republican Spain is today aiming at a real involvement and its booming foreign trade in war supplies [. . .] .

We who witnessed and were part of the magnificent unity of the Spanish people, bear a special responsibility for making sure that America is warned against such splitting maneuvers. Franco, with all his immense supplies of Italian soldiers and German munitions, could not defeat the Spanish Republic, but Chamberlain's agents,[46] Casado[47] and his junta of traitors, broke the unity of the Spanish people. This was done by an attack first on Spanish Communists, then on the trade unions, and finally and fatally against the Negrin Government and all who supported it.

In the same war the American warmongers are today using the Dies Committee[48] to try to smash all progressive and militant organizations [. . .] .

In fighting the Dies Committee we fight all our enemies at once. We fight the greedy war profiteers, who seek to break the backs of the unions and slash relief and social security. We fight [Father] Coughlin[49] and anti-semitism, the KKK, the lynchers and exploiters of the Negro people, and those who plan concentration camps or deportation for the American Foreign-born [...] .

Realizing full well that an America kept at peace is a blow to the warmakers and reactionaries all over the world, we call to the world with full hearts and at the top of our voices—THE YANKS ARE NOT COMING!

AIRPLANE FACTORIES
by
Langston Hughes

I see by the papers
Where the airplane factories still
Don't give no work to colored people
And it looks like they never will.
Yet it seems mighty funny—
Though I don't mean funny to laugh—
That they don't let no colored folks
Work in defense aircraft.
They let naturalized foreigners
And some without first papers
Work anywhere they want to—
Yet they start to cutting capers
If Negroes apply for jobs.
They say we're sabotaging defense
When we ask for equal rights and try
To get down off Jim Crow's fence.
I don't understand it cause
If we're out for democracy,
Why on earth then, Mr. Roosevelt,
Don't you give some to me?
Huh?

"Airplane Factories" is an unpublished poem by Langston Hughes that was sent to Lincoln Brigade veteran Bunny Rucker in March 1941. The poem was found with Rucker's papers when they were donated to the Abraham Lincoln Brigade Archives at the Tamiment Library. During the seige of Madrid, Rucker drove Hughes to the front so he could report on the war. (Courtesy Harold Ober Associates)

FROM AVE BRUZZICHESI

January 31, 1940

Dear Dr. [Leo] Eleoesser,[50]

In this letter I shall really try to finish my story of the evacuation from Barcelona.

I did not dream it would take so long and still there are so many things that one would like to talk over with you. If I can only write well.

As the refugees entered French territory their troubles and sufferings did not end there. Those who came in first had to continue another thirty kilometers or so to the camps that were to be their homes. They were considered "prisoners of war" and treated as such. Their valuables were taken from them and the army equipment guns ambulances etc were also taken over by the Daladier[51] government and not allowed to go to Valencia as the Spanish leaders desired.

I choose to call the camps where all the refugees were put Concentration camps because they were in my estimation even worse than the camps I had imagined the camps in Germany to be. They were nothing more than stretches of bare land, sectioned off by barbed wire and guarded by Senegalese guards. There was no shelter at all at least for the first month in France. It was February. The camps extended from Perpignan[52] to the Pyrenees near the Mediterranean. It was bitterly cold and the wind from the mountains blew over the camps almost continuously as did sand from the beaches. There was of course no sanitation. Herded together like so many animals these fine people had to eat, sleep, and defecate on the same little piece of land which was their home. In order to keep warm they dug holes in the ground & covered themselves with what blankets, twigs, tin or anything they might get to protect themselves from the cold wind. Four thousand refugees and the majority in the camps such as these. What an outrage!

It did not take long for typhoid epidemic to spread throughout these camps. Diptheria pneumonia, typhus, scabies too were very common and these poor refugees who were not killed by diseases often died from hunger and exposure to the cold.

Margaret Powell the Welsh nurse, having foolishly left her passport in Barcelona had to remain in one of the camps until we found her (and took her away unauthoritatively) as we visited the camps with Mission Britanica ambulance. (It took Rosita over a week to obtain this permission). She told us of a Catalan soldier who had a few francs and wanted to leave the camp to buy some food. They only got a dark liquid in the morning supposed to be coffee and soup in the evening for which they had to stand in line. This Catalonian boy could not make the Senegalese understand what he wanted and he innocently left the camp. The guard bayonetted him thru the abdomen. He died instantly.

Thousands of such shameful incidents happened which would take days to recount.

As I was working with the British mission then I can tell you of what happened to some of our friends. Do you remember the husky German doctor who became director of the hospital in Valencia after you left? His wife took charge of the nurses. I've forgotten his name (Glaser).

He had suffered from typhoid fever and like the rest of the Internationals without a country he too was put in the Argelese Camp. Women that we were (thank heavens) the French guards did not question our entrance and exits to the camp once seeing our permission from the camp. That is how we got the Welsh nurse out and Rosita with another friend got these doctors out. I did not recognize him when I saw him. He looked like a living skeleton. Once out, these refugees could make attempts to go to another country—but to get out was most difficult [. . .] .

All this happened after attempts to get to Valencia were squelched. The hospital train # 21 came into Cerbere filled with all the "enchufados" of the Sanidadad their family and furniture. In the entire train there were not more than 20 patients.

We stayed in Perpignan for almost a month and were sick at seeing food again which could not be shared. It took me over three months to learn to eat a small full meal.

Fund raising for the refugees still goes on. Many have found new homes as you know.

Please write and tell me if I can write more in detail about anything.

Sincerely,

Ave

FROM EUGENE DENNIS[53]

Notes on Some of the American Veterans of the International Brigade

There are one or more Vets in practically every district Buro and committee of the Party and YCL, as well as on the Central Committee. There are also a relatively large number of Vets who occupy responsible posts in the various leftwing and progressive mass organizations. These comrades constitute, on the whole, one of the politically strongest and most capable, reliable, and loyal sections of the Party and [Young Communist] League cadres. From among many comrades, mention should be made of the following:

1) John Gates: Member of the National Committee and Buro of the YCL and a member of the district Buro of the Party and state secretary of the New York State district of the [Young Communist] League (and a member of the district Buro of the Party). Gates was one of the first to re-orientate correctly after the outbreak of the present war. He has shown considerable firmness and political initiative and is perhaps the best organizer in the League. He is very vigilant and responsible, and is thoroly reliable. He has real authority in the League and in the broad youth movement and is very popular. Of the new leading cadres within the Party and the YCL, Gates and Bob Thompson are amongst the most outstanding and show great capacity for leadership and political development.

2) Bob Thompson: National vice-president of the YCL until January 1941 was state secretary of the League in Ohio; is now working semi-legally in the YCL center as deputy for Mac Weiss. Since the outbreak of the war, as well as before, Thompson has proved to be politically firm, reliable and vigilant. He has shown independent judgment and is an effective organizer. While he is not always sufficiently flexible in tactical maneuvering, Thompson is an uncompromising fighter for the line of the Party and the League.

3) Steve Nelson: Member of the Central Committee of the CPUSA state Buro of the Party in California and chairman of the county organization of the Party in San Francisco. Nelson is very dependable, devoted, and is a capable organizer. However, he does not always show sufficient political initiative and alertness. But he is politically

stable, is very responsible, is a capable mass worker, and has real mass influence. However, it should be noted that Nelson permitted his name to be used as co-author of a book review which took a friendly and favorable position towards Hemingway's book "For Whom the Bell Tolls." Nelson has recognized the seriousness of this action which is not characteristic of his work, for he is usually quite vigilant.

4) <u>David McElvey White</u>: A member of the national school commission of the Party and one of the best teachers in the national training school. Up till recently he was one of the leading officers and organizers of the Veterans of the Abraham Lincoln Brigade and the former Friends of the Lincoln Brigade, as well as very active in a number of national committees for aid to Spain. White is politically solid, is very responsible and trustworthy. He is an effective propagandist and is a firm fighter for the line of the Party.

5) <u>Bill Lawrence</u>: Organization secretary and member of the district Buro of the Party in New York. Prior to this, after his return from Spain, he carried on leading and responsible work in connection with the repatriation and rehabilitation of the Vets, and for a time also functioned as an administrative secretary of the Kings County organization of the Party in New York City. Lawrence is a very efficient administrator, is an effective Party organizer and is generally known as one who "can get things done."

6) <u>Carl Geiser</u>: member of the national committee and Buro of the YCL. At present is working in an airplane factory where he built up a strong YCL organization. Geiser is a good propagandist, shows independent political judgement, and is capable for leading and responsible work. He is thoroly reliable and loyal.

Some of the other Vets who have come forward in the recent period who are developing politically, who are doing responsible and leading work, and have proven to be loyal and reliable are: Irving Goff, national secretary of the Veterans of the Abraham Lincoln Brigade; Saul Wellman, district trade union secretary of the YCL in New York; Fred Keller, New York commander of the Veterans of the Lincoln Brigade; Irving Weissman (Wiseman?) secretary of the Jewish Council of the American Committee for the Protection of the Foreign Born; Ed Maki, state secretary of the YCL in Minnesota; Milton Wolfe, national commander of the Vets of the

Lincoln Brigade; Art Timpson, responsible for the agrarian commission of the Party in the New England states.

Tim Ryan
May 19, 1941
(PB of CPUSA)

FROM LOUIS GORDON

October 13, 1941

Gentlemen [VALB office]

I'm sorry not to have been able to answer sooner & acknowledge the package I received from you. The command here knows I was in Spain & it does not work to my disadvantage in fact I was kept over in this training camp as part of the cadre.

Most of the men & officers with some exceptions, naturally have a very healthy attitude on the Spanish war and discuss it freely. When I received the package I gave away a lot of it and told them who had sent it and the reaction was good.

In the future I would like to communicate more often & hear about other vets & where they are. I met Gabby Klein—don't know if any are at Eustis. If there are like to look them up.

Lou Gordon

FROM ROBERT NAGLE

Battery "C"
265th C.A. (H.D.)
Fort Brackett
Galveston, Texas
November 17, 1941

Dear Irving:

When I was last home on leave, Leny Levensen[54] told me to get in touch with you.—or rather get in touch with you in whatever work the Veterans is doing in the army. Needless to say I haven't kept the fact that I served in the I.B. [International Brigades] a secret; so that everyone knows about it.

Therefore, if you could send me, any literature that wouldn't off course jeopardize me too much, I could use it. After all, it could be passed around to some of the boys who are trade unionists.

All in all, they are interested in the war. They are intensely interested in the Russian campaign and seem to sense what a Red victory would mean. But they are equally outspoken in their hatred and condemnation of Great Britain. Naturally, getting only news that the press gives us on the actions of the British government, they too readily associate the people and the government as being in accord. So it becomes a rather painstaking duty to differentiate.

Morale on the whole is lousy. All of it naturally stemming back to the lack of political understanding of the role that we could play both domestically and internationally and the causes of the war. The officers are just as demoralized as the men and without sufficient training to be in charge of a group of men or knowledge of their jobs. And, of course, discrimination is rampant. Naturally, all the other items—petty things—like say leave, K.P. guard, unnecessary duty, not to mention only a few play their part.

But what I am particularly interested in getting the names and addresses of Mac Krauss—New York; Joe Barron of Klamath Falls, Oregon, Willoweit of Chicago, and Hewlett of Chicago sent to me so that I can correspond.

I am rather anxious to hear from you—so please with

Salud,

Bob Nagle

NOTES

1. John Gerassi interview with Milton Felsen, January 23, 1980, John Gerassi oral history collection, Abraham Lincoln Brigade Archive, Tamiment Library, Collection 18, hereafter cited as Gerassi.
2. Joseph Dallet to Mother, May 21, 1931, ALBA.
3. Peter N. Carroll, *The Odyssey of the Abraham Lincoln Brigade: Americans in the Spanish Civil War* (Stanford, Cal.: Stanford University Press, 1994), 9–20; Albert Prago, "Jews in the International Brigades," *Jewish Currents* (February 1979): 15–21.
4. Robin D. G. Kelley, "This Ain't Ethiopia, But It'll Do: African Americans in the Spanish Civil War," in Danny Duncan Collum and Victor A. Berch (eds.), *African Americans in the Spanish Civil War: This Ain't Ethiopia But It'll Do* (New York: G. K. Hall, 1992), 6; Langston Hughes, *I Wonder as I Wander* (New York: Holt, Rinehart, and Winston, 1956), 354.
5. James Yates, *Mississippi to Madrid: Memoir of a Black American in the Abraham Lincoln Brigade* (Seattle: Open Hand Publishing, 1989), 95–96.
6. Carroll, 107–24.

7. John Gerassi interview with Bill Susman, May 5, 1980, Gerassi.

8. As quoted in Carroll, *Odyssey*, 210.

9. John Gerassi interview with Maury Colow, April 15, 1980, Gerassi.

10. "The Yanks Are Not Coming!" campaign was organized by the Communist party in the fall of 1939 in order to oppose American entry into World War II. A number of Socialist party and pacifist leaders, including Norman Thomas, supported this effort.

11. For example, see the case of William Herrick, who later testified as a friendly witness before the Subversive Activities Control Board. Other veterans who became associated with the Socialist Workers party included Robert Gladnick, Henry Thomas, John Kenzierski, and Peter Sturgeon, ALBA. There was also a faction of the Socialist Workers party that followed the lead of Leon Trotsky and supported the Nazi-Soviet Pact, arguing that the defense of the Soviet Union was the primary concern.

12. Peter Carroll, "Premature Anti-Fascists, Again," *The Volunteer* 25 (December 2003): 5–8.

13. John Gates, *The Story of an American Communist* (New York: Nelson, 1958), 80.

14. John Gerassi interview with Milton Wolff, June 6, 1980, and December 8, 1980, Gerassi; also see Manny Harriman interviews with Irving Goff, August 24, 1980, and with Edward Lending and Vincent Lossowski, January 26, 1976, ALBA.

15. John Gerassi interview with Milton Wolff, June 6, 1980, Gerassi; Robert Colodny Papers, ALBA.

16. See Eugene Dennis, aka Tim Ryan, memorandum, "Notes on Some of the American Volunteers of the International Brigade," May 19, 1941, Communist Party of the United States of America, "Files of the Communist Party of the USA in the Comintern Archives" (New York: IDC Publishers, 1999–2000), reel 314; Harvey Klehr, John Earl Haynes, and Fridrikh Igorevich Firsov, *The Secret World of American Communism* (New Haven, Conn.: Yale University Press, 1995), 259–92 argues that this underground work did not begin until the fall of 1941 after the German invasion of the Soviet Union.

17. Quoted in *Stars and Stripes*, March 14, 1945.

18. Robert Colodny Papers, ALBA.

19. James Ramsay McDonald (1866–1937), one of the founders of the British Labor party, was elected prime minister in 1924.

20. Norman Thomas (1884–1968) was a leader of the Socialist party of America and six-time presidential candidate.

21. Brookwood Labor College Collection, Walter P. Reuther Library of Labor and Urban Affairs, Wayne State University, Detroit, Michigan.

22. Tucker Smith was the director of the Brookwood Labor College.

23. John L. Lewis was the chairman of the Committee for Industrial Organizations, later the Congress of Industrial Organizations.

24. Veterans of the Abraham Lincoln Brigade Collection, Bancroft Library, University of California, Berkeley.

25. *Mundo Obrero* was a Spanish Republican newspaper.

26. Almeria was a city in southern Spain bombed by the fascists in 1937.

27. Cooks Lit refers to the Thomas Cook Travel Agency and Mussolini being figuratively carried on a litter.

28. Karl Marx Hof refers to an apartment complex in Vienna built by the Austrian Social Democratic party.

29. Angelo Herndon was an African American Communist convicted for violating Georgia's criminal insurrection law after he helped organize an interracial hunger march in Atlanta in 1932. In 1937 the United States Supreme Court found Georgia's insurrection law to be unconstitutional.
30. Carcassone is a city in southwestern France.
31. Judas Maccabeus led a revolt against the Roman overlords in Judea. His victory in 165 B.C. is celebrated by the holiday of Chanukah.
32. Documents in the case of Don Henry, Records of the Special Committee on UnAmerican Activities, 1938–1945, Records of the U.S. House of Representatives, Record Group 223, Center for Legislative Archives, National Archives, Washington, D.C.
33. Dr. Edward R. Henry was a relative of Donald Henry living in New York.
34. Taurets are machine gun shells.
35. Juan Negrin was a Republican prime minister of Spain during the Spanish Civil War.
36. Dolores Ibarruri (1895–1989), known as La Pasionaria, was a Communist deputy in the Cortes during the Spanish Civil War. Her famous phrase "the fascists shall not pass! No Pasaran!" became the battle cry for the Republican Army.
37. This essay was published as a pamphlet by the Negro Committee to Aid Spain (1938).
38. Dijbouti was a French colony bordering Ethiopia.
39. Milton Wolff Papers, University of Illinois Library, Urbana-Champaign, Illinois.
40. Ibid.
41. Rolfe (1909–1954) was an author and activist. During the Spanish Civil War he was editor of *Volunteer for Liberty*.
42. Bennett Cerf was an editor at Random House.
43. "Quondam" means former or previous, creating a play on words since Random House was Rolfe's former publisher.
44. Batea is a small town near Madrid.
45. Published in *The Volunteer for Liberty*, January 1940.
46. Neville Chamberlain (1869–1940) was prime minister of Great Britain from 1937 to 1940.
47. Colonel Segismundo Casado was the leader of a group of anti-Nationalists who took over the Spanish government in the spring of 1939 and tried unsuccessfully to negotiate a peace treaty.
48. Martin Dies (1900–1972) was a Democratic congressman from Texas and chair of the House Committee on Un-American Activities.
49. Father Charles Edward Coughlin (1891–1979) was a Catholic priest from Royal Oak, Michigan. His radio broadcasts during the 1930s were enormously popular. They often combined economic populism with racism and antisemitism.
50. Dr. Leo Eloesser was a cardiothoracic surgeon who worked with Medical Aid for Spanish Refugees in San Francisco. He brought an entire medical group to serve in the Spanish Republican Army in 1937–38. Bruzzichesi was one of nurses in this unit.
51. Edouard Daladier was prime minister of France from 1938 to 1940.
52. Cerbere and Perpignan were towns in southern France where the French government established detention camps for Spanish refugees.
53. Communist Party of the United States of America, "Files of the Communist Party of the USA in the Comintern Archives" (New York: IDC Publishers, 1999–2000), reel 314.
54. Levenson was a Lincoln Brigade veteran.

CHAPTER TWO

AT WAR WITH THE ARMY

Since the German invasion of the Soviet Union in June 1941, the Veterans of the Abraham Lincoln Brigade (VALB) had been campaigning aggressively for U.S. entry into the war. In November, the organization published a pamphlet, *Western Front Now!*, written by National Commander Milton Wolff, advocating the invasion of Europe, perhaps as a way of liberating Spain from Franco's dictatorship. Wolff urged President Roosevelt to declare war on Germany immediately. The Japanese attack at Pearl Harbor gave the Lincoln veterans what they wanted. On December 8, 1941, Wolff sent a one-sentence telegram to the president: "We who fought the Fascist Axis in Spain proudly volunteer to march shoulder to shoulder with our fellow Americans for the final crushing of this menace to the independence and democracy of America and all peoples."

By then, numerous Lincolns were already serving in the military, having enlisted in defiance of the VALB's original nonintervention position or having been drafted under the national conscription laws. Like Lincoln veterans in civilian life, they expressed a sense of relief that the tensions between their political beliefs and national policy were over, at least for the duration of the war. During the following weeks, dozens of the veterans enlisted for what they were sure would be the final battles against fascism. Most were confident that the demise of Hitler and Mussolini would bring the downfall of their old enemy General Francisco Franco. By the end of the war, at least 425 Lincoln veterans had served in the U.S. armed forces and another one hundred in the Merchant Marine and nursing corps.

As they entered military camps for assignment and basic training, the Lincolns were pleasantly surprised at what they found. Nearly all commented on how good the food was, in contrast to their garbanzo bean diet in Spain. They also commented favorably on the abundance of supplies, the quality of their weapons, and the sophistication of the military organization. These advantages stood in notable contrast to their experience in Spain. The Lincolns would repeat these points throughout the war as U.S. industrial production soared to meet military demands and the army achieved what seemed to be logistical miracles in fielding invasion forces.

The Lincolns also felt satisfaction from their reception among the rank and file. Although they discovered that many soldiers knew little about the Lincoln Brigade and the Spanish Civil War, the fact that they were combat veterans put them in the spotlight, even among officers. Most of the Lincolns took these opportunities to educate their buddies about the antifascist nature of the war. They acknowledged meeting a mixed response to these efforts. Nevertheless, they remained optimistic that the average GI Joe, if properly instructed in the war's objectives, would understand why they had fought in Spain and why they had to defeat fascism in World War II.

These beliefs emerged clearly in the Lincoln veterans' participation in a study of fear in battle that was conducted during World War II by psychologist John Dollard of Yale University's Institute of Human Relations. Seeking to analyze the psychological attributes that made for good soldiers, Dollard had begun his research among World War I veterans at the American Legion post in New Haven. He soon discovered that the old doughboys had little experience with modern mechanized warfare ("the dive bomber, the Blitz, and the modern tank").[1] Dollard then approached the VALB. With financial support from the Rockefeller Foundation and the consent of both the Communist party and, unknown to the Lincolns, the Federal Bureau of Investigation, he interviewed twenty veterans about a variety of issues related to their war experiences.[2]

Dollard used the interviews to develop a 44-page questionnaire that took about five hours to complete, and he employed Lincoln veteran John Murra, a graduate student in anthropology, to survey three hundred veterans. The study was published in 1943 under the title *Fear in Battle* and later reprinted in the *Infantry Journal*. Based on the reported experiences of Lincoln veterans, the study described the varieties of stress and fear felt by combat soldiers and proposed strategies for controlling such problems. Besides receiving a favorable review from *Time* magazine, the project won praise from the Army's chief of morale services, who urged officers to use the research in training soldiers. The study's primary findings emphasized that fear among combat soldiers was nearly universal and therefore normal and that an intellectual understanding of why soldiers were placed at risk enabled them to control their emotions and perform well, despite their fear.

Underlying that conclusion was the major difference the Lincolns perceived between service in Spain and training in the U.S. Army: the quality of political education. Within the structure of the Spanish Republican Army and the International Brigades (of which the Lincolns were a part), each grade of the military organization, from the general staff and brigade headquarters to the battalion, company, platoon, and squad, had both a military officer with appropriate rank and a political commissar who was responsible for morale, education, and personal problems. Given the mistrust of the professional military whose leaders had rebelled under Franco, this double system protected the government from the army; the commissars technically outranked the military leaders.

Although in Spain, some rank-and-file soldiers complained about the political orthodoxy of the commissars, most came to appreciate the value of political education in strengthening the resolve of the fighting force. Once in the U.S. Army, they lamented the overall inadequacy of official instruction. As a result, in many cases, army commanders asked Lincoln recruits to prepare educational materials and to lecture to their fellow soldiers about the Spanish Civil War, the international conflicts that had provoked World War II, and the war's objectives. However, in many other cases, military officers disagreed with the Lincolns' participation in the earlier war and viewed these recruits as potentially subversive. As Saul Birnbaum wrote to the VALB office, "The Executive of the battalion is a stupid jerk who rabidly snarls that the Lincoln Brigade was not fighting for democracy."

Such negative attitudes soon became more apparent. Despite their realization that participation in the Spanish Civil War was politically suspect to government officials, Lincoln veterans were surprised to discover that the military had adopted policies that treated them as potential subversives. Instead of being assigned to basic training programs to prepare for war, many Lincoln veterans found themselves placed in limited service units, which included pro-fascists, Nazis, and German and Italian nationals who refused to fight against their homelands, as well as assorted misfits. "I hadn't looked forward to being in the Wehrmacht," veteran Jack Lucid wrote wryly from Camp Ripley, Minnesota, but "that is what I am in here." Angered and disgusted by such

circumstances, these veterans pleaded with their officers for trai.
into regular army groups, to no avail.

Other types of discrimination were less obvious, but equally frustrating.
Typically, army policy barred Lincoln veterans from officer training
school or did not allow them to graduate; denied them assignments to
combat units; and, often at the last minute, stopped them from
accompanying their units overseas. Such discrimination angered the
veterans, and they continually protested this unfair treatment through
military channels, as their letters amply document. In some cases, civilian
war workers encountered similar problems. Yet because a few Lincoln
veterans did manage to slip past the oversight of military intelligence
and received coveted combat assignments, cases of discrimination were
initially attributed to vaguely defined army policies or to the caprice of
particular officers.

By early 1943, however, VALB leaders had become convinced that orders
limiting the role of the Lincolns in the U.S. military expressed a government policy created in Washington. "It is simply and DEFINITELY A POLICY
established by the heads to effect [sic] us not as individuals under a
microscope, but as a whole on principle," concluded Milton Wolff, himself
a target of army intelligence. In January, VALB executive secretary Jack
Bjoze wrote directly to President Roosevelt to describe some incidents of
discrimination as well as examples of the loyalty of Lincoln veterans in the
war effort and concluded,

> We think it is now clear to all liberty-loving Americans that the cause of
> Spain was the cause of Democracy and was our cause. [If] This treatment
> of our Veterans, and there can be no other conclusion, is being meted out
> because we fought in Spain, then certainly some steps must be taken to
> correct this situation.

Gathering additional testimony from other veterans, including Wolff,
Moishe Brier, Jack Lucid, and many others, Bjoze went to Washington,
D.C., to meet with sympathetic political leaders, including Representa-
tives John Coffee (D-Wash.), Warren Magnuson (D-Wash.), and Secretary
of the Interior Harold Ickes, as well as the syndicated journalist Drew
Pearson, whose "Washington Merry-Go-Round" column appeared in
many newspapers. The result was a series of news stories, beginning in
April 1943, that described various cases of Lincoln veterans who had been

denied the right to fight as equals in the U.S. Army. *P.M.*, a progressive New York newspaper, headlined the problem in May 1943: "'Premature' Anti-Fascists Still in Army Doghouse." And a handful of congressmen publicly demanded that the army explain its policy.

Such publicity broke the dam, somewhat. To be sure, War Department officials continued to deny that political discrimination existed and cited as evidence the well-known examples of Lincoln veterans Bob Thompson and Herman Bottcher, who had served overseas and won medals for their courage under fire. But after Pearson's articles appeared, many Lincolns now found that their applications for regular service were approved and they began to ship out for overseas assignments. Nevertheless, the discrimination against Lincoln veterans in the military did not end in 1943, as many of their letters show. Through 1944 and 1945, moreover, outspoken members of Congress, including the House Committee on Un-American Activities, continued to challenge the commissioning of specific Lincoln veterans as military officers.

These contradictory experiences reinforced the Lincolns' self-identity as a special group. Whether celebrated as heroic "fighting antifascists," as their songs proclaimed, or hazed as "premature antifascists" by government leaders, the Lincolns understood that their service in Spain had made them unique. Many veterans saw themselves as exemplars of what a good soldier ought to be—militarily adept and politically astute. "All in all," wrote Jerry Weinberg, soon after entering the Army Air Corps in 1942, "it's a tough job living up to what's expected of a vet, but I'm trying." The persistent Weinberg would be shot down in a raid on the Ploesti oil fields in Rumania in 1943, manage to escape from an internment camp in neutral Turkey, and return to England to fly again, only to be shot down and killed in another raid, becoming one of the unsung Lincoln heroes of World War II. That some of their contemporaries opposed their principles and harassed their efforts to serve in the U.S. Army merely confirmed the Lincolns' distinctive identity. "And if I ever doubted whether I've done (and am doing) my share for progress," wrote the frustrated veteran Adolph Ross, "I no longer have any uncertainties. These reactionaries in Washington have reminded me that I haven't done so bad after all."

The letters written by Lincoln veterans during training reveal their changing attitudes as they learned more about U.S. military policy and the roles they could expect to play. They began by expressing optimism about contributing to the war effort and never doubted that the American people would sympathize with their antifascist stand during the Spanish Civil War. As they confronted obstacles to their participation in the war effort, they initially blamed individual officers for their troubles and endeavored to bring their cases to higher officials who, they were sure, would respond favorably to their pleas. Always the Lincolns assumed that if military leaders understood why they had fought fascism in Spain, the army would alter the policies that kept veteran antifascists from the war zones. For them, the Spanish Civil War was nothing less than the first battle of World War II. From the moment the United States entered the war, as Private Dan Fitzgerald wrote in the first letter that follows, the Lincoln veterans were determined to destroy fascism "once and for all."

I. WAR COMES TO AMERICA

FROM DANIEL FITZGERALD

Monday Morning

Dec. 8th, 1941

Dear Moe [Fishman],

Just a line to inform you that circumstances have changed that proposed date. I will have to postpone it to a later time—there is a little job to be done on the Axis in the meantime.

Whatever may come in the days ahead I intend to fulfill my obligations to my country and my ideals. I only hope that I will do nothing that will reflect anything else but credit upon those who have associated with me in the past. The memories and examples of Ray Steel, Doug Roach, [Hiram] Finley and Sam Levinger[3] are monuments to courage and inspiration at this time. I pledge myself to do my bit so we can smash the Axis once and for all. My best regards to the fellows.

Salud y Victoria

Pvt. Dan Fitzgerald

FROM LOUIS GORDON

Fort Eustis, Virginia
Dec. 8, 1941

Dear Moe [Fishman]—

Possibly recent events and the Declaration of War against Japan can best answer the question of my attendance at the Xmas dance. I'll try to have my wife attend for me.

Things are happening very fast in these parts, as you might well imagine. I believe the Army and Navy are geared high enough to cope with this and any future situation. Most of us here believe war with Germany and Italy will follow—also war between the Soviet Union and Japan.

There is a feeling of calm, quiet confidence in the air. No excitement, no running around, no joking—just a serious business which must be finished in the quickest possible manner.

Everyone feels that we are doing the right and only thing—and since the camp sent an enormous amount of men to Pearl Harbor, Schofield Barracks and other Near Eastern bases it strikes close to home, it's more personalized.

I guess most of our guys will be in the service pretty soon—those that can possibly make it. You'll probably have to hold up jobs for ten men yourself. You can do it, I'm sure.

I appreciate greatly your letters and I hope you'll find time to continue them.

Should I be transferred to any new place I will notify you of my new address. Also, remember how important packages are away from home. After all someone has to feed the censors!

Being in Anti-aircraft will probably mean plenty of action—of a new type to me, but I'm used to loud noises—if that's possible.

Manila is getting a taste of avion now. I'll close—regards to all around. Take care of yourself. If you want to know anything about anything to do with me, my wife is secretary and treasurer of the Paper Union Local 107- 54 E. 13th Street - Gr. 3- 1469. Pay her a visit—she's a good lookin blonde. (That should do it.)

Salud y Victoria
Lou

FROM WILLIAM AALTO[4]

December 9, 1941

[Fort Knox Kentucky]

Dearest Ed [Rolfe] and Maria [Mary Rolfe],

Un saludo carinosa del ejercibo americano éstá vez. [A heartfelt greeting from an American soldier, this time.]

In the armored force—our panzer division parallel. Am firing-sighting 75 mm. cannons, 37. mm.—30 cal. (=7 mm.) machine guns—and an American beauty. The 50 calibre[. . . .]

After 13 weeks (subject to C.W. notice) we'll probably go into active division, as we are a pretty intelligent compania. Not writing—seems after that end period in Conn. and NY—that I'm beginning to at last get to know—feel the American character.

My chauvinism is slowly being eroded by close contact with New Yorkers from all the lower classes.

Upon announcement of war, our captain declared

"Beat the living hell out of them"

and the previously cynical, antagonistic elements were submerged in really enthusiastic cheers and applause.

Morale is high—have snapped out of playing soldiers doldrums and are really het-up about winning the war.

Sorry I haven't written before, but our schedules here in this Armored Force Replacement Training Center leaves only 2 hours an evening to read (which I do constantly.) to write and to hold bull-sessions with the boys.

Spain gives me a good amount of prestige among boys. Could have become rating, but hate to push like ambitious b's do around here. I feel it's better to stay with the boys, officers heavily tinged with fascist leanings. German Army is their ideal prototype. The lads though are progressive in the main.

Someone has sent me Sunday [New York Herald-]Tribune sub. Clarina got me a daily PM sub and Ma sends me NM [New Masses][5] so plenty to read, together with [Herbert] Agar's [Louisville] Courier-Journal, which is competent job.

Any gossip of Hemingway, how's [Alvah] Bessies' book[6]—should I try to get it. Maria stronger and like Fritzie Kuhn,[7] how are your teeth, you old b——.

Bill Aalto

MEN WHO UNDERSTAND WAR-AIMS ARE BETTER SOLDIERS

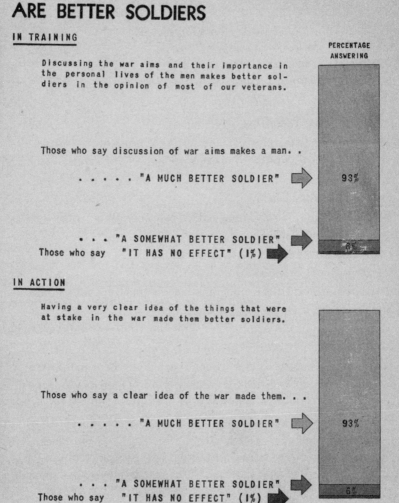

IN TRAINING

PERCENTAGE ANSWERING

Discussing the war aims and their importance in the personal lives of the men makes better soldiers in the opinion of most of our veterans.

Those who say discussion of war aims makes a man. .

. . . . . . "A MUCH BETTER SOLDIER"   93%

. . . "A SOMEWHAT BETTER SOLDIER"
Those who say   "IT HAS NO EFFECT" (1%)

IN ACTION

Having a very clear idea of the things that were at stake in the war made them better soldiers.

Those who say a clear idea of the war made them. . .

. . . . . . "A MUCH BETTER SOLDIER"   93%

. . . "A SOMEWHAT BETTER SOLDIER"
Those who say   "IT HAS NO EFFECT" (1%)   6%

From John Dollard's *Fear in Battle*

2. EARLY RESPONSES TO MILITARY LIFE

FROM MIKE FELLER

Feb. 2, 1942

Dear Moe [Fishman]:

The letter you sent to Camp Upton reached me today at the Army Air Base at Selfridge Field, Michigan. It certainly was swell to hear from you.

We are treated rather nicely out here. The food is excellent. We don't get any "garbanzos" or "lentajes [lentils]."

I have been assigned to the Headquarters Squadron of the 3rd Air Base Group and according to the Lieutenant I should be very proud to be in it because I am "handpicked," to use his phrase.

Quite a number of men out here are learning for the first time who the Lincoln Brigade vets are. Others are beginning to realize that if Hitler & Co., were quarantined then, in 1937, it would have prevented the outbreak of the present war. Unfortunately, we don't get the proper reading material out here.

According to the semi-official reports I should be on the move sometime this week and shortly thereafter shipped overseas.

But you know the way the saying goes; "C'est la guerre"—.

Mike Feller

FROM SAUL BIRNBAUM

Fort Bragg, N.C.

March 1942

Dear Fellows

Just a short note to thank you for sending me Harold Smith's little manual[8] and the Auxiliary paper.

The moral[e] here is O.K. It seems that the Coughlinities,[9] Isolationists and other traitors have made very little impression on the average soldier.

The instruction here is excellent and the commanding caliber of a very high order.

The only shortcoming that I can see is that we need a fuller consciousness of the fact that we are a citizen army and that we are fighting for existence as a democracy. In short there should be lectures assigned us for education in democracy just as we receive education in fighting.

Appreciate very much getting as much news as possible and would like to have you send me ten copies (all I can spare out of 21.00) of Harold Smith's manual. Please give him my regards, the rest of the boys too, plus wives and children. We have many wives, haven't we?

Fraternally,
Saul Birnbaum

From Lawrence Lustgarten

Jefferson Barracks
Missouri
[1942]

Dear Hy,

I was extremely pleased to hear from you. I'm stationed here in Jefferson Barracks permanently as a drill instructor. This is the largest Air Corps Replacement Center in the country and new men keep arriving daily. My work keeps me fit and healthy as I'm out in the open all day. Moreover I have extremely refreshing contact with hundreds of men daily. These men are new recruits in our Army and as a drill instructor I feel I can be of no small service to them as this is their first introduction to Army life.

I'm known quite widely as a Vet of the Spanish War and for awhile literally hundreds of men plied me with questions on Spain and the war. Though they display very little knowledge of what occurred there, to a man they are extremely friendly and occasionally one of them has heard of the Lincoln Battalion and the International Brigades.

The men here are from all over the country and on the whole are typical of the average American youth. Many are quite backward but one and all evince a deep hatred of the Axis.

The first thing that struck me about our Army upon enlisting was the comparatively high degree of organization that exists and of course the excellent facilities that exist here compared with what we had in Spain. I've gotten over it by now but I'm sure every vet felt as I did when he enlisted.

I've just applied for an opportunity to become a flying cadet—to go to school to learn to fly (either as a pilot, bombardier or navigator). Whether I'll get the chance or not is another matter but I feel I have a halfway decent chance to go.

The general topics of conversation here in the camp are Gen. [Douglas] McArthur, who is looked up to by the average guy as an idol. The proposed pay raise for soldiers and the daily military events in the Far East, Southwest Pacific and the Russian front. It must be confessed, however, that the average guy here knows very little about what is happening as few read the newspapers.

Well I'll close now Hy. I'd like to hear from you again. Tell Hal Smith I don't quite get that crack of his but suspect the worst. And give him and his wife my sincerest congratulations and heartiest regards. Tell Tom Page that here you either shave daily, or else! (you regret it!)

Regards to all the boys

Sincerely, Larry Lustgarten

From Jerry Weinberg

Air Corps Technical School

Keesler Field, Mississippi

May 8th [1942]

Querido Amigos

Well they can't keep a good little man down. I qualified for Radio operators school and for Aerial Gunnery. I took the Aerial Gunners physical and passed. That means I'll be leaving for the Gunnery school shortly and I'll be flying soon. I always wanted to get back at some of those bastards who strafed us.

The fact that I was in Spain has won me the respect of all the men here, including those who are Pro-Franco. Those last mentioned show a silent respect by not daring to say any thing bad about the Brigade, at least in public. All in all it's a tough job living up to what's expected of a vet but I'm trying.

I still can't get over being in the air corps and the fact that I'll be part of a bomber crew. I wish all the boys could get this opportunity.

The Air Force is probably more "offensive" minded than any other of the service branches. This is so because of the nature of the weapons used,

The Washington

Merry-Go-Round

By Drew Pearson

Heroes of Lincoln Brigade Complain of Discrimination

TODAY in the State Department many of the reactionaries will admit they made a tragic mistake in boycotting the Spanish Loyalist government during the Spanish Civil War.

Had the career boys not thrown the United States on the side of Franco—and indirectly on the side of Mussolini and Hitler who were supplying Franco with arms—the American Army in North Africa today would not have to keep troops marking time on the borders of Spanish Morocco, worried over a Fascist thrust from Spain.

Even more important, many diplomats now believe that had the dictators been crushed in their practice war in Spain; had the United States shown it meant to throw its weight firmly behind democracies, the present war might never have happened.

Believing this even at that time —in 1936 and 1937—several hundred American youngsters went to Spain, enlisted in the famous Abraham Lincoln Brigade, fought for the freely elected Spanish Republican Government against Franco. Many of them were wounded. Many were killed, among them the son of Ring Lardner, famous American humorist. Those who came back, possessed a first-hand knowledge of modern warfare—warfare which many West Point graduates who ran the United States Army had not then tasted.

One Who Caught On

IN GERMANY, Hitler used the Spanish Civil War to test out planes, tanks and men.

But in the United States, most of the men who risked their lives to fight in the Lincoln Brigade against the dictators have experienced a peculiar fate. When they enlisted in the American Army, they say they were discriminated against, cross-ques-

tioned as if they were social outcasts, and many of them thrown into service battalions, which means kitchen police, cleaning stables, and doing manual labor for the duration.

Those few Spanish War veterans who have been given a chance have used their previous fighting experience to great advantage. Capt. Hermann Battcher, called the Sergeant York of the Pacific, rose from sergeant to captain, has been awarded the Distinguished Service Cross and the Purple Heart with Clusters..

However, Battcher is not an American citizen. All who volunteered to fight in Spain lost their citizenship at the instigation of the career boys in the State Department. Furthermore, Battcher got into the war early, before the War Department clapped down a thinly veiled discrimination against veterans of the Lincoln Brigade.

From Lieutenant Colonel To Private

For instance, here is the experience of several youngsters who fought against fascism in Spain and who wanted to fight against it in the American Army:

Approximately one year ago John Gates, a lieutenant colonel of the Fifteenth International Brigade in Spain, enlisted in the United States Army. In Spain Vincent Sheean and Herbert Matthews of the New York Times cabled back dispatches on his bravery. In the United States Army he joined the Fifty-ninth Armored Artillery Battalion, Camp Chafee, Ark., where he became a sergeant. Then as his unit was about to go overseas, his commander received a telegram from the Adjutant General in Washington ordering Gates transferred to a service unit—which means no combat service throughout the war.

No explanation was given. Two lieutenant colonels thought so much of Gates that they inter-

vened. But nothing happened. There was only mysterious silence in Washington.

Finally Gates sent a letter to President Roosevelt.

"There is no greater honor," he wrote, "than to fight for one's country. Am I so base that I should be denied that right? What better way to prove one's loyalty than on the field of battle?

"I am supremely confident that if the board of officers were to review the case, or a special investigating officer appointed, the recommendation would be to return to my former unit. Our men are fighting gloriously in Africa and the Pacific. I only ask to take my place alongside them."

But the letter got no further than the War Department. No board of review was appointed. Apparently Sergeant Gates had committed the unforgivable crime of fighting for Loyalist Spain.

This is only one of many, many cases. George Cook, a lieutenant in the Lincoln Brigade, entered the Fort Benning, Ga., Officers Training School, Twenty-third Company, last December. All his mail was opened and read. He attained a high standing in his class, but suddenly in the eighth week of training, he was yanked out and transferred to the medical department along with over-age men. No explanation was given and no board of review granted.

"Some Unseen Hand"

ANOTHER case is that of Sergt. Irving Fajans, also in the Fort Benning Officers Training School, Twenty-ninth Company. He had been wounded in action in Spain, attained high marks in officers' school, had been permitted to buy his uniform and make all preparations for receiving a commission.

But one day before graduation, he was suddenly told he could not graduate and was transferred to the Fourth Service Command, Atlanta, where he will work out the war.

Again take the case of Pvt. Alvin Warren, who after three months' basic training at Fort Knox, was asked by his company commander to remain as cadre training personnel. He had fought in Spain for a year and a half and his experience was considered valuable by his immediate superiors.

Then suddenly he was transferred to Fort Benjamin Harrison, Ind., to a company of limited service men including Italians, German aliens, and others not allowed to enter combat units.

Then there is the case of Morris Brier, who entered Officers Training School at Camp Croft, Seventeenth Company, was rated second in his class, but on March 23, three days before graduation, after purchasing his officer's uniform, was told for some mysterious and unexplained reason that he could not graduate. He was transferred to a headquarters station complement.

These are only a few of many cases where some unseen hand, similar to the influences found in both the State and War Departments in the past, have reached in to penalize the youngsters who were far-sighted enough to see what was going on in Spain and to risk their lives to stop it.

Meanwhile the War Department has commissioned as a major, Harry Brown of York, Pa., even while he was indicted for tax frauds (late convicted); and also commissioned as lieutenant colonel, Freeman Burford, of Dallas, Tex., previously indicted on a charge of conspiring "to defraud the United States" and paying $148,000 in one-dollar bills to Seymour Weiss and former Governor Leche of Louisiana. Leche and Weiss pleaded guilty, were imprisoned, but Burford managed to block extradition from Texas to Louisiana, and now has been rewarded with a lieutenant coloneley in the United States Army, while youngsters who fought the battle of Spain remain privates.

THE WASHINGTON POST: WEDNESDAY, APRIL 14, 1943

ISSUED BY THE VETERANS OF THE ABRAHAM LINCOLN BRIGADE
100-5 th Ave., N.Y.C.

Drew Pearson, "The Washington Merry-Go-Round," reprinted by The Veterans of the Abraham Lincoln Brigade from the *Washington Post*, April 14, 1943 and, although the air force is divided into two groups, Combat and Interceptor commands, which are offensive and defensive respectively, everyone speaks of the offensive. Our chaplain spoke of bombing Tokeo and then going straight on to Berlin. It should be the other way around but I won't argue with him now. The thought is still a good one.

I could make a few criticisms. One is that none of our lecturers, up to this time has mentioned the Red Air Force or pointed out the lessons of the Eastern front. I wouldn't question him because he might be [a] rat and his answer could do more harm than not bringing up the matter at all. We discuss it in our barracks. The Red Army has certainly won the admiration of the men. With few exceptions the boys are all in favor of opening up a "Western front" now, to aid the Red Army.

I would like to have Jesse Wallach's address and if possible will you send my address to Marty Hourihan. Tell some of the boys to write to me.

I'd also like to hear from Milt Wolff. Tell him if its necessary I'll study up on my Spanish and French.

Regards to all,
Jerry Weinberg

FROM MILTON WOLFF[10]

6/29—42

Darling! [Ann Wolff]

Today we got the works. We were uniformed, inoculated, vaccinated and interviewed. At the interview Jerry [Cook] and I got what was expected. But for me it does not matter—as you know.

I didn't do so bad on the tests—106 + 118. Very strange that I should do better in the mechanical aptitude than in the other. I really don't think that we shall be here very long.

I don't look too bad in a uniform. Soon as we can we shall take pictures and send them along.

What is new on the house? On B, the wolf? & etc.?

The interview tried to determine the following:

1. was I a C.

2. did I know any

3. who sent me

4. why did I go

5. why now

6. How did I become a Major

And an assurance that I would have a rank in this army—such assurances aren't worth much. [. . .]

    Love,

    Milt

From Peter Reiter

7/21/42

I am sending my best wishes to the Abraham Lincoln Brigade Veterans.

I am getting along swell. I like the place and I am in a good outfit. I am feeling happy and we are all feeling happy. I am proud to be an American, and there's no dirty yellow dog take my "liberty" away that dirty rotten son of a bitch, rotten Hitler, and rotten Mussolini take our liberty away, that will never be done. We are going to destroy all those rotten son of a bitches off this earth and we will never stop till there wiped out clean. That rotten son of a bitch took our liberty away from us in Austria, Hungary, Czechoslovakia, Yugoslavia, Spain. now that dirty son of a bitch try to take the American "Liberty" away. But it will never work. We are going to destroy all these Cock Suckers. We will never stop before they are all gone.

I volunteered for service in the U.S. Army to help win the battle.

I don't want to run around in a city as a coward, and when we have destroyed the yellow dog, Hitler, and Mussolini we will have peace all over the Universe.

I am sending my best wishes to all of you. I am proud to be in the American Army, and I am proud of our president and our highest officials in our armed forces who will lead me in the battle.

I went into the war in 1914 in the world war till 1918. In 1919 I fought in the Hungarian army for liberty. 1937–38 I fought in Spain to free our selves from all dictatorships.

1942—I am in the U.S. army, the army that I like. The leaders are awful nice to me from the highest to the lowest.

    Peter Reiter

FROM DR. SIDNEY VOGEL

[Camp Rucker, Georgia]

Wednesday, Aug. 26, 1942

Dear Ethel and Lisa [Vogel]:

[. . .] Now to here. As I told you this week our C.O. (Commanding officer) arrived. He has been to work organizing us and to-day for the first time we had something to do so that I did not lie around reading all day. As C.O. he must organize the future hospital so that we are trained and organized to set up when we get to where we are going. Incidentally we had a pool of all officers, $1 per head, number with country picked out of hat (14 countries) as to where we are going. I picked Iceland so that I have small chance of winning. All we do know is that from here we go. To get back to my story. I was placed on the medical side and my major put me as head of psychiatry—neuropsychiatry. Why? because I know a little and no one else knew anything. It really isn't important and I don't mind—that we'll discuss some other time. Incidentally all the men are competent— and the head of surgery is a trained surgeon and his assistants also well trained—better than me—but that too is not part of this story. He has also mapped out a plan of training—drills, gas, tents, marches, etc. and to-day I saw two swell training films—one a German one—apparently confiscated— on parachute troops and the other on anti-aircraft protection—this sure is a real army—everything from soup to nuts—and I am learning. As other part of this training period each of us were assigned certain studies— things to read—and we are to present it—so that all of us will know what makes a hospital in the army tick. My topics are one lecture on the organi- zation of the neuropsychiatry department and the other on sanitary control of a hospital. Others have different topics etc. (When I see all there is to know and learn I realize what a big job I did in Spain.) My C.O. knows about my previous experience—and one other guy that I have been friendly with. But otherwise the problem or rather topic has not been brought up. And you know how quiet and unassuming I can be. Anyhow, at to-day's conference—we have one three times a week to discuss what we are doing, plans, suggestions etc. the question of morale was touched on in a superficial but sincere way by the C.O.—just in passing. To-night at dinner we all happened to be together and the C.O. opposite me, suddenly at dessert asked me my opinion re certain things based on my experiences. Suddenly I found the whole table of officers had stopped talking, had crowded closer and were listening to me as I held forth with mouths agape (this quiet guy had all that experience and we never knew it) and the C.O. kept me going, and wants me to talk to everyone re all these things such as morale etc. hospital, surgery in war etc. so that "we who have had no experience will be better prepared from having been told what to expect etc. etc." And I asked him if I had his permission to draw on my experience when I give my talks on Sanitation and the organization of the neuropsychiatric division he said by god yes—we need it. And as we walked from the table I could see them all look in childish amazement at me. And I could see that my stock was up since I had not talked about it to anyone. So you see it cropped up. I was waiting and wondering when.

So that's all for the bedtime story.

Love to you and Lisa (don't tell her that I would rather be in your bed than hers).

Our C.O. is a swell guy.

XXXX Kisses for Lisa

Sid

FROM DR. SIDNEY VOGEL

[Ft. McClellan, AL]
Saturday
2-13-43

Dear Ethel [Vogel]:

[. . .] I must tell you about the 'short arm' inspection, which I already mentioned to you[. . . .] Yesterday I did it again and so can give you a better report. Well it seems that 1x a month by AR [Army Regulation] # something, men (enlisted) get a 'short arm' inspection. Actually it is supposed to be an examination for everything but it resolves itself actually to contagious diseases—especially venereal. Since I am given an hour to examine over 200 men you can imagine how thoro it is. The men are lined up by a tough 2nd Lt. and are undressed except for a coat. I sit on a chair and as each comes to me he opens his coat and lifts his arms so I can see his arm pits (crabs, etc.) and then after a quick glance at his chest & belly we get down to the short arm. And since they don't know at this stage of their training how to adequately expose themselves for this inspection, I have to repeat almost 200 times "do this," "do that," and "next," so that I must have suggested a phonograph record for the next time. The 200 men seemed like 800 to me even tho the Lt. helped by bellowing instructions. Well, with this picture, and the shyness of men exposing themselves in this way, I'd like to make a few observations. Altho I am a doctor and have seen parts of bodies before, I have never seen so many of the same part in so short a time. And it is surprising to see the variations in size, color, form, contour, and associated characteristics of surrounding parts. It surprised me as a doctor, and I think a paper ought to be written. True my judgment may have been warped by the speed up of the work and I was rather tired afterwards, but I think I am right in saying that there are red ones, pink ones, blue, orange & yellow; long, short & medium; twisted, straight, curved; symmetrical & asymmetrical; efficient looking and non; disproportionate; etc. ad infinitum and not ad nauseam. This impressed me so much (and also the Lt. who had his nose right in it in a rather unscientific 2nd Lt. way much to the embarrassment of the men) that I suggested the use of these variations instead of fingerprints and am going to suggest the same to [FBI Director] Edgar Hoover. There just aren't 2 alike, which observation probably isn't very acute of me.

As I told you the 2nd Lt., a swell tough guy with a Polish name, and speech, and warm understanding young face, had that face right into the source of my work, much to the annoyance of the men. He too must have been amazed and he kept asking me various questions re each one as his wonderment increased. I of course had no time to answer all. He also made rather pertinent general observations which I too could of made, but I had work to do.

One case of crabs aroused an exclaim of excitement from the Lt. and he insisted on a personal exam. And when I told him I had had them 2x etc. he broke down and openly told me how he had had them, and a warm bond between me, himself and the patient developed. And that's all. And that's why, in overcoming my insomnia, I no longer count sheep. So good night little boys and girls until to-morrow at 6 P.M. (If Allan had been writing this story he would have drawn pictures, which would have made the story 'Short Arm' sound better.) [. . .]

All my love,
Sid

FROM EDWARD LENDING

Friday the 29th

1943

Hola Camaradas!

Furlough's over. Back at the old post, Anti-Aircraft. 40 mm Bofors Guns and 50 cal. MG's. This outfit is a jig-time producer of crack batteries. Have been assured by Battery Officers we'll be shipped within 5 months.

It's a comparatively soft—if busy—life. The regime is plenty tough. But the physical conditions are so infinitely more comfortable that you appreciate in a fresh light how tough we really had it. And the familiar, nostalgic beefs and gripes make you chuckle inside.

I'd be a model soldier, I think, if I weren't so incredibly absentminded. Take yesterday, for instance. Yesterday, amigos, was one for the books!

All day long we prepared us—persons and huts—for inspection. We washed and scrubbed and scoured and polished. Then came the big moment.

The door flew open. In strode the Top Sarge, Two Looeys, and the Battery Captain.

"Attention!" I barked as I snapped into same and saluted briskly. Holding the salute, I sounded off stentorially, "Sir—Private Lending in charge of Hut 13."

I saw consternation capture every face in the hut-officers and bunkmates! For what couldn't have been more than 10 seconds—but what felt like many hours—I was just deeply bewildered.

AND THEN I KNEW . . .

The brisk salute I was holding ended in a clenched fist. So help me modesto!

Thus ended the cozy anonymity I had been enjoying. What probably saved my soul from being dispatched by the firing squad at dawn was the fact that I had reported I.B. experience at the induction center. So it was on my service record which had been transmitted here and my explanation was plausible, if not relished.

What followed was an invitation to see the Old Man, "in his office, suh."

We had an interesting talk tho I couldn't ascertain his sympathies. In any case, I broached the question of morale, respectfully unburdened myself of some opinions on the subject. He invited me to put them on paper, which I've already done. In addition, he insisted that I write up our evening's experience for the "Add to Prize Boner Dept." of Camp Hulen Searchlight. Said he'd welcome any other stuff I might submit on Spanish War Experience. [. . .]

Ed Lending

FROM MILTON STILLMAN

May 27, 1943

Dear Comrades:

It's been a long time since I last heard from you or I last wrote to you. The Volunteer For Liberty you first sent me sure made me feel good. I would like to know why I do not hear more oftener from the organization. I sure would like to know what is going on in our organization. How are things (I am down in Texas in an Internment Camp that has war prisoners yes nazi prisoners that were captured in N. Africa. The prisoners that we have here at present are very young nazi they are from 14 years of age up to about 25 years old. Yes most of the prisoners are only about 14 or 17 years old. They believe that by next year we will be their prisoners. They were told by Hitler that their air force had bombed NY so much that it was ruined. They could not believe their eyes when they landed in NY from N Africa and saw NY had not been bombed at all. They also believe that Russia was finished off because most of them were transferred from the Russian front to N. Africa. They sure are treated swell out here. They are not made to work hard. They seem to be very happy to be captured but you know the fascist one can not trust them at all. We are given orders to shoot to kill if and when they try to make a false move. So far they have not given us any trouble.) I would like to here from the organization more often. Lets here what the vets are doing with you. So until I here from you. I remain vet.

Milton Stillman

3. DISCOVERING PROBLEMS

FROM JOHN GATES

Fort Sill Oklahoma

Feb, 12, 1942

Dear Milt [Wolff]

Couldn't pick out a better day than today to write to you, altho I'm plenty sore that this day that is so important for all Americans and for us who were part of the Lincoln Brigade, and that is so full of meaning now both in general and in particular with respect to the imminent fall of Singapore, went completely unobserved in this U.S. Army post. It may be that a big "reason" was the fact that we're in the South and the presence of so many southerners here (altho that's the best reason for observing it), but I wonder in how many northern (!) posts the day was observed? I think rather that the failure to recognize this great American day is due mainly to the continued lamentable separation between national and military policy (as the Roberts[11] report pointed out) and so a great opportunity is lost that could have been used to build morale further and help accelerate the building of the American army of victory. This would have never happened in Spain, but that was a "foreign" war of course, as some people who should have known better still think, and who still question the loyalty to America of those who fought in Spain, because of their political beliefs. As you probably know, I was recommended by my battalion for officers school but turned down by the examining board despite the fact that I was more qualified from the point of view of previous education, military experience, and present record than many others accepted, only because as I must assume, of my political beliefs. But just as many people have come to understand many things (and the most important things) they did not before, so they will finally learn that just because of such beliefs there can be no greater loyalty to America. At least we commemo-rated Lincoln's birthday, both in word and deed.

Of course, I don't need to tell you who know me so well, that all this only has the effect of spurring me on to be still a better soldier for Uncle Sam and to do my best to prove to the powers that be that their opinion was wrong. Nor does all this alter the fact that, looking at the picture of this war in all its vast entirety, the correct strategy is being and will be carried thru by the United Nations, compared to which cases like mine are like a drop in the ocean, as the poet says. Still, the army builds men, but it is also true that men build the army, and many things little and big remain to be done that will finally add up to victory.

The kind of letter you wrote is exactly the kind I want to receive. Contrary to your surmise I am not getting as newsy letters from other sources, more informed or otherwise, so keep it up.

I was extremely sorry to hear about John Kozar. I knew him fairly well, in fact had a quite a bit to do with his rehabilitation when he returned from Spain—he was a very good guy. I think something ought to be done to perpetuate his name, a memorial plaque or something—along the style of the things done with regard to Capt. Colin Kelly.[12]

It's a great idea—the open letter to our Canadian buddies. If not already sent I would appreciate your sending me a draft copy, and if the officers here agree, I would be more than glad to sign it. I think it's a great patriotic act. I assume it will be a very tactful tho blunt letter, since we do not want to appear as meddlers in the affairs of other nations.

With respect to the [Arthur] Munday-[Lou] Gordon argument, all modern guns of all calibers, from 37 to the highest are being made with split trails—it gives greater stability and facilitates greater elevation.

I don't know when the Memorial banquet is coming off, but in case this gets to you before then maybe you can use this little message from myself and [Samuel] Slipyan: "Now it is clear that the Americans who died in Spain did not die in vain. Like those who died at Gettysburg, they helped to make possible the United Nations, whose firm unity, gallant armies, and self-sacrificing peoples, will destroy the fascist axis, and thus forever guarantee that government of the people, by the people, and for the people shall not perish from the earth."

Let me know of other occasions and whether you would want any messages from me. You better hold on to my vets card and see that my dues are paid up. I leave here about the beginning of March. Where—? But I hope its Ireland. Regards to all.

Yours,
Johnny

P.S. No I am not Napoleon but if the artillery helped to make him what he was, it might help me a little bit too, or do you think it's hopeless?

Fort Dix, NJ

July 27 1942

Darling [Ann Wolff]—

[. . .] We went to see the sgt in charge of shipments and after an hour's search for our records he was ready to give up—but we slipped him a hint or clue—by saying we were in Spain. "Oh! That's a different story!" said he and off he went. In 10 minutes he was back. "I know the story on you two."

"Yes, but we don't." said I.

"Oh, ho," laughed he, "don't worry, you'll be shipped soon. Come around Thursday and [if] your not shipping over the weekend, I'll fix you a three-day pass."

All together he was very nice and respectful to us. Me he gave several knowing looks. So what?

Just as we are getting over the "crabs" a professional thief raided three barracks, including ours. He made off with $150 in cash (according to rumor) and sundry watches.

Corporal said he would never bring his wife to live near an army post. "Why"? I asked.

"No morals in post," says he. "All these army wives lay like rabbits."

"Grossly exaggerated," says I. "And besides a wife who would two-time doesn't need any special locations for the act." "Furthermore," I warmed to it, "she could be unfaithful much easier at home." And cruelly, "if you won't bring your wife here because you fear promiscuity how in hell can you trust her back home."

I think I crushed him.

Met the first guy here who knew anything about Spain and who is definitely liberal and pro-loyalist. He was a newspaperman in Utica NY. Had a good talk with him. What a relief, I was beginning to think Spain never happened. [. . .]

Love,

Milton

From Milton Wolff[14]

August 15th, 1942

Darling [Ann Wolff]—

[. . .] I became a squad leader and now there is talk of my becoming an instructor—but not for me—not down here anyhow!

I know my letters are getting less frequent—but that is because the days are crowded right up to the hilt—and pfft, pfft—they fly right by—

We have gotten about 6 lectures on the war and I'll be dammed if anyone of them was worth a damn. Our little corporal made the best speech of all when he said "we are fighting for our freedom which is threatened by the rulers of Germany." period. First one to make a distinction. (Since then I have oiled my rifle).

I am in a Battalion of misfits, enemy aliens, and suspected nazis. I should say the Batt. includes the above categories. There are also other aliens and sundry others who seem to be regular. At my reclassification—I was practically forced to promise to take the officers test—so we're off to the races again. As soon as I become eligible I shall take it—tho I know that nothing will happen.

If you have trouble with B[ailey]—call Ivar Bryce[15] at the same number and ask him—"what the hell?" [. . .]

all my love, my love
Milton

From Gerald Cook

Camp Wheeler, Ga.
U.S. Army
[c. August 1942]

Dear Jack [Bjoze],

I don't know if Milt [Wolff] has written you of our change of locale. I can't remember his mentioning it so will presume he hasn't. A week ago we were shipped down here in the heart of the hottest country this side of Brunete. Georgia certainly can give off heat. (Perhaps that's why the governor is so full of hot air.) Day and night we're bathed in sweat. We use so many salt tablets that all our clothing is caked with the whitish stain of dried salt.

Despite that however our stay here is proving to be very interesting and instructive. Every day except Sunday we're on the field at work. A welcome relief after rotting at Dix. We've both been placed in charge of squads and are used in our platoons to help with the instructions. Feelers have been put out to estimate our attitude towards remaining here after our basic training period as instructors. But naturally we want to get to a permanent outfit (not a training center) and do some work there.

Indications of one sort and another point to the probable necessity of your launching a campaign on our behalf. Milt's battalion (he's in the 10th and I'm in the 11th) have been interviewed again and each man informed of the nature of his future work. Milt was told that because of his experience as a shipping clerk he would, in all likelihood, be attached to a quartermaster's outfit. His experience as a shipping clerk! Not a word of his experience as an infantry battalion commander. Of course he protested and will try to obtain a transfer to a combat infantry training battalion. I've yet to be interviewed but from the ages and types of men in my outfit it looks as though I'll be in the same position. In addition to all this I've neglected to add that of all the men who left Dix in our group Milt and I were practically the only citizens. And the group was liberally sprinkled with enemy aliens, some of whom stated at their interviews that they objected to fighting in the U.S. Army, against their own countries. Whether our being sent with them was coincidental or designed we can't stay. Or can we? So if you have any strings to pull—pull them!

Write and give us the low down on what's going on in town among the guys. Regards to everyone.

Salud

Jerry

From Daniel Fitzgerald

Hq Det 3d Bn. 47th Inf.

A.P.C.9

Fort Bragg, N.C.

August 29th 1942

Dear Moe [Fishman]:

This is to acknowledge a bit tardily it is true, but here it is; the package and letters you have sent.

The delay was caused by the false alarm that happened here—we thought we were heading for action, got all keyed-up and then—phooey, back to 4–6 more months of stagnation—Looks like some more fancy stalling on the 2nd Front. It is tough to get my perspective on the beam so much messing about is going on.

I have tried to get foreign or overseas duty—no soap—I tried to push my air cadet application and found out that they have tied a big can to my tail. I have sought a transfer to an air squadron which is due to go over—no soap.

Moe, I wish you would take this up to the Exec board—I mean the running around we are getting in the service. I was speaking to Syd Levine who passed thru here a while ago and he has the identical story. Definitely and concretely here is a concrete case of discrimination—my own. I apply for air cadet (bombardier) just after Pearl Harbor, I have as references [Representative Vito] Marcantonio [ALP–NY] and Blackie Myers;[16]—with flying colors I pass my physical exam; I score a 129 in the mental test where 90 is passing. I am accepted and on March 13th orders are received from Post Headquarters (originating in 4th Corps area) transferring me to Kelly Field Texas; just as I am to leave a phone call comes thru ordering my name deleted—this phone call and its message are confirmed in the special orders of the day March 17, 1942, issued by Post Headquarters Fort Bragg, over the signature of Col Kennedy, Post Commandant, and his adjutant, Capt. V. Robertson.

Now I appreciate the need for Vigilance and Investigation of all who receive commissions so I have waited for them to rescind that bit of discrimination but in vain—I cannot get to anyone to present my case. I have a clean record here, excellent, I have no police record, no felonies etc. Why the hell should I be denied a job I am qualified for just because I am a militant anti-fascist? The rightfully necessary laws and regulations against the 5th Column are being subverted by appeasers and defeatists to wreck morale, and fighting unity of our army.

Today I understand the Vets are working on a scheme to do certain work in co-operation with the army. Surely in all justice to our membership that projected scheme must be viewed alongside of this treatment we are receiving. I feel it is my responsibility to bring this to the attention of the leadership. We are fighting a 2 front war—one, against the axis armies, and secondly against all appeasing, defeatist, confusionist policies that hamstring our efforts for Victory—for example the fight against Jim Crow, for a mixed regiment, for the 2nd Front; for production etc etc. We will fight fascism under <u>all</u> circumstances under <u>all</u> obstacles. Yet we have the responsibility to smash all obstacles that are preventing us from mobilizing our full resources in this most desperate hour.

I am sorry I have to put this into correspondence but while I was in the City I failed to see any person in the office, only the girl was there.

Please write me confirming the receipt of this letter, and what is the opinion of the Executive Board.

Fraternally Dan Fitzgerald

From Eugene Morse

October 9, [1942]

Dear Moe [Fishman],

After all my other letters written to you in a carefree, happy vein this one must be a bit dour. As you know I had been very happy serving my country in the armed forces and had but one objective, to master the art of being a good solider, an efficient, effective, ruthless, disciplined soldier, whom my officers could depend upon in any emergency. I felt confident that together with my fellow soldiers wherever and whenever we went into action we would justify the confidence of our officers and our country. I feel it is a privilege as well as a democratic right to be in the United States Army and if the fortunes of war so decreed would gladly lay down my life in defense of our democratic way of life.

A great change has taken place during the past few weeks. Just about 3 weeks ago while I was out in the field with my old outfit, the 31st Engrs., I was called into the orderly room, told that I was transferred, and ordered to move out as soon as I had packed my belongings. No one knew anything about the transfer. Neither my commanding officer or anyone else. They only knew that I was to be "broken" as a private first class to a buck private and was to go into a quartermaster corps. Now I had volunteered for foreign service and I had a bare hope that this was an intermediate step. I couldn't imagine that I, with not the slightest experience in quartermaster work and an expert weapons and combat man, could possibly be permanently transferred to a Q.M. outfit.

Now I don't want in any way to disparage the Q.M. branch of our service.

It is just as vital to the winning of the war as any other branch of the service.

Without any efficient Q.M. Corps, the servicing and supplying of our troops would be impossible, and no arm of the service could operate efficiently. In this branch, as in every branch, soldiers who master their jobs and do their utmost, are doing their share toward the winning of the war.

To get back to the 358th Q.M. corps the one I am now a member of after being here three weeks I have a fairly good idea of what's what. This is a very unusual, I might even say mystery outfit. Here I am hesitant to write in detail as I do not wish in any form to violate any regulations as to secrecy which it has been necessary to establish to prevent any important information getting into enemy hands. However I will write about those things which are common knowledge in the community around here, and which, since nothing has been done to stop them, I presume are not military secrets.

First—this outfit is not attached to any group or regiment. Since it is a service outfit this is strange, since what or who are we to service? To date we have been doing odd jobs around this camp such as cleaning up for other outfits, collecting and sorting garbage and scrap, etc. No rifles or any other type of weapons have been issued up and although we drill 15–30 minutes each morning our main function is common labor. As you will see when I write about the men that compose the outfit that is unusual because many experts in different fields are here.

Now the most unusual feature of this outfit is the men who compose it. The majority of the men are foreign born, about 75% of them, most of them German, a sprinkling Italian. Now there's nothing definite that these men are pro German or pro Italian. What is definite is that these men are not enthusiastic about our struggle to defeat the axis. Many have relations in Germany or Italy and are obviously relieved that they are not in a combat outfit and presumably will not have to bear arms. Also amongst them are some few who are American born of German nationality who have been former members of the Bund.[17] Only one in particular do I know of definitely. His name is Katzmann and he was a Lemke[18]— Coughlin candidate for Congressman in Chicago. Now all of this group seems very satisfied and content to remain in what the general belief here is to be a labor non-combatant outfit[. . . .]

This in spite of the fact that many are from different branches of service, Air Corps, armored division, cavalry, infantry, signal corps, etc. And many are experts of one form or another. Some having had ratings as high as tech sergeants. Quite a few were buck sergeants.

On the other hand I cannot accustom myself to the idea of playing a non-combatant role in this war. I have been a consistent anti-fascist fighter all my life and I feel that my place is in the ranks of those troops who will come to death grips with our axis foes. I hope you will not feel this individual bravado but that on the basis of my combat experience in Spain, plus my training here, I am qualified to term myself an experienced, combat soldier. This of course is not enough, besides this a soldier must have the will to win, the discipline to obey orders, and an overwhelming desire to destroy the enemy even tho this cost his own life. All these I feel I, along with all other American soldiers, possess. I hate like hell to write in a manner which may make me out a conceited, pompous ass. But this thing is so very important and vital to me that even if you do get that impression, I've got to let you see the facts as I view them.

Now I can't speak for any of the other fellows who are here. But there's about a dozen, and more arriving daily, all native Americans, who I suspect feel somewhat like I do. They come from all over. From every branch of the service. One or two I knew in civilian life. They too are very bewildered and like myself, are becoming shocked and indignant as the suspicion arises in our minds that this company is one whose "members" are suspect of their allegiance to our country.

Because if this is not so—why so many unusual things? As a soldier I will obey any and every command of my officers without hesitation. It is not up to me to question any order, no matter what my views on it are. If I'm told to dig a ditch with my bare hands, even tho a shovel were besides me, I would do it without the slightest hesitation. If I'm called on to do anything that's my duty and my job to do it. But to do it as a soldier of the United States Army, proud of the noble heritage and tradition of our glorious nation and confident by marching arm in arm with fellow soldier who feel the same as I do. But if I have been placed here because of my political past, because on that basis someone responsible for my transfer has made the grave mistake of suspecting my allegiance, then I cannot, nor ever can accept such a status. Now the only way open to me to ask for a transfer to a combat outfit is to ask my company commander. To see him I must first obtain permission from the top-sergeant. I asked his permission and it was refused. I shall continue to ask for an interview hoping it will be granted. Meanwhile of course I do what every soldier does,—do my job to the best of my ability and contribute as much as I can toward the defeat of the axis.

The past few days two more vets have been transferred here. One is Jack Lucid from the west coast and Emil Churchich from Milwaukee, Wis. Same story as [mine]. Same feelings.

Thanks a lot for the package. Greatly appreciated it especially the book. Give my regards to all the boys my new address is Pvt Eugene Morse

> 358 L.M. Co-Service
> Camp Ripley
> Little Falls, Minn.

From John Lucid

October 14 [1942]

Dear Archie [Brown],

Didn't get a chance to see you when I dropped by on my way out. At the time I was considerably cheered up because it seemed that I would stop putting on fat as my contribution to the defeat of fascism. Altho I knew the outfit here was a Quartermaster company, even truck driving or warehousing is better than sitting on your ass—if you can't stay in a combat outfit.

However, I hadn't looked forward to being in the Wehrmacht. And that is what I am in here, in effect. Altho it is called the 358 Quartermaster, it consists largely of German nationals or people of German extraction. There are a few Italians. Moreover, these people are I am sure not a cross-section of German-Americans. Anti-semitism is the core of their intellectual processes. Not all of them perhaps, but most of them certainly. One bastard, perhaps the smartest character in the bunch, ran for congress with Coughlin backing some where in the middle west. He is a veritable sewer of Fascist ideology. Another guy, a well educated bloke! apparently, spent the hour before lights out last night spewing out filth that marks him as a careful student of Streicher and Goebbels.[19] And from down the line of double-tiered bunks came appreciations of his efforts.

There are also some anti-fascists here. Besides a small cadre of soldiers assigned to start the company—it is only a month or so old—there are three veterans of the International Brigades—you may know Morris, for one. And there is a guy named Spencer from Philadelphia who was active in the unemployed movement. And one from Wisconsin, a left-winger in the youth movement is here—his name is Hudson. Altogether ten or a dozen anti-fascists I think.

So, naturally it is necessary that these Nazi sympathizers and so on be put on ice. I would even say they are getting too good a deal here, as most of them are quite glad to be out of danger. There is little enough to do, and the sonsofbitches are far from downhearted. But, of course, the handful of antifascists want to do our part in the war and hate like hell to rub elbows with such a bunch. Or so I think.

Best Regards,

Jack

From Milton Wolff[20]

January 11th, 1943

Darling [Ann Wolff]—

[. . .] Of course I can understand why Jack called Dinah[21] on this business. . . . But that is all wrong. The only place for the thing, if they want to do anything about it, is in the open. So with Dinah contacts D.— right. He is the biggest fish in the bunch and he couldn't get commissions for three of his own men named F, G & A[22]—so what have you?

As for your idea of this being a test of our morale or something—I think that is utterly ridiculous—and pompous in a way. We are not so important as to have the big guns toy with us to test our endurance.

It is simply and DEFINITELY A POLICY established by the heads to effect us not as individuals under a microscope, but as a whole on principle. The principle itself being nothing new, nothing recently concocted for our benefit. It is the old, reliable "Keep 'em down" principle that holds good. No "hokus-pocus" to look for.

So it must be treated that way and fought out on that basis—just like the "anti-lynch" or "Poll-tax" business, only so much less important.

Fortunately for us a few guys like [Bob] Thompson & [Herman]

Boettcher and [Dan] Fitzgerald slipped under the wire and are doing a grand job.

For the rest—listen to this.

Irv Fajans writes,

"When I got back to McClellan I was appointed to Station Complement which means that as a Corporal I will have some petty chore to do. All the officers and men here look down at me as a "Benning failure". I can hardly explain to them. I don't know them—they don't know me.

"The other day I was interviewed by intelligence. In reply to my pointed questions they said that it was army policy not to give guys like me commissions—to reclassify them a 1B—and that I was probably stuck at McClellan for the duration!"

Thus ran his letter, not word for word—but that is the gist of it. [. . .]

So you see? They are putting the boots to us—and that's that.

No. I don't think that Dinah or her channels or her likes will pull us out of this one. It will take a fight. A fight linked up with the I.B'ers in N.Africa. Our dealing with Petain and now Mihailovetch[23]—it's part of the old pattern I outlined to you before.

And that is all my love

    Love as always
    Milton. . . .

FROM ALVIN WARREN

                            Jan 14, 1943
                            [Fort Benjamin Harrison
                            Indiana]

Jack Bjose [Bjoze]
Executive Secretary
Veterans of Abraham Lincoln Brigade
100 Fifth Ave
New York N.Y.

Dear Jack:

I am very sorry that I have not gotten the details of my situation to you earlier than this. I have been waiting to find out definitely as to the disposal of my request for a furlough to New York. It has been definitely refused, with the statement that I would not be permitted to enter any coastal areas. However, they are permitting me to travel to Chicago. So I guess you will have to answer all questions and act as my representative in N.Y. Below is a statement of the facts starting from the date of induction.

I was inducted into the Army June 8, 1942. I was held at Camp Upton, N.Y. for one month before being sent to a Replacement Training Camp. I arrived at Fort Knox Ky July 7 1942. Here I received my three months basic training attached to a gunnery platoon. During my training period, I was interviewed by my superior officers and recommended for Officer Training School. At that time I was the only drafted man out of my entire company to be so recommended. Later on I also received the highest recommendations for officers not specifically attached to my organization. (During that period I was promoted to Squad leader.) The company commander asked if I would [like] to stay on as a cadre (training personnel) after the training period was completed. I told him that I would rather not as I preferred to join an active division or enter one of the tank technical schools.

Near the end of the training period I was called in by the Battalion commander for an interview before going before the Officer Candidate School board. This interview lasted well over an hour, when the usual interview of this type lasted only about ten minutes. During the discussion many questions were asked about my attitudes toward labor unions, Harry Bridges,[24] my political affiliations etc. Several days later I was ordered to appear before the Medical Board for a physical examination for officers school. This in itself was unusual as it was customary to go before the Officers School Board (and if accepted, then go for a physical examination.) The examining officer turned me down because of certain alleged defects. I was told at that time, that the findings of the medical officer would not affect my status as an enlisted man and that I would be sent out to active service. From then on, until I was transferred, I functioned as acting cadre on the company training staff. The Commanding Officer told me at that time that I would soon go to a division or to one of the technical schools.

On October 27, 1942, I received a War Department order to entrain for Fort Benjamin Harrison, Indiana. Here, I entered the H.Q. and H.Q. Post

Company, 153oth Service Unit. Let me tell you something of the character of this company. It is composed of I-B or limited service men, many of whom, in my opinion, are malingerers. Further, there are Japanese, Germans, and Italians in this company who are not allowed to go to combat outfits. Some are suspected of Fascist-Nazi leanings. In addition there are deserters, A.W.O.L.s, drunkards, and general troublemakers. It was until recently, staffed by non-coms who have been rejected by regular outfits and many of whom have been in the guardhouse at one time or another. The main function of the company is that of a work outfit. There is no military training carried on at all. It supplies K.P.s, sentries, prison guards, work details and a host of other non-descript details. It has all the characteristics of a dumping place for undesirables and problems. You can well imagine the state of morale in such an outfit. Then there is this further fact. My mail is censored along with that of the foreign born and the suspects.

Upon my arrival at Fort Benjamin Harrison, I immediately asked my first sergeant if he knew why I had been sent there and what steps could be taken to secure a transfer into a combat outfit. He told me that he didn't know the reason that I had been sent in, but that more than likely it would fall into one of the three categories.

1. Physically unfit or limited services
2. Being of foreign origin, with relatives in the land of my nativity
3. Having participated in labor or progressive activities, such as my background as a member of the Abraham Lincoln Brigade during the Spanish War 1936–1938

I asked if he would attempt to find out from the Personnel Division, Post Headquarters what was the reason and what I do to effect a transfer. He said he would. The result was, as he stated, that H.Q. did not know the reason why, that I had merely been transferred in on a War Department order. He further suggested seeing the Post Chaplain to see what he could do about the situation. This I proceeded to do. The Chaplain told me, as a result of his inquiries, that I was there because of physical condition. He suggested as the next step, that I apply for a physical examination to find out the exact nature of the alleged deficiencies and take the necessary steps to correct them. I did this. The medical findings were that I was perfectly fit for full and active duty. With this information I went to the head of the Personal Division, Lt. Thomas, to find out what my exact status was and how I could be transferred out to combat duty. He told me that he did not know nor could he find out what the exact reasons for my being sent to this post were. This was in contradiction to the findings of Chaplain. He stated further, that there was no way I could be transferred to other services. The only developments since then is that the Military Intelligence has been visiting many of my former friends and employers, soliciting information of a political nature, about me.

In closing I want to remind you of certain facts which I think are important. You know that the Army is desperately in need of technical men. I have five years experience with Diesel engines. To make that experience more valuable to the Army, the year previous to my induction, I attended a Diesel Engineering School so that I could qualify as an expert in my field. This knowledge is needed by the Army now. Further, my two years experience in Spain has provided [me] with knowledge that can be very useful in the combat services of our Army. I feel that I can help achieve successes with a minimum of cost in life and blood. All I want out of the Army is the chance to serve like any ordinary American soldier to be able to go overseas to participate in the battles which will bring the downfall of [my] countries enemies. Any source of action which you may decide upon has my full agreement. You may use my name and the facts in the case in any way you see fit.

Fraternally Yours
Pvt. Alvin Warren

From Lawrence Lustgarten

Hotel Edison
"The House of Hospitality"
46th Street to 47th Street
Just West of Broadway
New York
4/43

Applied for OCS (Armored Force or Infantry) in July, 1942. After interview by Officers Board was rejected. Upon inquiry of the Lieut. in charge (in Miami) was told I didn't have enough experience in the Infantry of the Army of the U.S. Managed to see the file on OCS applicants in Lieut. Piavarnik's office in Miami—(National Hotel). My name had under it "not favorably considered upon recommendation of S-2."

Applied for Aviation Cadet in July 1942, several weeks later. Had all necessary papers—birth certificate, 3 letters of recommendation, and other data. After a month went by with no reply I inquired of the M/Sgt. in charge of Message Center in National Hotel, Miami what had happened to the papers. After checking, he told me S-2 had taken them. I inquired of a Capt. in S-2 about it but he replied he knew nothing about it.

While attending enlisted bombardiers school in Carlsbad, New Mexico, in October 1942, without a word I was conducted to the Provost Marshal by my C.O. Lieut Dunlap, who took me right out of school, and there was thoroughly searched and placed in the guardhouse. I remained there for a week without a word of explanation and then a Capt. from Intelligence told me that the facts they had about me were that I fought in Spain as a pilot under the alias of "Larry Lindbergh." That I enlisted in the Marines and was subsequently discharged for fraudulent enlistment. He stated they were convinced these facts were not true and he said I was to be released, which I was later that day.

In March, 1943 after fully qualifying as an aerial gunner I was placed on a combat crew in my squadron. Prior to this about a dozen gunners, I included, were being used as temporary instructors with the under-standing that as soon as we were placed on a crew our responsibilities as instructors ceased. About half a dozen of us were put on crews. Two days after this I was removed from the crew—none of the other gunners were. Upon inquiry of Capt. Willis my C.O., I was told that I was going to be used as an instructor since they needed them. I inquired of Lieut. Stanley, in charge of the school concerned, whether he had asked for me to act as an instructor and he replied, no, that as far as he was concerned the agreement whereby we would cease being instructors as soon as we were put on crews still held. Since Lieut. Stanley would obviously be the one to have me used as an instructor and since Capt. Willis doesn't recommend instructors normally, obviously my C.O. Capt. Willis had received orders to remove me from a crew. Lieut. Stanley and I had a discussion in which I told him I believed that the only reason I was taken off the crew was because I had fought for the Spanish Republic. He promised to inquire of Capt. Willis as to the reason and did so but said he could receive no information though Capt Willis did imply that my being a Vet was not the reason. This despite the fact that I was the only gunner so treated. I inquired further of various officers in my squadron. Capt. Wood in charge of Operations, Lieut Holmes, my Adjutant, who said they knew nothing of the case.

Larry Lustgarten

FROM MILTON WOLFF

[April 1943]

Jack [Bjoze],

Here is the story from the beginning and I hope that it will answer all your questions.

On June 26th, or was it the 27th? I enlisted in the AUS. My enlistment was not without incident, however. Before I was finally sworn in I was closeted in a side room in Whitehall Street with a man dressed in GI clothing and holding the grade of Private. He was obviously of the FBI; clean-cut, college, pleasant, and so very sympathetic. After a few aimless questions we got down to the business of who sent me to Spain and why? After making it clear that I went on my own and that I joined the Brigades in Spain via Paris, the interview was concluded. I was sent to Fort Dix. At this reception center, it is the usual procedure for the newly inducted men to be processed in three days and then, sent away to a camp for basic training.

After I had spent two weeks in Dix I went to see the Operations Officer with the intent of discovering the cause for the delay. A very cooperative officer he was. He commenced a search for my records which tell all. He could not find them. They were not in the usual files. How come, he asked me? I volunteered the information that I had been in Spain fighting with the Republican army. "Oh," he ohed, "that's different." Whereupon he went to special single cabinet file and extracted therefrom my card, gave his head a confirming nod, turned to me and assured me that I would be going after awhile. I was not destined to spend my time in Dix. Four weeks later I got the call to pack the old barracks bag. I was just beginning to feel at home in Dix and had about convinced myself that that was a good place to fight the war from. As good as any so far.

On the train to our secret destination I found that I was among as select a group of disgruntled men as could be found anywheres in America. Or was it America? The language I heard spoken on all sides of me was Italian and German. Whenever I caught a snatch of Italian that I could understand, the resemblance to Spanish, you know, or of German, which resembles Jewish, which I also understand a little, I learned that the train was being beefed about, Dix came in for some choice cuss words, and finally America in general did not fare too well. Before you get the impression that I was in a group completely made up of Nazis and Fascist sympathizers, let me inform you now that it later turned out that only 80 percent of them fell into that category. About 18 percent were aliens whose opinions of world affairs and politics and war equaled those held by the average American at that time. The other 2 percent were Americans, too, and aliens who were proven in one way or the other to have been rabidly anti-fascists for as long as they could remember . . . who had fought Hitler and Mussy and whatever other native fascists to hand they could root out, with everything they had.

After I had taken in the situation I was convinced that we were on our way to a concentration camp. Several times I entertained the notion of leaving the train at some way stations and making my way back to America. What kept me where I was I can't imagine, unless it was the discipline I learned in Spain.

As you know, we did not go a concentration camp. We were deposited, instead, in Camp Wheeler, the largest and best Infantry Training camp in the Country. I was delighted. Infantry. My baby, what I knew most of, it was wonderful. My joy was short lived, however, for I soon discovered that we were in Branch Immaterial. In other words, we were in for the snappy six weeks basic instead of the thirteen given to combatant units, and that afterwards I would wind up in Quartermasters.

I was put in the Company D of the tenth Battalion. Captain Shallington was my commanding Officer. He would keep calling the men together and telling them that they had better speak English in the barracks, that they better stop receiving clippings from foreign newspapers, that they were being watched, that they better not try to start anything here, and such stuff.

When we appeared for reclassification it turned out that some eighty of the men refused to give any information to the interviewers at all and that some even announced that they had no intentions of "taking up arms

against their brothers in Italy and Germany." In my interview with a
sergeant I insisted that I be transferred to a rifle battalion. My loud
demands for action and the Infantry attracted considerable attention.
It seems that no one had ever requested the Infantry before . . . that is in
their right mind. I was looked upon as something of a freak. Well, never
mind, it did get me before the commanding officer of the Reclassification
center in Wheeler and he promised to get me transferred.

Once I asked Captain Shallington what I was doing amongst such a
collection of men, and he said, "Well, you are Spanish, aren't you? You are
not an American citizen." Me . . . borned and raised in Brooklyn, USA, so
to speak, a former Democrat and an ardent fan of the Brooklyn Dodgers,
not an American Citizen??? I have heard a great many derogatory remarks
about Bensonhurst and Flatbush, but never have I heard that they are not
part of these United States. As for being Spanish, if two years of a strict
Garbanzos diet has given me Spanish blood . . . then I am Spanish. The
ideals for which I fought in Spain were not peculiarly Spanish, they were
first of all American. They are the Four Freedoms for which I would like to
fight now.

Well, the Captain looked puzzled. "Beats me," he said. I will help get you
a transfer, he said. And so me and a Scotsman were transferred to the
Fifteenth Battalion Company A. We were among Americans, at last.

In the Fifteenth Battalion everything went smoothly until I was asked to
put in for Officer Candidate School. Behind this there is a story you should
know. My original score on my IQ test was 107. That did not qualify me
for an OC. However when I gained that interview with the Captain of
reclassification, he asked how come such a low mark. I explained that on
that damned infernal answer sheet where you must match the number of
the question with the answer, I had doubled up on one question and thus
misplaced some fourteen answers before I detected the mistake. By time I
got through erasing and tracing the misplaced answers my time was up.
My only excuse was that I was suffering a miserable head cold aggravated
by a combination of every injection known to medical science having been
poured into me. At least three, anyhow. Anyhow, I considered it a small
miracle that I had gotten even 107 . . . I was expecting something like .07
perhaps. So the Captain insisted that I take a retest. (I wish I could
remember his name.) He said, "Wolff, we need men like you. We need
officers who have been under fire. Right now," he added grimly, "you

know more about handling men and infantry fighting than any officer in Wheeler". So what could I do? I accepted the retest even though I argued that I would not get a commission. I was basing myself on what had happened to other Spanish Vets at Fort Benning, you know. However, he succeeded in brushing all those arguments aside.

In the retest I scored 141. Quite a score, if I do say so myself. You know how I am on tests??? Never can get quite the right answer to those silly questions about how many bushels, etc. So I became eligible for OC.

Captain Butler was my commanding officer. He was a first lieutenant then. He also insisted that I apply. Lieut. Col. Ross my Battalion Commander joined him and so I eventually appeared before the Board and passed and went to Fort Benning as a Corporal.

By the way, did I tell you that I appeared on "The Pass in Review" radio program while in Wheeler? Spoke a brief paragraph about how I had fought Fascist Franco and wanted to fight again and how wonderful I thought the Infantry is. They tell me it was on a nation wide hook-up. Did you hear it?

No sooner do I arrive in Benning than my good friend and comrade in arms, Irv Fajans is denied his commission after brilliantly completing his course at school. "What the hell," I think, "is that what is going to happen to me." What a waste of time, money, etc. Might as well quit now and get shipped across to do some fighting as a corporal. Why wait another three months . . . I have been in the army six months already. With this in mind I get to see my new Battalion Commander, Lieut. Col. Rosma, 3rd Battalion, First Student Training Regiment. I explain to him why I think I should quit at this point and get sent to a port of embarkation. He is very much surprised and annoyed. "What kind of an army do you think this is," he roars. "This is a Democracy, a democratic army. Do you think that we would send you here and then pull such a raw stunt? This is America and after all you fought on the right side as far as I can gather. You will get a fair deal." He then promises to look into the case, he urges me to keep up my good work and dismisses me.

Who am I to doubt the word of my superior officer. In the next eight weeks I received repeated assurances from him as well from Captain Reid, who is my company commander, that I will graduate. In fact, Capt. Reid rates me as the top man on his list for graduation. This in spite of the fact that I am not doing remarkable things with the graded tests. You know how

I am with tests. However, I am passing academically with a comfortable margin and in Voice and Command and Practical Work I am way up there on top. Though I do have a few disagreements in tactics every now and then. But nothing serious, mind you. Nothing drastic.

Comes the sixth week and thirty odd men are dropped from the class. Couldn't make the grade so they appeared before the school board and after an interview they are dropped. I learn that you must appear before this board before you can be dropped. About this time the Battalion Commander calls me in and asks me if I am an American. He has my birth certificate in his office and he asks me if I am an American. Of course, I say. "Do you believe in this war?" He asks. "Yes, I believe in this war," I answer, "that is why I have left my home, wife, and daughter to do some fighting. I am not a light hearted adventurer."

"I have had some men watching you," he says, "and all their reports are very favorable to you." He waves a sheaf of paper at me. "As far as I am concerned," he adds, "you will graduate." So. . . ?

So, they are watching me, the men who sleep next to me are watching me, my mail is being opened and every word recorded. Such attention, and why?

On the eighth week I am called off the field into the Company commanders office. Captain Reid looks at me and says, "We have just received orders from the Fourth Service Command relieving you of your duties and transferring you in grade to Station complement." I am stunned. Station Complement. The home of the misfits, the limited service, the WAACS and the civilians . . . the rear guard.

Naturally, I protest. Where is the Board meeting I am supposed to get? Capt Reid says, "No board for you and you have two thirds of a day to get to Wheeler so you'd better start now." He sighs, opens a draw, and pulls out a bulging file. He waves it wearily at me, "I have done all I could to keep you. As you see I have reams of material on you and every word of it is in your favor. But, what the hell can I do? I am only a goddamned Captain in this man's army." With that he waves me out and goodbye. As I open the door to leave, he adds, "If you ever need a recommendation call on me. As far as I am concerned you are the only goddamned soldier in this class."

Thanks.

Now I am in the Station Complement, Camp Wheeler, Georgia. I am in Chemical Warfare Branch. I have put in an application for the infantry and one for tank destroyers and one for combat-engineers. I am still in Chemical Warfare, Warehouse number five.

A high ranking officer, whose name I cannot give, who is interested in my case helpfully suggested that I lean over backwards to prove that I am not a Red because I fought for Loyalist Spain. He hinted that that would help him help me get overseas to do some fighting.

I didn't get the connection. I still don't. I do not want to fight for Franco, or Vichy, or Bergonzoli[25] . . . so why should I lean over backwards to prove anything? It seems to me that I have leaned forwards enough to prove to anyone that my one desire is to fight for all the good things that America stands for, to fight against the Nazis and the Fascists and the Japanazis who want to destroy these good things. That is how I fought in Spain and that is how I want to fight now. That is how I want to be accepted into the fighting ranks of the American Army in North Africa, in the South Pacific or in the forthcoming battle for the liberation of Europe.

Maybe you can tell me, whether I am right or wrong.

Yours for a speedy victory

Milton

FROM IRVING MITCHELL

Tues—May 5 [1943]—8 P.M.
Camp Swift, Texas

Dear Toots [Irving Fajans],

Got your post-card of Apr. 13th as I was going into El Paso on a Monday afternoon. I had a pass from then until Wed. night. (Passover) I had to get away for a few days. Was in a hell of a state of mind. The first column on the Vets by Pearson was in Apr. 14th. I had read that one and the other shorts that followed.

Delayed writing since I expected the letter you said would follow. I heard from Arty Silverstein. He's at Buckley Field, Colorado. Bob Thompson is in a hospital nearby with a bad case of T.B. Leona [Thompson] was out there. He had malaria overseas. Arty says [Herman] Boettcher is back in U.S., I was surprised since I thought he had recovered from his wound. From Steve Levine out in Amarillo, Texas I hear that Joe Gordon and Tom Rissanen went down on a merchant ship. Also that Lt. Richard [Robert?]

Klonsky is wounded—and is at Percey Jones Hospital—Battle Creek, Michigan with a fractured back. Or do you know all that?

Johnny Perrone is still at Camp Pickett, Va. and looks as if his outfit may go. I hope he gets to go with his outfit.

As I wrote in the opening, I was in a lousy frame of mind—still am for that matter. Two weeks just before my outfit left I was transferred. I had been sure I was going. Had made quite a few talks on Spain. My conduct etc was tops. Was o.k'd physically. The Chaplain told me that he and the Colonel had [been] talking about what a fine character and a good influence I was—this just several days before I was transferred.

I had all the forms made etc when on a Wed. eve I was told to hand in rifle etc. My C.O. being at B'n H.Q. I went there to ask why the transfer. When he saw [me] he spoke to an officer while I waited nearby for a half hour. Obviously he wanted to avoid talking. Finally the Colonel came and asked if he could help. When I asked why the transfer he said that no one in the outfit was responsible. I asked if there was anyone on the post I could see. He said no, that the order came straight but didn't [know] from where. I saluted and left. Don't ask how I felt that night.

(I realize that you and the other Vets who went to O.C.S. got it double. Not only denied your commission but put in limited service. But I feel that you, Milt, etc can look at it more objectively. Did you?)

A staff sgt. went up to the C.O. that night and asked how come? He told the sgt. he knew of it only 5 minutes before I did and felt so lousy he sent an orderly to tell me.

I got transferred to ordinance for rations and quarters the next night and my outfit left. Remained at Ft. Bliss 2 weeks and then sent to join the 82nd Chemical Bn, formerly of Ft Bliss and now here at Camp Swift. Am not assigned to any company as yet. I think that I'll probably be put into a limited service. The reason the 3rd Cmp. didn't transfer me was lack of time. It certainly would be a fucking to have to go thru training again and be transferred if this outfit goes.

Today the fellows who were transferred mostly sick etc—went before the B'n Dr. Almost all were trying to get limited service. When he started to examine me, he asked what's wrong. I said I was perfectly o.k. However he sent me to the hospital to have my kidney operation scar looked over. A Lt. Col asked how it was and I said I felt great, that for the past 6 months I had no trouble. He said he would reclassify me if I desired but I said no, that I was o.k. for combat duty. I have a feeling that my old outfit will be short and will send for men to be rushed to the P.O.E. And that former members will be taken first. A pipe dream, eh? Anyway I'm hoping.

When this first happened I wrote to my brother and asked him to see Jack Bjoze. If I'm left I'd like to see what I can do to clear my status. Felt it would be best to ask Jack. There was one strange factor. In our Bn but in another Co. there was a fellow by name of Stimson or Stinson[26] who was a Lincoln Vet. He's 41 now and was from the West coast, tho since his return from Spain he's been in Reno because of his health. Had typhus in Spain. He left Ft. Bliss with the outfit. He may be dropped at P.O.E.

When sober he knew the score fairly well. However he was a heavy drinker and in the P.X. he'd get soaked in beer and sometimes shoot off his mouth about 'Political Commissars', etc. You know the type. I usually avoided him on such occasions. When sober he once told me that the non aggression pact had soured him, etc.—Do you know him? Anyway went along. I suppose my working as a guard [at] the building could be partially responsible.

What with moving around etc. I've had no letter from my brother about seeing Jack. But my mail is all fucked up now. You can write to me without a Co. address. I'll get it.

If you haven't written do so. Is Milt Wolf at your camp? If so give him my best.

    Salud

    Mitch

4. HOME FRONT DISCRIMINATION

FROM GEORGE CULLINEN

98-25 65th Ave

Forest Hills, N.Y.

1/5/44

Dear Comrade Jack [Bjoze],

Here is a very brief account of my activity during the past ten years. I believe it covers the most important things that the Gov't definitely knows about me.

George Ambrose Cullinen

Born October 29, 1914, at San Francisco, Calif.

Active in trade union movement in marine industry from 1934 to 1937.

Applied for and received a passport in March 1937 at San Francisco. Did not take any oath regarding Spain. There was a pink slip of paper inserted in the passport on which it was stated, "this passport not valid for travel in Spain."

Arrived in France O.K. Arrested and imprisoned in Toulouse on orders of French Gov't. Charged with attempting to cross the Spanish frontier along with 29 other Americans. While we were in jail the American Consul from Bordeaux came and collected our passports from the warden. He didn't bother to come and see us. We were sentenced to 40 days and ordered to get out of French territory within 8 days after our release.

We finally arrived in Barcelona on a Spanish ship from Marseilles. We didn't have our passports but the Spanish Gov't. knew the reason and was glad to have us.

Upon my return to Paris in October 1937, I waited a month for my passport which had been in the American Consul's office all the time I was in Spain. When I got the passport it was stamped, "only good for return to the USA."

When I arrived in New York a federal agent boarded the ship and took the passport. After that I shipped out and became an active member of the N.M.U. [National Maritime Union].

In April 1938 while in Wash. D.C. as an N.M.U. delegate to the American Youth Congress, I was arrested for protesting the Nazi invasion of Austria in front of the German Embassy. There were about 30 of us altogether. We were in jail a few days and then were bailed out to wait trial. About a month later, after pleading not guilty, I was convicted and given a 30 day suspended sentence.

After this I shipped out and continued my N.M.U. activity aboard various ships until May 1941 except for a brief visit to Mexico early in 1940.

Got married and went to work in Beth[lehem] Steel Co. shipyard in Hoboken, N.J. Became an active member of C.I.O. shipyard workers union. Fired once for union activity and reinstated.

Quit the shipyard job in December, 1941 and went to New London, Conn. to get a 3rd Mate's license. Shipped out as 3rd mate in June 1942 and sailed steady until November. Applied for a Seaman's Passport in June 1942 and have not received it yet.

Hired by American Export Airlines as an aerial navigator in November 1942.

Applied for a passport in December 1942 and promptly had $10.00 deposit refunded with a refusal stating that a passport could not be issued to me "at this time."

I went to Washington and managed to get nowhere fast. A certain Mr. Nicholas of the Passport Division suggested that I get some letters from prominent citizens vouching for my loyalty to the U.S. Govt.

Since that time I have been working on the case with the knowledge of several influential people who have intervened personally on my behalf. Among them are James Eaton and D.G. Richardson both Vice-presidents of American Export Airlines Inc.; B.H. Anglin, Labor Relations Mgr. for the Texas Co.; and Col. A. Woody, U.S. Army Air Corps, General Staff, G-2.

In March I made another application which was also turned down in almost exactly the same words, but this time they did not refund the $10.00 deposit.

I went to Wash. again in April and this time Col. Woody went along with me to the Passport Division. We were referred to the same Mr. Nicholas. Col. Woody put up a strong argument in my favor but to no avail.

Before this I forgot to say that I had been investigated by the Army and Navy Intelligence. A certain Mr. Dolan of Army Intelligence reported to Mr. James Eaton that my whole past record was just "reeking with Communism" and that I had quite frankly admitted to him that I was a communist. He based this remarkable assumption on the fact that I told him I was proud of having fought against Franco and considered that fight to be the same one we are carrying on today against the axis nations. As a matter of fact I told him I would consider myself a traitor to my country today if I turned against the things I fought for in Spain. This probably got under his skin because he deliberately lied in order to have me fired. His little scheme didn't work though because Eaton and Richardson are both pretty fair minded individuals and besides they need navigators.

After that I went to Blackie Myers of the N.M.U. and had him write a letter to Mrs. Shipley, Chief of the Passport Division. He also spoke to her about the matter during one of his trips to Wash. She promised him to issue me a passport if the N.M.U. officially requested it. This was done but she went back on her word.

That was about 5 months ago and practically nothing has been done since then. I have been working at La Guardia Field, in charge of the navigation instruments on all the planes, a job that is just as important as flying.

About 2 months ago the company's Wash. representative put out a feeler on my case and decided that I should try again after the first of the year. I'm supposed to get in touch with Richardson on the 10th of January in order to plan my strategy when I go to Wash. He doesn't know yet about the "Vets" going to bat for me but I'm sure it will be O.K. with him.

Hope this letter serves the purpose. Will keep in touch with you. Salud y victoria.

George Cullinen

FROM ROY SHEEHAN

November 2, 1944

Dear Harold [Smith],

Some of our boys have been having trouble out here. George Haggerty, a sheet metal worker has been working at the Naval Ordnance Testing Station at Inyokern for over three months when he was suddenly escorted from the area under armed guard. The same things had previously happened to Joe Vaughn who had been working there about a month. The reason given was "security" without any explanation.

We have several other recent instances of similar discrimination against veterans. In discussion with the executive committee I was instructed to ask for your help in compiling a list of such happenings elsewhere in the country. We must publicize and expose discrimination against people who have demonstrated their loyalty and antifascist convictions, while America Firsters,[27] bundists and native fascists are holding jobs without their loyalty being questioned. In other words, we want to fight—and need all the help we can get.

At our last meeting our guest was Helen Fisher of the JARC,[28] who spoke on the program of the JARC. The Post resolved to continue working with the Committee, and in addition, directed the treasurer to pay the sum of $7 monthly for the support of a child at the school in Mexico City. The new records were played and were very well received. Perlman will send you an order for the albums before the 15th. Incidentally, they are swell.

At this meeting also a new exec. Committee was elected composed of the following: Will Carroll, Ben Goldstein, Art Landis, Ben Richman, and Joe Vaughn. The Post officers remain as before.

As you know we had an emergency meeting of the exec. com. when the news from Spain broke. Because of the scarcity of news and conflicting reports we decided to be very cautious in issuing statements or in taking any actions. However we are prepared to swing into real activity for aid to the Spanish republicans when advisable. We would very much appreciate any information, bulletins or other coverage you can give us on Spain. There is only one decent newspaper here, the Daily News, and as it is a tabloid all news is cut to a minimum. Enclosed is a copy of the letter sent to each veteran in this area last week.

A letter has been send to Isadore Tivin extending the condolences of the Post to him and his family on the recent death of his father.

There have been several complaints about not receiving the Volunteer. My last letter contained an up to date list of addresses, so will you please have your mailing list checked against this. Also enclosed are more addresses to add to this list.

We are celebrating the 8th anniversary of the defense of Madrid with a dinner for veterans and friends on Nov. 10. (Also to celebrate, we hope, the election returns.) A full report of the event will be sent for the Volunteer.

Salud
Roy Sheehan
Ex. Sec.

5. SEEKING REMEDIES

FROM JACK BJOZE

January 15, 1943

Honorable Franklin Delano Roosevelt
President of the United States
White House
Washington, D.C.

Dear Mr. President:

We are addressing ourselves to you as Commander-in-Chief of the armed forces of our nation in the hope that you will intervene in a serious problem which has developed within the armed forces. Our organization is made up of Americans who fought in the Abraham Lincoln Brigade on the side of the democratic government of Spain. Most of our members have had military experience in actual combat.

At the present time approximately five hundred of our members are in various branches of the armed forces. An additional three hundred of our members are sailing the ships as part of the Merchant Marine. Eight of our members have given their lives since the war in an effort to keep the ships sailing.

Immediately after Pearl Harbor, we offered the full support and services of our organization and membership. On December 24, 1941, we received the following letter in reply:

> "The President has asked me to express his appreciation of the fine spirit which prompted your offer of service during the present emergency. It will be brought to the attention of the Adjutant General of the War Department immediately."
>
> Sincerely,
Wayne Coy
Special Assistant to the President

The fact that eight hundred of our members are in the armed forces and the Merchant Marine is the living embodiment of the pledge we made to you, our Commander-in-Chief.

For the past several months, we have received reports of serious discrimination against our members in the armed forces, particularly in the Army. As reports of these cases of discrimination have piled up on our office, it had become quite clear, and even admitted in certain quarters of the Army, that members of the Abraham Lincoln Brigade are barred from combat duty and from advancement in the Army. A number of Veterans were separated from their combat units and transferred to camps together with Fascists, Nazis and pro-Japanese elements. We have a list of some of these cases and will be glad to submit the names and complete data to you or to anyone you may designate. We also cite to you, not because they are exceptional but rather as an example, two cases in which this discrimination took other forms.

We refer to the case of Technical Sergeant John Gates, presently assigned to Headquarters, 59th Armored Artillery Battalion, Camp Chaffee, Ark. Sergeant Gates, for no known justifiable reason, was transferred on receipt of a telegram from the Adjutant General's office to a service unit.

Sergeant Gates was one of the outstanding men of the Abraham Lincoln Brigade in Spain. He was ~~Commissar~~ Morale Officer of the 15th International Brigade. Vincent Sheean and Herbert Matthews have written of his courage and skill in combat.

Another case is that of Corporal Irving Fajans #32315745, Hq. Fort McClellan, Alabama. Corporal Fajans was a member of the Officers' Candidate Class, 130, 29th Co, 3rd Student Training Regiment, The Infantry School at Fort Benning, Ga., which graduated on December 19, 1942. On the eve of graduation, he was informed that no orders had come through assigning him to active duty. Some two weeks after graduation, he was transferred back to Fort McClellan without his commission. There has been no explanation for such unusual action made to Corporal Fajans or to anyone else. Corporal Fajans like Sergeant Gates had an excellent military record in Spain.

It would seem obvious that the discrimination practiced against Sergeant Gates and Corporal Fajans and the other discriminations (of which we have record) which have developed throughout the armed forces originate in Washington and have become a policy of the War Department. It is this fact that makes the situation a serious one not only because of its threat to national unity, but because it is holding back experienced and proven anti-Axis fighters from contributing their abilities and their lives if need be for the defense of our country.

Those members of the International Brigade who have not been discriminated against and have been assigned to combat duty have proven their worth. Two of the outstanding heroes of the New Guinea campaign are former International Brigade members. We refer to Captain Herman Bottcher and Sergeant Robert Thompson. We quote from a release issued by the Australian Information Bureau:

> "THE DISTINGUISHED SERVICE CROSS has been awarded by General MacArthur to Captain Herman J.F. Bottcher, U.S. Inf., who, when a sergeant, led a unit which drove a wedge between the Japanese forces at Buna Village and Buna Mission. Captain Bottcher has gained fame as America's one-man army, and the story of his deeds in Papua has been told throughout the world."

The story of Sergeant Thompson can be found in the United Press Dispatch of Jan. 3 from New Guinea.

".... Sergeant Thompson, who yesterday led an attack which knocked out four Japanese pill-boxes....

Sergeant Thompson, 27, is a veteran of the Spanish Civil War. He said he volunteered because he hated Fascists....

I heard about Sergeant Thompson first from the General commanding this sector who knew of his daring leadership and fighting qualities."

We do not understand why men like Gates and Fajans, and the others who have been discriminated against—all of the same courageous caliber as Bottcher and Thompson—have been held back from fighting our enemies. These veterans have much to offer in defense of American Democracy, yet the War Department has apparently seen fit to prevent them from doing so.

All this is serious enough, but an added infamy and disgrace is the treatment accorded those of our members who have been placed in labor camps alongside of Nazis, Fascists and Japanese sympathizers.

We think it is now clear to all liberty-loving Americans that the cause of Spain was the cause of Democracy and was our cause. [If] This treatment of our Veterans, and there can be no other conclusion, is being meted out because we fought in Spain, then certainly some steps must be taken to correct this situation.

May we meet with you or someone designated by you to present the facts and to discuss the problem so that an early solution may be reached.

Very sincerely yours,

J. Bjoze

Executive Secretary

FROM DAVID ALTMAN

Borden General Hospital
Chickasha, Oklahoma
Feb. 21, 1943

Dear Jack [Bjoze]—

Received your welcome letter and realize I should have written you.

I was thrilled reading the newspaper accounts of Bob Thompson and [Herman] Bottcher. They have set us a splendid example.

Herman Bottcher, 1944

With the smashing Russian offensive and the allies getting ready to strike, I can't help feeling disappointed at my position in the Army. Being classified as Limited Service, I am denied all opportunities of getting into a combat unit. I've tried my damndest in the three camps I've been in to get into combat, but the medical classification says otherwise. At Fort Sheridan after hearing about Spain, the interviewer went to the sergeant, and the sergeant to the captain to see if I could make the parachute troops, but no go.

Having no choice, I was sent here and am assigned to a surgical ward in the hospital. The chances of getting transferred out of the medics once your in are very slim. I've requested active duty here about five times and told them of my experience in Spain. The last time they told me they may be able to do something for me to get into field work, but to work in the ward in the meantime since that training would be useful in field work also. The best I can aim for is stretcher bearer or first aid man. We start a medical school training tomorrow. Half a day school and half day work.

Salud & Victory Greetings
Dave

FROM HARRY HAKAM

859 Commerce St.
Miami Beach, Florida
April 8, 1943

Dear Jack [Bjoze]:

I have been down here now for the last three weeks trying to get some work but taking it easy generally. I was down to the Navy Recruiting Office here and have applied for enlistment and they seem to be different sort of people down here altogether. I put my cards on the table and told them about Spain and about the sad experience that I had in the Navy yard in New York. In the opinion of the navy men down here that guy in N.Y. who gave me all that trouble should be kicked out of the navy and they feel that my experience in Spain should even qualify me for a rating. This sure don't sound like the navy, but that is just what happened. So I applied for enlistment and have passed a stiff physical that they give for the navy. Now I have to go up within 10 days for a rating and they want me to bring a letter of recommendation substantiating my service record in Spain. I told them about the Lincoln Vets and they said a letter of recommendation from them would be a fine reference and that it would be a good idea to present such a letter when I go up for a rating next week. So send me at once by return mail a letter commending me about my service in Spain also any clippings that you have on hand about Herman Bottcher—whom I cited an example of a vet in action—If necessary please go out to the newspaper and get back number to clip and I'm enclosing 1 dollar to cover any such expenses. Please Jack, don't neglect this a single day since I must have this stuff and the reference back by the 18th of April as I have to appear on that day for a rating.

It would be wonderful if I could get a rating on the basis of my Spanish experience plus my technical background—especially so in the Navy—and there is every chance that I will so don't fail me as it means as much for the Vets organization as it does to me and is the best possible answer to those rats who gave me that trouble in the navy yard. Sounds hard to believe but that is what the set up is down here and I aim to make the most of it. As you probably know I was at the Jarama front right on through to the Ebro offensive. I was never sick a day while I was in Spain and I was never wounded and at the time I left Spain for Paris on that first leave in Sept 1938, I had over 14 months active service in the front lines. 2 months I spent on leaves and rests and 2 months I wired up for electricity a big hospital in Mahora a town near Albacete. Also was in the first telephone squads to be organized by the Brigade. So put it on thick but in a modest way—you know what I mean Jack—because a lot depends on that letter I hope?

So Long and lots of luck?

Harry Hakam

P.S. Don't forget those clippings on Herman Bottcher—They are very important too—

From Moishe Brier

Camp Croft South Carolina
Monday April 12, [1943]

Dear Jack [Bjoze],

Well here I am again back in my old camp doing my bit to win the war. Of course a man with my battle experience and seven months training in infantry tactics in the American army had to be given a job in keeping with his ability and training. So they gave me that job—I am working in the Sales Commissary as a bookkeeper. My duties are of most importance and varied. I add the bills and price the foodstuffs that are sent to the mess-halls. Milton said that he also serves who stands and waits—so I guess I also serve although I sit and wait.

When I got back I was called into the office and told that as long as I was a bookkeeper I would work in the Commissary, I said that I don't like bookkeeping and want to be sent to a combat outfit—the answer was hmm-hmm—a couple of more hmmm's and that I was not attached here or assigned here but to Atlanta and Atlanta will decide. . . . In brief I am now a bookkeeper.

There is one break my work is easy and very little of it so I have plenty of time to read and write so I'm taking advantage of it and am studying American History and any military books I can get ahold of. Besides I am with Bill Mich of the Dept Store Union so we study together. Anything to prevent a case for Section 8 and besides we are doing something that I always wanted to do.

I hope the work is getting along O.K. I've been reading Pearson's column every day but haven't seen a word as yet. How about a bonfire under his can.

Have met Zero [Mostel] here and spent Saturday nite with him—what a character he is—always acting even over a glass of beer. I hope the hell he would stop it as he becomes annoying but is sure funny. He put on a performance Sunday at the Jewish U.S.O. there were some 450 people there, the largest crowd ever and Zero was very funny although very tired and sick.

Jack, I would like a copy of Hamilton's book and send me any copies of the volunteer as they come out. I'd be careful of any letters you send as I still think my mail is being read.

Got some work to do, for awhile, so I'll close with

SALUD

Moishe

P.S. I feel like I am doing the work of a 4F in the clothes of a 1A.

From Irving Fajans

[4/43]

Dear Jack [Bjoze],

I was interviewed by the Post Intelligence Officer today. By "accident," there was a civilian sitting in the office who after a short period of time took an active part in the questioning.

Ostensibly I was being interviewed because of the many letters I had sent through channels and which the Officer was now going to clear up for me. Actually, I got no direct information from the interview except that "the way had now been cleared" for me to be transferred to combat and that I would be transferred soon.

The tone of the interview and the kind of the questions they asked do not make me very hopeful of any real or general change in attitude, at least not yet.

Some of the questions were—

Who had "sold me the bill of goods" which induced me to go to Spain? "We're realists—your saying you went to fight fascism isn't convincing realistically."

The same old standby, "What would you do if the United States went to war with Russia?"

On the opening of my mail he didn't say they weren't doing it, but advised me to read a "Message to Garcia."

On the commission, he said, "What are you worrying about, you're going to combat aren't you?"

Although both were extremely well-informed about Spain and the recent developments in the newspapers, etc., they conveniently "don't know" the reasons for any of the things which I asked,

When I asked about not being interviewed for advanced college training even though I passed the exam, he said he didn't know I had taken it. Later when I got back to the Detachment, I was told I was being interviewed tomorrow (Tuesday). I don't think it means anything except for the record.

To repeat, although everything was ostensibly "palsy-walsy," I don't think the attitude has changed a bit and what's happening now is a business of covering up any real glaring errors in routine handling of the Vets rather than a change in policy.

Salud,

Irv Fajans

6. WASHINGTON MERRY-GO-ROUND

From Leonard Grumet

Medical Detachment
Camp Irwin, Calif.
April '43

Dear Jack [Bjoze],

Am writing this to let you know that I am another Vet who has been suddenly transferred and sent to this outfit which is one degree better than an internment camp. SCU 1964 is composed of 90% limited service men (the maimed, halt and blind) and 10% of enemy aliens, Bundists (suspects) labor organizers, etc. As far as I know I am the only Vet here. Have been told, in confidence, by an officer here, that I am being kept here to be watched!

Have read Washington-Merry-Go-Round in which Drew Pearson tells of similar experience of other Vets. Seems obvious that there is a concerted drive to get us out of combat. Base this on quite a few cases I know of personally.

My record (15 months) in the army is spotless and have had nothing but the highest recommendations from my commanding officers wherever I've been. [. . .]

Please Jack, write me at once giving me some advice based on the experience of the other Vets. Would it do any harm to have influential persons write to Washington in my behalf?

Thanks.

Salud y Victoria

Leonard Grumet

From Joseph Hecht

Jun./43
Sunday

Dear Jack [Bjoze]:

The following is a brief history of my life in the army. Use whatever part of it is of value.

I was drafted in Feb. 1942 at Camp Upton. I gave the classifications clerk the information that I had been in Spain etc. When he asked me my rank there I did not tell him that I was a company political commissar but gave the equivalent military rank, that of captain which he entered on my qualifications card.

I was put in a medical outfit and sent to Camp Lee for basic training. There I was interviewed by a public relations man and given a big write-up in the Camp Lee Trainer. The Petersburg Virginia paper and the Army Times carried the same story! all very favorable. The Richmond Times Dispatch later carried another story also sent out by the public relations office. I spoke on the Camp Lee radio program, addressed a chamber of commerce meeting and a U.S.O. Forum. Finally the Lt. Colonel in command of our Battalion (the 7th med. Tn'g B'n.) arranged for me to speak to the whole battalion on my experiences in Spain. The Lt. Colonel's name was Wolowitz—I think he is now in North Africa.

After my 2 months of basic Training, I was made a corpsman and was kept over in cadre to train new men coming in.

In August I met Capt. Ziff in charge of qualifications [?] for Camp Pickett (Camp Lee Med. dept. had transferred him) and convinced him that I would be of more value in a combat unit and about 2 weeks after our conversation orders came through for me to [be] transferred to an armored at Ft. Knox. The morning I was to leave those orders were rescinded. No explanation.

In Sept. I was sent to the Officers Preparatory School at Camp Picket for Med. Adm. Corps. I finished the course but was not passed despite the fact that 2 others from my own company at the school with whom I had studied and who had leaned on me for some assistance had passed among the highest in the school.

I reported back to my Company Commander Capt. Russell Wilgh, he told me that it wasn't because of marks that I had failed but his guess was that G 2 wasn't satisfied with my past. He also told me that he knew that orders from the Service Command had come through for my transfer. I was to be transferred to the . . . General hospital in Oct. For the first 4 months my work consisted of cleaning, mopping etc. The last 2 months I have spent doing routine clerical work.

After I had been at the hospital about 2 months I put in another request for a transfer to a combat unit. My Detachment Commander Lt. Davies agreed to it but it was turned down by somebody higher up. I made inquiries among some of the boys working in the Personnel Office & was told "unofficially" that my qualifications card is marked "not to be transferred out of the Third Service Command."

To-day one of the boys working at the hospital showed me a Milwaukee paper in which Drew Pearson has a column on the Vets. It's good.

I would appreciate it very much if you kept me in touch with any new developments—remember that I am one of the boys "frozen" for the duration. If any of us are ever sent out I want to be included.

Salud y Victoria

Joe

7. "THE SAME OLD TALE"

FROM ADOLPH ROSS

June 16, 1943

Wednesday Evening

Dear Jack [Bjoze]—I received the Book About Mendy[29] and am deeply grateful. I did not answer immediately as I had to look up the information you asked for.

The officer who made the statement that I'm being withheld from overseas shipment is Captain George E. Harrison. He is C.O. of the recruit detachment at this Camp. He told me this statement was made to him (to be told to me) by Captain Willard Clements, who is in charge of Unit Personnel (S-1) for the Post.

Later I saw Captain Clements myself and he said: "Did Cap't Harrison tell you why you are not eligible for overseas duty?" By this question he implied that Cap't Harrison had told me his message.

The S-2 officer has not yet received an answer from Washington. He told me so on June 10, 1943.

Capt Clements also told me that he could not ship me out of Camp Luna since I'm in an overseas Pool and that therefore the only way I could get overseas or assigned to a squadron in the States would be by a direct order from Washington mentioning my name. I'm afraid such a state of affairs will have me rot here in Camp Luna indefinitely.

Milt Wolff wrote me a very encouraging letter about all our guys finally getting overseas. This was something I hadn't known. It sort of convinces me that I'm being held for the same general reasons that Johnnie [Gates] is being held up.

The Book about Mendy recalled all the things I've gone thru at Home and abroad. It seems unbelievable that we've gone thru and done so much. We truly are the ones who are full of life. It takes but a pause and a bit of reflection to realize it.

And if ever I doubted whether I've done (and am doing) my share for progress, I no longer have any uncertainties. These reactionaries in Washington have reminded me that I haven't done so bad after all.

Along with the suffering that always affects people like us whenever we are forced into idleness there is the negative value of learning the art of patience, and also the pride of knowing the strength and dignity of our deeds.

Pardon me for waxing elegant, but I just had a few Beers and am in the mood. I do hope the info is specific enough.

Salud,

Adolph

From Sam Nahman

S/Sgt Sam Nahman
Tampa, Fla.
MacDill Field
June 7, 1943

Hello Boys,

Well the axe has descended, chalk up another hit for the defeatists. Following are some of the sordid details. I don't know why but some how I felt I was going to get thru. What an optimist!! Here goes.

On June 3 I was to get transferred to another field for further training and inside of a month or so I was to be overseas. That morning orders came out promoting me from a sergeant to a staff sergeant. All packed up and ready to go I went to receive orders at combat crew headquarters. There I heard that a rumor had cropped up that I was not going. I went to the officer in charge and asked if he had heard the rumor, he said no but would check up on it. He then called his superior officer on the phone and asked about me. The officer (a major) said yes I was to be knocked off the combat crew. I asked why I was knocked off, my pilot was very satisfied with me, I was rated one of the best engineers in my sqdn. I passed my combat physical and I had the necessary technical schooling. I told him I would like his permission to see the major. He then said it would do me no good to see him as it was done by "intelligence" and was out of the major's hands. I then told him why I thought I was knocked off by intelligence and he was surprised. When he heard intelligence cut me off he had thought the worse. All he could do tho was express regrets. I told my pilot and crew and they were mad as heck. My pilot went in to talk to the officer but of course of no avail. I then went back to my old sqd'n. I told my engineering sergeant about it and he said he had heard about it and he heard I was a communist. When I asked him who told him that he said they (with no further explanation) had come around saying that. Boy by that time I was hopping mad. I went to see my first sergeant and asked permission to see the C.O. and explained the situation to him. Altho he has the authority to grant permission he said I would have to see the personnel officer. I went to him, explained what had happened asked to see the C.O. in order to find out officially why I was taken off the combat crew and also where I now stood. He seemed to know all about the case. I told him I felt I was being discriminated against because I fought in Spain, that I felt I was qualified to be on the combat crew and only that morning I was promoted from sergeant to staff. I told him that I had been engineer-gunner for five months here and 3 months in B-25, the oldest engineer here. I also told him I volunteered to be an engineer gunner and volunteered also for the combat crew. He got very mad and indignant and said he would not give me permission to see the C.O. and anyway he continued, "the captain couldn't do anything for you" (meaning that the matter was not a local one). I told him I'd like to see some one in base headquarters. He kinda exploded then and said, "I order you not to go over my head and see anyone in base." I then asked if I was to continue working as an engineer in the sqd'n. He answered I would and added "for the time being until we receive further orders and at that time we will inform you."

Well I wasn't going to stop then. The following afternoon I went to see the Jewish chaplain as he is the one person (and very influential) I can see with out getting permission. I told him my case and he was astounded at the raw deal I was handed. He told me he had read about what had happened to other vets in Drew Pearson's column and various magazines and papers. He told me quite frankly he would help me if he could. Speaking plainly he said this is a hot issue and most effective way to help me was to do it in connection with a national organization. He told me he was going to new york during the week and that he would take it up with the anti Defamation league of the Bnai-Brith (I think that's the way you spell it). Rather than first taking it up with the base which he said would liable to make me get transferred to Shenango, Penn. (Is that the place where most of the vets were sent to) he could do more by raising it that way and any way since the policy seems to be a national one it would get better results. I will drop in to see him from time to time and will keep you informed as to results.

Well that's the whole case as to all that happened and all I did. Write and let me know if you have any suggestions as to what I should do or what some of the other fellows have done. I will keep in touch with you. Write to me at Sylvia Nahman 2906 - 13th St. Tampa, Florida it is easier getting mail there.

Salud and Victoria
Sam Nahman

FROM HARRY FISHER

Sept 25. 1943

My Dear Sweetheart [Ruth Fisher]:

[. . .] Now hon, I have some news that's going to make you very blue, just as it did to me. I learned this morning that the radio gunners who shipped out this week, are now at Fort Monmouth, N.J. I was supposed to be with that gang. When I heard of that this morning, my heart went way down to my shoes. I was debating with myself whether I should tell you this, knowing it would make you feel rotten and sad, but I can't hold anything back from you. And furthermore, I was not shipped because I'm being "investigated." That much I know definitely—but I can't tell you any more of this now. Anyways, after thinking it over all day, I've planned on some action. This is what I'm going to do. I'm going to see an officer of my training group Monday. I'm going to tell him that I'm the only radio gunner of the entire training group (a training group has about 1500 men) who has not been shipped, which may mean one of two things—First—a mistake—and second, a change in classification. Since I'm supposed to be notified of any change in my classification, I'd like to know if this was done. If I have been reclassified, I'd like to know why and what my classification is. If I have been reclassified to something I don't like, I'm going to ask permission to see the major, my J.G. commander. I think it's best that I do all this hon. I feel lousy that I should be investigated because of Spain and working for Tass.[30] I have my heart so set on defeating the lousy nazis and Japs—I'm so damn anxious to do my share—but still I have to be investigated. Of course I can't say that I know I'm being investigated, because I'm not supposed to know. It's a hell of a situation, isn't it my dear. I'll keep you 100% informed on what takes place from now on. I'm doing my best to be a good soldier, and no matter what happens, I'll continue to do my best. After all, I'm in no position to complain. Look at what happened to John Gates. Four groups that he worked with were sent overseas, and he was kept back. Here he was, an experienced soldier, with plenty of battles behind him, begging to be sent to a front yet he was kept behind. By the way, where is he today. And then look at all of the other Spanish vets who were sent to O.C.S. and were flunked out on orders from Washington. Now they really had something to complain about. I know they would have made good officers. I can understand how badly they felt, yet they took it like good soldiers, and begged to go overseas, so's they could take a crack at the enemy. Look at all of our boys who went overseas and made good at the front. My friend [Herman] Bottcher, now a Captain. The paratroopers who are now officers. Milt Felsen, a prisoner. By the way, have you heard any more about him? Bob Thompson, who was recommended for a captaincy by his commanding General. And many more cases. To think that I'm being "investigated" because I fought against Hitler & Mussolini five years ago. It's hard to believe, but it's true. [. . .]

You know I felt as low as I ever did in my life when I learned all this early today. I just laid down for an hour and couldn't say a word for an hour. I felt sick to the stomach. To think how close I would have been to you! But then I thought it over. What am I—a baby? I've taken much worse blows in my life and got over them, I saw some of my best friends die in Spain. Whenever I think of those boys, I feel a pang in my heart. But I kept on going and fighting. I didn't act like a baby, and I'm not going to act like one now, and neither are you. Ruthie, my sweet, I never cared much for pep talks and I don't like to give them, but hell we're really lucky, very lucky. I'm still alive and healthy, healthier than I've ever been in my life, thanks to the army. Chances are I'll still get into radio, for I have a good record so far. I'll have a chance to learn a trade that will come in handy when the war is over. It's even possible that I'll be in Fort Monmouth yet. I think I'll know soon. So why be despondent and blue. And Ruthie—look at the news today. The Red Army has taken Smolensk. Do you see what that means? The Germans will be forced out of Russia. Anything may happen now. This news helped cheer me up considerably. Ruthie, I felt low this morning. But this afternoon, while marching, I sang louder than I ever did before. The war news is wonderful.

You want to know why Gen. [George C.] Marshall says we'll have five million boys overseas by the end of next year? You put two and two together and say that this means Gen. Marshall expects a long war. I thought I explained all this to you once before, but I'll do so again. Our Generals and strategists must plan on the war going on for years. I can assure you that if Gen. Marshall figured the war might end in two months, he would still prepare for next year and the year after. Not only that, we may need millions of soldiers to police the world after the war. And chances are fathers won't be included among them. So don't worry about that hon. Do you remember I told you about the allied General in 1918 who said the war would last for years, and then ended two weeks later. In a war, anything can happen. You never can tell. Right now the lousy nazis are taking an awful beating in two places, Italy and Russia. Perhaps soon in France! Again dear, anything may happen. Let's hope. [. . .]

I must tell you about a movie I saw. It's "The Fallen Sparrow" with John Garfield. A wonderful picture, dealing a lot with Spain and the vets. You must see it and tell me what you think of it. Will you hon? I don't want to tell you the story. I'd rather have you see it. I'm pretty sure it's playing in N.Y. My only criticism of the picture is that it should have been a bit clearer. The names Franco, fascists, Loyalists, Lincoln Brigade should have been used. But of course, Hollywood was more interested and emphasized the thriller part of the story rather than the political. See it by all means! It's well worth it. I've gotten a lot off my chest tonite sweet, and I'm glad I did. I feel much better about it now. I hope you feel better too. Things may turn out well in the long end. In the meantime I promise you, I'll keep my chin up and I'll be a good soldier. You do the same thing. Your health right now means more to me than anything. You must continue to take care of yourself. Only too well do I remember us singing "Let me call you sweetheart." We sang it at the range the other nite and I remembered. And I also remember the night we played very softly the Russian records. What a warm feeling I get when I think of it. Now dear, as soon as I learn anything about the business I wrote about, I'll let you know. I'll try to get it settled Monday. The officers here are a pretty good bunch, and I think they'll help me. Take care of yourself sweet—I love you.

Harry

FROM LAWRENCE CANE

Oct 12, 1943
[Camp Clairborne, La.]

Dear Jack [Bjoze];

Just thought I'd sit down and write you what's been happening to me the last few months.

It's the same old tale of woe. Yes, it seem they've decided to give me the same old treatment meted out to most of the boys.

If you remember, last March I graduated from OCS—at the top of the class too.

I was then sent to the Army's military intelligence school for a couple of months. While there, I lectured on several topics including Spain—from a military angle.

I also graduated from that place pretty high on the list.

While there, I wrote to Washington and asked for an assignment to the airborne engineers.

They were supposed to be frantic for officers for the airborne outfits then, I never heard anything about it.

After hanging around there (it was Camp Ritchie, Md.) they sent me here to Ft. Belvoir, Va. to an Engineer Officer's Pool.

After being at Belvoir for exactly a week, I was ordered to a Cadre Officer's School on the post and assigned to an Engineer Dump which is in Camp Clairborne, La. to which I was supposed to go after a month.

There I was not knowing a damn thing about trucks, not even knowing how to drive them.

A Dump Truck Co., incidentally, is a kind of labor outfit which hauls materials for construction purposes (dirt, gravel, bricks, etc.)

So, I sat myself down and wrote another letter to Washington asking for assignment to any combat or airborne battalion or any Port of Embarkation shipment.

The letter was bounced back at me by the General at Belvoir with a reference to some War Department regulation which prohibits requests for overseas assignments.

There was nothing left to do but accept my fate and decide to become the best damn lieutenant that ever rode a dump truck.

On to Clairborne I came, a little bitter, I admit, but determined.

As soon as I got down here, I wrote another letter to Washington asking for combat or airborne.

I was made supply officer of my company and placed in charge of all combat training. That included training in all weapons, tactics, etc.

That wasn't too bad. At least I was helping to train men in combat subjects, even if they were probably never going to go into battle.

But, I didn't reckon with Claiborne. It's a place where incredible stupidity and inefficiency prevails.

And, the Major who commands my provisional training regiment is a four-star jerk if there ever was one. He is distinguished chiefly by a riding crop, a dalmatian dog, a beer-belly, and a complete inability to do anything right.

My troops are Negroes and I'm not boasting when I say that I became quite popular with them. Perhaps too popular for my major's approval. He has the standard attitude towards Negroes.

In any event, I had several reprimands from him, not about my work or my handling of the troops—oh no. But crappy little things.

For instance, one day he caught me driving a 2 ½ ton truck. He asked me if I had an operators license. When I told him that I was trying to learn how to drive the vehicles I was in charge of and that I had tried to do it through official channels but that the red tape was so thick that I couldn't get anywhere, and that I had taken matters into my own hands, he damn near bust a gut telling me never to do it again.

When I asked him what a guy was supposed to do if he had the misfortune to be assigned to something he didn't know anything about— He had no answer. Particularly to my remarks about the necessity for an officer to know his stuff before he can expect to command the respect of his men.

Anyway, the upshot has been this—

The other night he called me in and told me that I was to become ASSISTANT MOTOR OFFICER OF THE REGIMENT!

What a laugh!

The regiment expects to receive a fleet of three hundred trucks in the next few days—and I'm expected to be in charge of their maintenance, dispatching, overall care.

This is a verbal order and doesn't countermand my original assignment to my company, which comes from Washington. Yet, I'm taken away suddenly and must not, explicitly, his orders, have anything to do with the training of troops in my company.

I don't know a thing about vehicles. But nothing. And there are plenty of officers in the regiment who are graduates of army motor schools, and who would be only too glad to have my job.

So there I am, rated by the Army as a "Very Superior" combat officer, and also as an expert in demolitions, reconnaissance, all weapons, and all phases of combat engineer operations. That's all on my classification card.

Add two years of Spain, and a lieutenancy in the machine-gun company of the Mac Pap Battalion. What have you got?

Just another sad sack for your files.

It may be that he's putting me in a spot where he expect me to bungle, and then have me reclassified for incompetence. But, he's nuts. That'll never work.

I want a combat assignment so hard it hurts, but I'll never give in to their crap. I can take more than they'll ever dish.

But, Jeez, Jack I sure would like to see action against the Nazi bastards again.

Yours, Larry Cane

FROM ADOLPH ROSS

Tuesday, November 9, 1943

Dear Jack [Bjoze]—Your letter was quite a revelation. It did my heart good to know that the boys are getting somewhere and doing things. And yet at the same time it makes me feel lousier than ever that I'm laying around these last 18 months.

I went to San Francisco on a 3-day pass and saw Archie [Brown] and Lushell [Luchelle] McDaniels. We had dinner and went to a Dance run by the N.M.U.

On Saturday, Oct. 30, I helped with the running of a conference for aid to Spain, run by the Joint Anti-Fascist Committee of San Francisco.

The representation was good and I enjoyed doing something useful for a change. The petitions seem to be going out by the looks of the conference.

Today I got a bit of bad and good news. I was called down for a physical recheck for Cadets and failed to pass it. It was just as well as I had previously passed with a few breaks and sooner or later they would have caught up to me.

Immediately I went to see the S-2 officer and asked again for overseas and combat duty. I told him I was tired of all this after 18 months. He said he has no record of me except what I told him.

He asked me if I believe in Communism. I said I did.

"Do you believe in overthrowing the Gov't."

I said that I would work for my program by democratic means and was an upholder of the Constitution, but that should a Dictatorship take over I would work to overthrow it as then democratic means would be impossible.

The other officers present asked about Spain and what the content of the meetings were, held by the Political Commissars.

Finally, after a bit of bullshit, the S-2 officer told me that my C.O. said I was O.K. and that I was getting a kicking around.

The funniest thing of all came when he said I was not a communist even tho I thought I was one.

Then he agreed to go to bat for me and try to get me transferred to a combat outfit in the tank, Field Artillery or Infantry. And he told me to come back in a few days to check up on it.

He advised me to forget about O.C.S. as it would take too long and besides I might run into the same old political difficulties. I agreed heartily as that would be a delay. All this doesn't mean anything yet but it's the most hopeful sign I've had.

My regards to Dave Smith and Rip Markowitz. I'll try to get to the Dance.

Salud!

Adolph Ross

FROM MAX KIRSCHBAUM

Pfc. M. Kirschbaum
#4204458
North Camp Polk, La.
[1944]

Dear Vet:

I'm recording some facts which I believe you may be familiar with as undoubtedly you have received reports from other Vets and so honestly "Yank" Magazine has written of the injustice that some of us boys have to contend with.

I came into the Army in Oct. 43, I made mention on my record that I fought in Spain. At my reception Center I was interviewed for ½ hour. Questions and my answers were taken down verbatim. The only thing I wasn't questioned about was how I came into this world.

Being held in Camp Upton for a month I was sent to Camp Blanding . . . into the Infantry. While there I discovered that the investigation was continued as my hut mates were questioned in regards to myself and one of my officers supposedly having me in consideration advised me to refrain from any political discussion as I was "accused" of being a Communist.

At the completion of my basic all the boys were sent P.O.E. I was transferred in Camp as a Cadre. Being Cadre I was recalled after two days and returned to my original outfit and held there for more than a month sitting on my behind at the behest of G.2. which information was posted on the orderly bulletin board. I was finally sent to my present outfit at that time located at Cp. McCain Miss. After being a week there I [was] called before the Cp. Hqs. G.2. section and questioned again and information about me was read off. At one time I lived in Cincinnati and I was investigated also so called reports about my actions back in 1934 was mentioned. My employment on W.P.A. [Works Projects Administration] and my membership in the Workers Alliance,[31] my employment in Chrysler, my membership in the C.I.O. My conversations with my fellow employees was raised to me and lastly my registration in the elections which I thought was an American citizens private affair. This renewed questioning was conducted by the Counter Espionage section of G.2. Before the questioning started I was informed that I could refuse to stand this investigation but being that there is nothing in my actions in the course of my life which I have to hide that may prove criminal intent I willingly stood their questioning. When the interview was over which was taken down in shorthand I made a statement of protest against the line of questioning insofar that my political beliefs and also that my voting record is again my private affair and also the political parties or party I am being questioned about are recognized as legal political parties. And also this continued investigation will not improve my morale and therefore let it be established once and for all either that I'm a criminal and treat me as such or recognize me as an American soldier who can make a definite contribution, to the war effort and respect me like the average soldier.

The battalion G 2 officer assured me the case was closed and I could ease my mind. Two weeks later my C.O. appointed me as Company Mail Clerk. This appointment I had for two months and over and last month I was made Pfc. Two weeks ago my C. O. informed me that Hqs informed him that I was a communist and therefore unfit to be a mail clerk. He assured me that him and the 1st sgt. were extremely satisfied with my work but he had to act on orders.

I've spoken to the Bn. C. O. and he says he has orders from higher Hqs.

Before this incident I was recognized a capable soldier regardless of where I functioned whether in the field or office but now I can see no purpose in continuing as a soldier.

I mentioned this to the C.O. and he sympathized but he could do nothing about it and told me that I would continue to be a soldier regardless at which point I disagreed.

Please advise me if I can remedy this situation.

Salud

Max Kirschbaum

8. CLEARED FOR ACTION

FROM HARRY HAKAM

April 19, 1943

Dear Jack [Bjoze]

Hold on to your hat and get a load of this—Went up for a rating today and got a C.P.O—Chief Electrician Mate. That is top rating and all in all pays around $200 a mo. To get this rating they require a minimum of 15 years technical experience and do not give it to anyone under 35 years of age— As you know I'm only 30 and I got the top rating only because of my military experience. Your letter helped a great deal. I showed the Lt. Commander a copy of Drew Pearson's column on the discrimination against the Vets and he gave me the rating anyway—In fact he enclosed your letter with my enlistment papers in order to explain to them in Washington why he gave such a young fellow—such a high rating—So I leave on the 28 of April for Camp Blanding to be sworn in. Keep your fingers crossed—because this navy officer is sticking his head a way out on my case. I still wont believe it until I'm in uniform wearing my stripes.

I'm telling you Jack they are different down here. In N.Y. I get kicked around. Down there they think that I'm a great guy—Keep your fingers crossed—and double crossed for here is the payoff—The Navy is conducting a War Bond Drive and is giving a program at noon hour in front of Burdines (which is the equivalent of R H Macy) on Flagler ST & Miami Ave. (which is like 34th St & 6 Ave). The busiest corner in town. There will be a stage platform on a gigantic trailer truck with the band from the carrier Yorktown which was sunk—a Chinese and a Russian chorus and three featured speakers two torpedoed seaman and Yours truly billed as a Spanish vet who has been fighting fascism since 1936—and has now found the navy no less—There will be pictures, newspapers and my speech will be broadcast over the largest radio station in Miami. I feel a bit leery now and am afraid somebody in Washington will hit me with a monkey wrench—

Once I get sworn in and into training they can only remove my rating via court martial and if they pull anything off this time I'm going to holler blue murder—Keep your fingers crossed again and again for I still don't believe it. Keep this story to our own bunch for the present and Ill send you the results of the Bond Rally—(I'm flabbergasted) with any publicity out on Thursday—but don't release any thing about this until I get sworn in and into the training camp—Then I'll really know what the score will be— not before—I Hope—(drawing of fingers crossed) I hope

Salud

Harry Hakam

Chief Electricians Mate-To-Be

FROM MORRIS KORNBLUM

Thurs Dec. 30, 1943

Dear Vets:

Many thanks for your gift of the "Seventh Cross."[32] I've just finished it and its effect on me is better than anything else I could have gotten for Christmas. Also thanks for the "Volunteer."

Even if I might have thought that my experiences in Spain were dead things, that the passage of years would obliterate the memory and that people wouldn't give a damn, events just don't work out that way. The discrimination against some of the boys in the Army, the heroic fighting of others, the awarding of honors and medals, the leadership shown by volunteers of other countries,—Italy, Yugoslavia and its genius—Tito etc; bring home again and again a feeling of accomplishment both past and present and pride for association with such men of character—even though I was not a fighter but a medical worker.

I expect to be in New York next week and will try to drop into the office. Good luck and best wishes for a victorious New Year.

Salud Morris Kornblum

FROM EDWARD LENDING

June 30, 1944

Dear fellers—

A report for the record. It may be of interest.

A year and a half of investigation into L'Affaire Lending Culminated. The decision: Cleared for overseas duty, granted right to ship with my outfit. But enjoined from holding any job or using any material listed as restricted, confidential, or secret; or entrance to OCS or other specialized training schools.

I may be a telephone operator—that equipment's no longer deemed secret.

The news is so damned good, it's numbing! Cherbourg and Vitebsk and Viyenni and Saipan and the CIO Political Action Committee—We had to encompass it all.

Salud,

Ed Lending

NOTES

1. Peter N. Carroll, *The Odyssey of the Abraham Lincoln Brigade: Americans in the Spanish Civil War* (Stanford, Cal.: Stanford University Press, 1994), 251.
2. Transcriptions of these interviews are in the Abraham Lincoln Brigade Archives.
3. These were Lincoln volunteers killed in Spain.
4. Edwin Rolfe Papers, University of Illinois Library.
5. *PM* was a left-wing New York afternoon newspaper; *New Masses* was a left-wing monthly magazine.
6. *Bread and a Stone* (New York: Modern Age Books, 1941).
7. Kuhn was head of the pro-Nazi German-American Bund.
8. Harold Smith, *Attack for Victory* (New York, 1942), a pamphlet published by the Veterans of the Abraham Lincoln Brigade.
9. Charles Coughlin was a Roman Catholic priest famous for his radio broadcasts that opposed U.S. intervention in World War II.
10. Milton Wolff Papers, University of Illinois Library.
11. The official U.S. government report on the attack at Pearl Harbor was directed by Supreme Court Associate Justice Owen J. Roberts.
12. Kelly flew the first U.S. combat mission against Japanese naval forces after Pearl Harbor, losing his life.
13. Milton Wolff Papers, University of Illinois Library.
14. Ibid.
15. Wolff refers to two British intelligence agents for whom he recruited Lincoln veterans to work on secret operations.
16. Myers was head of the National Maritime Union (NMU).
17. The German-American Bund, founded in 1934, was a pro-Nazi organization.
18. William Lemke (R-N.D.) ran for president in 1936 as the Union party candidate, allied to the anti–New Deal politics of Father Charles Coughlin.
19. Julius Streicher and Joseph Goebbels were leading Nazi propagandists.
20. Milton Wolff Papers, University of Illinois Library.
21. Dinah Sheean, wife of journalist Vincent Sheean, was Wolff's private link to Col. William Donovan, head of the Office of Strategic Services (OSS).
22. Irving Fajans, Irving Goff, and Bill Aalto were Lincoln veterans in the OSS.
23. General Henri-Philippe Petain, head of France's Vichy government, and Yugoslav guerrilla leader General Draja Mihailovitch collaborated with German occupation forces in their countries.
24. Bridges, allegedly a Communist, was head of the San Francisco waterfront workers' union.
25. Annibale Bergonzoli was an Italian officer captured in Libya in 1940.
26. Chester Stewart Stinson was a volunteer in the Lincoln Brigade.
27. The America First Committee, founded in 1940, was the largest group opposing U.S. intervention in World War II.
28. The Joint Anti-Fascist Refugee Committee worked to rescue and assist Spanish refugees, some of whom were in concentration camps in Europe and North Africa.
29. Joseph Leeds, *Let My People Know: The Story of Wilfred Mendelson, "Mendy" (August 17, 1915–July 28, 1938)* (New York, 1942).
30. TASS was the Soviet news agency.
31. The Workers Alliance, founded as a socialist organization in 1935 and later merged

with the Communist party's Unemployed Councils, attempted to unionize workers in the federal government's Works Project Administration.

32. Anna Seghers' *The Seventh Cross* (Boston: Little, Brown, 1942) was an anti-Nazi novel.

CHAPTER THREE

PROBLEMS IN RED AND BLACK

"Spain was the first place that I ever felt like a free man," remembered the African American veteran Tom Page, a native of New York City. "If someone didn't like you, they told you to your face. It had nothing to do with the color of your skin."[1] The southern-born Crawford Morgan explained that in Spain "people didn't look at me with hatred in their eyes because I was black, and I wasn't refused this or refused that because I was black. I was treated like all the rest of the people were treated, and when you have been in the world for quite a long time and have been treated worse than people treat their dogs, it is quite a nice feeling to go someplace and feel like a human being."[2]

In their struggle against fascism in Spain, the members of the Lincoln Brigade had resolved to eliminate the racial animosities that limited democracy in the United States. Among the nearly three thousand volunteers, more than eighty were African Americans, a half-dozen identified as Native Americans, two were Chinese, and one was Japanese; there were also Filipinos, Puerto Ricans, Cubans, and at least sixty different European white nationality or ethnic groups represented in the ranks. That brigade leaders kept such detailed records indicates that the Lincolns saw themselves as a self-conscious melting pot organization. Viewing itself as a "people's army," the Brigade created fully integrated military units, from officers to foot soldiers. Captain Oliver Law, killed in action in 1937, was the first African American battalion commander to lead predominantly white troops into battle. And when, despite official policy, racist comments did occasionally emerge, as they might in any army, brigade leaders acted decisively to stifle such outbursts.

These antiracist commitments contributed to the pride of the African American veterans who offered their services to the U.S. Army after the outbreak of World War II. When the Japanese attacked Pearl Harbor on December 7, 1941, Vaughn Love went the very next morning to volunteer for the army. "I didn't ask anybody because I knew that that was where I belonged. I knew since the end of the war in Spain that we would have to face these bastards ourselves."[3] Of the African Americans who survived the Spanish Civil War, nearly twenty served in the U.S. military, Merchant Marine, or health services.[4]

The U.S. military treated the black Lincolns, like their white comrades, as a distinct species both officially and informally. Their unique combat experience gave them a favorable status among the white officers and black soldiers. Some, like the former officer Walter Garland, were invited to give public lectures about the battles in Spain. Indeed, Garland's expertise as a machine gunner enabled him to make a mechanical improvement in the army's machine gun sights for which he received a military commendation. Others, like Vaughn Love, became respected instructors who trained African American GIs for combat roles, even though black troops were not expected to fight the enemy with weapons. Within the ranks, their personal prestige made the politically mature, battle-hardened veterans a steadying force to bolster the morale of their fellow soldiers. Yet despite their favorable impressions, the black Lincoln veterans typically faced the same political discrimination that confronted other Spanish Civil War veterans. And like other Lincolns, the African Americans waged a two-front war in the army, seeking opportunities to persuade the white leadership to give them meaningful assignments to hasten the defeat of fascism.

Such possibilities were drastically limited by the racially segregated system within the U.S. armed forces, a stark and omnipresent contrast to their circumstances in Spain's International Brigades. White and black Lincoln veterans alike frequently commented on this anomaly, and it remained a persistent insult to the ideology and personal feelings of those who faced both political and racial discrimination in a war ostensibly fought against the Nazi "master race." Nothing better reveals the resulting indignation than a letter by Bunny Rucker to his wife, describing his journey by train from New York City to his assignment at Fort Bragg, North Carolina:

> The unpleasantness of the Jim Crow ride was offset by the obvious contrast to the purposes for which all the passengers Negro and white were traveling. In spite of the harsh abusiveness of the conductor who made us change coaches in Washington, D.C. His manner defeated the purpose of Jim Crow. The long parade (some demonstration it was!) of

Negroes through the coaches to the front coach, with bags, parcels &
children was bound to be uncomfortably similar to lines of refugees, in
war areas. It suggested a deeper kinship between all oppressed peoples.
It's unbelievable and impossible that a nation can exist half-slave and
half-free. It's much too obviously true today for anyone with a spark of
honesty to deny it or remain complacent about any feature of Jim Crow.[5]

Rucker's image of refugees with "bags, parcels & children" evoked the
photographs made by Robert Capa that showed Spanish civilians fleeing
Franco's troops in 1938–39 and foreshadowed life in the segregated, Jim
Crow army.

Lincoln veterans, who had fought with weapons in Spain, deeply
resented their exclusion from combat roles in the U.S. army. Some
rationalized whatever contribution they could make to the defeat of
fascism, but many admitted that the waste of their skills infuriated them.
Such disappointments afflicted other segregated troops as well, as Rucker
indicated in another letter. Having seen the film *Stage Door Canteen* he
noted the contrast between "the advance of democracy and the backward-
ness of Jim Crow conditions in which the soldiers here were able to see the
movie." He was affected, though not surprised, that a black soldier had
attempted suicide.

> He has long been unable to make sense out of the situation and had
> developed a bitter resistance to the whole thing. A good mechanic and
> willing to work if only allowed to work unmolested by the general harass-
> ments of military Jim Crow life which is what it all amounts to. Given a
> 30 day sentence for not wearing the proper headdress was the cracking up
> point for him. He found some lye in the guard house, ate it then ate some
> laundry soap and cut his wrist with a razor blade. He made a messy
> unsuccessful job of it. His way of fighting. We must say it was ineffective,
> but so many other things he was doing are bound to have seemed
> ineffective to him. His skill, his life would be worth much more to the
> army if he were allowed to use it effectively. It certainly has not been used
> effectively.[6]

Besides such routine discrimination, Lincoln veterans were quick to
react to overt instances of race prejudice. When white military police
called one of Walter Garland's friends a "black bastard," the former officer

joined in the ensuing fistfight and was arrested. But he stood his ground and persuaded superior officers to pardon the alleged offense. Similarly, the Texas-born, white veteran Julius Deutsch used his political skills to transform an accidental incident of desegregation in the barracks into a more permanent situation. Other Lincoln vets happily observed these occasional violations of segregated military protocol.

The San Francisco white veteran Archie Brown had never seen Jim Crow before he was sent to Texas for training. His repugnance and sense of social justice came through clearly as he told his wife about a 1944 bus ride from Dallas to Camp Maxey, Texas:

> A white woman half paralyzed got on the bus and rode for some distance. She had great difficulty moving one foot. I didn't see her condition at first. She sat on a canvas stool in the aisle along with others. Some time later the bus discharged a number of people. Those remaining of course have the choice of the seats before anyone else is admitted. There was a space in back for a person—and the driver suggested she take it. But she was so prejudiced that even in her condition she refused to sit there. It was then I noticed her condition. My partner wanted to offer his seat—but I told him not to. She remained sitting in the aisle.
>
> In Fort Worth they have separate waiting rooms and toilets of course; over the drinking fountains are big signs saying "white." It made me sick to my stomach.
>
> Anyhow things are looking up. The Dallas papers are writing articles of how important the Negro vote is becoming.[7]

Lincoln correspondents also reported numerous instances of racial violence on and off base, particularly in the southern states. Black veterans feared assignments in the South and often stayed on the bases to avoid trouble. Some, like Jimmy Yates, noticed improvements in race relations from his earlier days in the South; Burt Jackson was delighted to be reassigned near Detroit. Northern whites like Milton Wolff were appalled by examples of public terror near Camp Wheeler, Georgia, and compared antiblack sentiment to fascist racism.

Black volunteers saw such racist treatment undermining the war effort. In his later oral history, Vaughn Love described his discovery of an elaborate scam by which white military police near Chattanooga, Tennessee, regularly arranged to prevent black soldiers from boarding buses back to their base, then arrested them for being Absent Without Official Leave (AWOL) and transferred them to Fort Oglethorpe, Georgia, where they were kept in an empty jail. "Every morning they would take them out and farm them out to these Georgia farmers," said Love.

> I got seventy or eighty affidavits. . . . They had an investigation and found out it had been going on all the time, only this was the first time anyone had complained. Now this was the difference with a first sergeant like myself. I didn't take any crap off these bastards. . . . They were selling the labor of these guys they took into custody. Here we are trying to win a war and these sons-a-bitches are taking soldiers away from their military duty to work on farms.[8]

Despite this hostile environment (or because of it), the African Americans pulled every string they could to obtain transfer into combat units. "I feel quite rested after my long furlough," wrote the optimistic Burt Jackson, "for that is all the interval between Spain and the return to the front is." Although assigned to a "pick and shovel outfit," Tom Page exulted upon his arrival in a war zone in North Africa. Sergeant Vaughn Love proudly led his quartermaster group, which he had personally trained for combat, overseas in 1944, though an injury kept him out of action. Bunny Rucker, utterly disgusted with segregation, eagerly transferred into a medical unit, if only to get to Europe. Once there, he volunteered for combat in northern Italy and Germany, where he finally got his chance to fight, but was seriously wounded in 1945.

None achieved greater heroics than Sergeant Edward Carter II. Although his military record in Spain is sparse, Carter boasted of combat experience in a 1942 interview with the army newspaper at Fort Benning, Georgia. He had enlisted the previous year, two months before Pearl Harbor, and took basic training in Texas, where he expressed shock at racial conditions in the South. Although Carter was an excellent marksman, the army placed him in a quartermaster truck company and shipped him overseas in 1944. The German counteroffensive in December, known as the Battle of the Bulge, compelled the army to use black troops in combat situations. Like Bunny Rucker, Carter seized the opportunity. Coming under attack in Germany while riding with his rifle squad on a tank in March 1945, Carter bravely fought off a German squad, killed at least six enemy soldiers, and captured two, despite receiving multiple wounds. The army awarded him the Distinguished Service Cross, the highest honor given to any African American during World War II. Fifty years later, in a ceremony held at the White House in Washington, D.C., President Bill Clinton added to the laurels by awarding Carter, along with six other African American soldiers of World War II, a posthumous Congressional Medal of Honor for his valor in Germany. By then, only one African American Lincoln veteran, Frank Alexander, was still alive; he died in 1996.

The correspondence of the African American veterans reflected their anomalous position: fervent antifascists, but obliged to serve in a segregated military that seemed to mirror the racial values of the enemy. The private letters of Bunny Rucker to his wife that appear below reveal the tremendous anxiety, frustration, and rage that followed from that paradox. But Rucker's emotional outbursts, spoken intimately to the only person he truly trusted, appear to be exceptional among these letters. Walter Callion voiced no particular anger when he wrote, in the first letter to reach the VALB office in January 1942 and printed below, "I am colored so we are in a different outfit." He assumed that all Lincoln veterans understood the absurdity, shared his frustration, and yet would remain as committed as he was to stay in the fight against the common enemy. Indeed, that restrained, matter-of-fact voice steadies most the correspondence of this chapter.

I. ENTERING THE SEGREGATED ARMY

FROM WALTER P. CALLION

Jan. 25, 1942

Hello Friends:

I am a soldier in the artillery unit here in Fort Sills, Okla. My name is Walter P. Callion. I was in Spain 14 months in 1937–38. Today I went over to the 29th Battalion to see a friend of mine John Gates. I heard he was here in Fort Sills. He sure looks well and little as ever. We talked for about an hour so I left.

I am colored so we are in a different outfit. I have been in the army for four months and now I am in the regular Army.

Gates wants to go to the officers training school and get in the tank regiment. I want to go to the officers school too and I think I have a good chance to go.

Friends; my home is in St. Louis, Missouri. The reason I am writing to you is because I want to keep in touch with the Lincoln Brigade and meet some of the old boys. So will you please try to answer this letter for I will be looking for an answer.

Salud,

Walter P. Callion

FROM WALTER P. CALLION

March, 6. 1942

Fort Sill, Oklahoma

Dear [Moe] Fishman

[. . .] There is not much going on down here. A few of the boys are leaving here for the 29th. Quartermaster Corp. in California as truck-drivers, the Battery commander said he was going to keep me here to start this new Anti-tank outfit we are going to have one 37mmgun it is A small cannon A 50 cal. machine gun and A 20mm machine gun. This Regiment was using the 155mm gun, a very large Artillery gun, and now we are going to use the French 75mm. instead of the 155mm.

Listen Fishman I do not like the American Army as well as I did the Spanish Army some of these officers and I seem to agree to disagree but we will make it all right I guess they all ways want to holler at some one like a fool until they found out that I was in Spain and they seem to get interested in me all of a sudden I can get along fine now so far so good.

You know I do not get very much mail and sure would like to get more letters I do not have much to write about because there is no news down here, but I would like to know what is going on out in civilian life this place is just like the jungles same thing every day I have not been off this camp in three month there is a little town called Lawton about three miles from the post it is so small you can walk through it in fifteen Min. so there is no place to go, they should give Oklahoma back to the INDIANS. It is no place for me.

So I will not say good by but so long till I hear from you. [. . .]

WALTER P. CALLION

From Crawford Morgan

Camp Pickett, Virginia

9-2-42

Dear Elsie—

[. . .] I am some place down in Virginia three miles from a little town name [B]lackstone, population 1800 and our camp has over 40,000 troops here.

I came here last week and began school this past Monday. The hours are 5:45 a.m. to 5:30 p.m. complete then you are on your own until 11 p.m. You are free most Saturdays at noon until 11 p.m. Sunday, not so bad if it wasn't for the very, very bad transportation. So we [?] the most of us don't go any place over the week-ends.

The training period is for eight weeks. We don't spend all of our time in school, we drill and do a lot of other things.

I am in a Medical Battalion. I don't use a gun. I was mad as hell when we just arrived here from Dix last week, but I have got over it. There are not many negroes here but of 40,000 there are one Negro Engineering Div. I don't know what kind of officers they have, negro or white. We have 17 Med. Battalion here one are negro with negro noncoms and all white officers.

The boys here say you have a very good chance here of going to the O.T.S. but once you get four bars they send you away very quick.

All in all it's not bad here, it was very good in Dix. All of the negroes there was in the K.P. including myself every day. [. . .]

Salud

Crawford Morgan

From Burt Jackson

Southeast Air Corps

Training Center

Tuskegee Army Flying School

Tuskegee, Alabama

Oct 1, 1942

Hi Fellows;

I was quite pleased to hear from you. I still feel ashamed at the way I take my time about writing; but you fellows aren't bad either.

I know that it's dull on the home front, but I am sure you fellows are doing a swell job.

When you get blue and miss the guys in khaki, well just remember that "En el retroguardia si esta muy buena a ti."[9]

But no staff fellows. The Air Corps is the berries. For some reason or other every other soldier you meet seems to be a 2nd Looie or a Staff Sgt. I am a three upper and a one downer my self (Staff Sgt.)

However, the real joy of being a member of a fighting anti fascist army again is dulled and some time sorely tried by being so near "Montgomery cradle of the confederacy" (at least that's what the road signs say outside the capital of Alabama).

However, I am sure that we will soon get a chance at the major perpetrators of racial superiority. God but it will do me good to be at the other end of air attacks. And think how "der Fuehrer" will feel when he sees his prized air force knocked out of the sky by people he has taught his "aryans" to despise.

Anyhow say hello to the fellows that are still in the big city and drop me a line when you get time.

Till Victory
Burt Jackson

From James Yates

Sunday 22
11/24/42
Pvt. James Yates
427 Sig.C. Rm. Co.B
Davis Monthan Field
Tucson, Arizona

Hello Vets

Well here I am out in the west, after a few months in the army. I was 2 w[ee]ks at Fort Dix one day I was told to pack up and go, and the train headed west [to] Pitt. Pa. Well all the boys was happy that we was not going to the South land but we forgot that one could go South in the army from Indiana. Which we did and landed in Fort McClellen, Ala. for a 6 wks cycle of training, had to get in 6 wks what other before us got in 13 wks. A beautiful camp is Fort McClellan, surrounded with beautiful mountains, we started marching when the train reached the camp and it was on the go until the Captain says you must pack and go you can't stay here.

But truly no joke I did like my stay in dixie. Camp life was better than I expected, food was fair. I got a chance to see my Mother who I hadn't seen in 10 yrs. And a few weekends in Birmingham, Ala.

I have lived in the South before in fact I was born there. And I can already see a new South with a great change, taking place among its people, a very hopeful sign of progress.

Our trip from Fort McClellan to Arizona was quite a pleasure. A Pullman train with diner, 3 days & nights through Miss. La. Texas, New Mex and we arrived in Arizona on Sun. I was placed in the Sig. Corps. in the Air force. We have a swell outfit. Part time we are in classes and the rest out in the field. It['s] lots of fun out in and under an Arizona Sun, Oh, we always have to be on the watch out for rattlesnakes which we do quite well. Some of the boys ran across a few wild hogs in the mountains. We had the day off (Sun) and a few of us went rabbit hunting.

Our camp is just 5 miles from Tucson which is a beautiful place. Also we can get passes every nite if one wishes.

I am just about getting use to the air planes flying over at night. It was very hard to sleep my first week here.

My Lieut. told me the other day that he had noticed on my record that I had served in Loyalist Army, and as soon as he gets a chance he wanted to talk with me about my experience in Spain.

I think every man in my outfit welcomes the Africa offensive but realizes only an offensive in Europe will be the real thing.

Say hello to all the boys and write soon.

Yours friend Vet.

From Walter Garland

Company "D" 731st Military
Police Ba.
114th Inf. Armory, Camden, N.J.
December 20, 1942

Dear Jack [Bjoze]:

I received "The Great Offensive"[10] this morning, and it is difficult to say how completely grateful I am for it. Gosh, it made me hold my breathe.

Somehow, you really feel being cut off from all discussion and to be able to sit down to read such a book (if it is at all like "Military Strength") it is a real treat.

Just as I was opening the package, the company commander walk[ed] up behind me and asked to see it. I, of course turned it over to him, anxious to get his reaction. (Not because of any interest in him but rather that he seems unusually interested in the fact that I read considerably and I supposed he wants to know more "WHAT") Well he seemed to know quite a bit about Max Werner. And had read his first book. He thumbed thru the fly leaf to see who published it and checked how many copies had been sold. He is a former intelligence man. He saw the Vets seal and wanted to know was it an order. Of course I explained to him that it was made up of those who served in the Brigade in Spain. Being a Floridian and a staunch Rotary man I felt sure that seeing the name Abraham Lincoln might cause quite a rise but he finished up his remarks by saying the "what America needs is one opinion about the war and quit (name calling), just as in Lincoln's time all kinds of mud was slung at him."

I certainly look forward to many a happy hour thumbing the pages of this book.

Perhaps Elsie or Pat [Garland] has told you of the M.G. Sight that I have been working on. As you probably don't know the tests on it were highly successful and greatly improved the accuracy of the Browning Light M.G. when it is mounted for firing from the M3 Scout car. A model is now being prepared by the Bn. Colonel and The Co. Comm.; when it is finished he promised that we would take it to Washington for the powers that be.

Best regards to [John] Murra, who, rumor has it, is now in the office. Ask Elsie to write when time permits.

Walt

FROM JOE TAYLOR

Sgt. E.J. Taylor
730 Med San. Co.
Camp Mackall, N.C.
May 17 1943

Dear Jack [Bjoze]

I am some what ashamed of myself for not having written you & the "Vets" before now. I will try to do much better in the future.

I want to thank you and the staff for sending me the "Volunteer for Liberty." The copies I've received have been swell. Even my company commander has on two occasions read it. Not to mention the guys in my company who [every] month ask for it and for me to explain to them, some of the things in it. As a matter of fact the Volunteer is my only means of knowing what the guys are doing both on the International & home fronts.

Crawford Morgan was with me both [in] Va. & Miss. but he is now in Tenn. doing OK I understand. As for myself I have been in Medical unit every since I've been in the army for the past 8 months I have been what is called a Medical Sanitary Company. Our job is Mosquito Control in Camps on this side so far. This is quite a let down when you think those of us who went to Spain fought in the Army. Well they say it takes everything to win the war, so until something better comes along I'll do my best in this outfit.

I have been here in North Carolina for about a month. We don't expect to be here long any way it is a hell of a lot better than Miss. I hope I never have to go there again.

Well Jack when you get time drop me a line or two and you can be sure I will answer it. Give my regards to all of [the] guys when you see or write to them.

So until next time I'll sign off, hoping to hear from you soon.

As Ever Fraternally

Joe Taylor

2. POLITICAL DISCRIMINATION

FROM WALTER GARLAND

Sunday Mar. 27, 1943

Dear Jack [Bjoze]—

The following is a statement you requested. Its briefness will save you time and make it easier, it is hoped, to conduct your important work.

As you know induction took place at Ft. Jay May 26, 1942, immediate transferal followed to Camp Upton. It was at this time that the experience and activity in Spain was made known to the Army Intelligence. Reasons were clear—a demonstration of good faith and an honest desire to make what ever small contribution possible towards winning the war.

I was then assigned to 731st Military Police Bn at Ft. Wadsworth, Staten Is. My C.O. at that time admitted that a telegram had been forwarded, in advance of my arrival, warning the[m] that I was a communist and a veteran of Spain's struggle for freedom from Fascist Slavery. At that time there was a fairly free talk about what any intentions were. He accepted my statement and never had any reason to think that my role was anything but that was directed towards welding a tighter organization making whatever offering possible towards building a unit ready to grapple with those monsters.

The past ten months have been passed in trying to make as much as possible positive a contribution to the army. I taught a map making class, ran a Bn Scout Car School, a Bn Mortar School. Participated in the training program in Machine Gun instructions. Offered for consideration that Machine Gun Sight Aid and received commendation from the N.J. Military District Commander for it.

All proposals for transfer to a combat organization have been either covertly or openly refused.

Trusting this will be of some help.

Walt

P.S. The "Sight Aid" is supposed to be confidential, do whatever you feel is wise!

FROM JAMES YATES

> Cpl. James Yates
> 47 Aviation Sqdn.
> Davis Monthan Field
> Tucson, Arizona
> 2/20/43

Dear Vets

It maybe interesting that you know I have been transferred out of my old unit just before they left for duty, although, I enlisted in the Army. And have had only one interest—and that was becoming a good soldier in

James Yates

my outfit. I am buying one bond each month. As one means to help win the war.

It had been my greatest desire to have stayed with my unit whom I had learned to love. It was as much a shock to the boys and officers as to me. Although since I have learned from good sources it was because I fought in Spain.

Well I going to keep plugging and trust that some day I will be able to take up the fight on the battlefield against fascism.

My regards to the Vets

Yours Jim

FROM JAMES BERNARD (BUNNY) RUCKER

Fort Bragg

North Carolina

March 12, 1943

My Darling Wife [Helen Rucker]:

It did happen. Just as I was at the height of preparations for playing at least a definite and positive part in this phase of the war, a special order from the Ft. Bragg Post Headquarters came down which transferred me to the Post Detachment, under the provisions of an order that requires me to be re-classified for "limited service." I've already moved. My new organization does maintenance work around the Post. Trash disposal, beautification and care of the grounds all over Ft. Bragg, etc. I'm not in the same work as Winnie, which is to unload freight cars, but my area is immediately adjacent to his. All in all, it's a lousy outfit as far as I can see. I am transferred with my present rank. How long I will keep it I can't say, because I won't let the prevailing conceptions of ranks and ratings prevent me from expressing my thoughts about a lot of things. It just doesn't make sense, although it's clear what is behind such prejudicial actions. And it's more than disgusting with its degenerate motivations. However, it does stand to reason that these motivations will never have successful results, regardless of what it may do to me personally, and I admit that it is having and will have a strong personal effect on me. I was hit very hard a truly foul blow if there ever was one, taking into account the whole picture of what I have tried earnestly to represent my whole career in the army and before, I took personal pride in that I acted on the basis of my hatred against Hitlerism at all times, and I had personal hopes that I'd be given by my own country even a limited opportunity to express that hatred through some measure of participation in our armed forces. This has been effectually denied me by my transfer—from an already Jim-Crowed "Separate" organization into non-combatant limited service on a Jim Crow basis. Even my own commanders recognized the insult and expressed their regret that they had to give me an explanation at my own request. They were very convincing in their proof that they were not a part of giving the order and I have reason to believe they were sincere. It is a policy which is being practiced in such cases since Sept. 11, 1942.

As it is I have a very undecided attitude toward the career that awaits me. It's impossible for me to be sincere about it. "Limited Service" is not that at all. The limited part is O.K. but it's certainly not Service. It's an absence of Service and a limit to the desire of some people somewhere to use policies that will win the war quickly. More than my personal case is the fact that this is an over-all policy which is being used by a nation that is in the midst of a life and death war with the most ruthless, most destructive enemies of mankind in all the history of the world. So what is indignant in me is just the reactionary affront to just plain common sense and the fact that it's so easy to be put over the American people. If this can be, what of Jim Crow, what of the Four Freedoms, what of Democracy, what of all the things for which the American People are fighting with their backs to the wall.

The boys in my old company are very disturbed about this element in the nature of my transfer even without my having ventured to discuss it with them. They are discussing and are doubting and I can't be there to re-assure them about the real nature of the war which they are in. My C.O.'s expressed plainly their concern for this question when I discussed my being transferred.

My new organization, I can see is organized with some of the worst features of plantation organization and personnel techniques. I'm sure that I'm going to rebel vigorously against a lot of them and regardless to how well advanced progressive democratic leadership is (or is not) in respect to this big question mark blot on American Democracy. I'm just about fed up with "carrying the torch" when there are so many others who need the light of that torch as well as I and who are surely in a better position for carrying it than I could be expected to be under prevailing circumstances. That's being personal perhaps, but personally I am a human being with no less sensibilities and self-respect than any other.

I'm going to try very hard in the next few days to see everything in its true perspective, but I am going to fight somehow, if only against the limitations which prevent my entering fully into the fight against the main enemy. Although that will consume a lot of energy which could be put to better use. [. . .]

Bunny

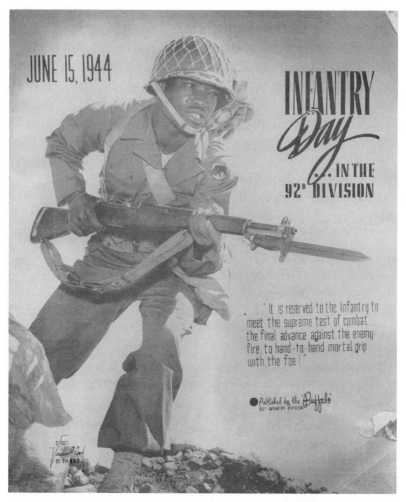

Bunny Rucker served with the segregated 92nd Infantry Division.

3. CHALLENGING JIM CROW

FROM WALTER GARLAND

---

10 February 44

Dear Anne [Brier]:

[. . .] That really wasn't sarcasm about the fox holes of Camp Upton. Some M.P.'s referred to a Negro soldier as a B—k B—d. A fight ensued! Several of us were arrested. However, as a result of some straight talking (and reviewing officers with democratic inclinations) we were absolved of all "guilt."

Salud y Victoria
Walt Garland

That "Sight" of mine is now on exhibit at the Chrysler Bldg. on 42nd Street: If you are around that way—drop in.

FROM JAMES BERNARD (BUNNY) RUCKER

Fort Huachuca, Arizona
April 26 [1944]

Darling [Helen Rucker]:

[. . .] I think I'll be building my reserve back in a little while. They've had me scraping the bottom lately. I don't know what's been lacking, but somehow I haven't been allowing things to work themselves out. I've been pushing and straining pretty hard. A left-handed way of being without confidence. The trouble is in the nature of the work I do and I don't look at it in a broad enough view. I made an analysis of such an outfit as this. Even the army makes an official distinction and is correctly objective in making it. The medics is a service force, not an arm. Tactically we are considered as without arms. (None are provided). It isn't even mentioned in the partial list of services given in the manual. This provides the key to understanding a lot about such a unit and one's own attitude and allowances should be made for the distinction when individual evaluations come up. My trouble is that we all generalize too freely as to what our outfit does and its relationship within the forces of victory. The army command does not generalize. It makes the distinction. We fail to make it with inaccurate results in our way of thinking. So when we resent being patted on the head we misdirect our resentment and fall into traps. For me, it's a special problem. I have never liked this kind of work, I have no special capabilities to suit it. And I'm conscious that I'm only trying to make the best out of a bad situation in which I will never be satisfied. My problem is to keep this dissatisfaction from being a source of antagonism toward those who are adapted to or like, or specialize in this work, or toward anything in any general way. That is, to be able to see the whole picture all the time. I have no means of protest. I haven't thought of anything I might do individually that wouldn't make matters worse. It's a case of eating humble pie and liking it. That's what the army is like. I read in P.M. how Don Gentile's creed was the air corps or nothing. Well . . . that's not B. Rucker. B. Rucker had to challenge Federal laws signed by the President himself, before he was able to give what he could in the fight against Hitler. He had to violate the international neutrality agreement by crossing the French border into Spain in the night. Sneaking past internationally constituted guards. Now the picture is bigger and B. Rucker must carry out his ordered assignments whether he likes them or not. But he takes an awful beating, not only from his dislike of the assignment, his preference for others that he could carry out as well if not better, but from the taxing of all the military morale he can muster. I'm not ashamed that it is such a difficult assignment. I'm just recognizing the fact, because at any moment, in any day, I'm strained to the utmost and left with only the tiniest bit of reserve. This makes it harder for me to approximate and appreciate the attitudes of my fellows, for which I need that tiny reserve. So I have none for myself many times. That's the bargain. Willingness to give everything to the "last full measure." It would be much easier to give it all at once. Many times I can think with pleasure that it would be a relief to swallow that last gurgle of blood. It would be warm and sweet and restful. I never think of death on the present battle-fields as being unpleasant. I can always think of many more unpleasant things that I've seen since I've been in the Army. It's easy for me to volunteer for overseas duty. I don't deserve any credit for that. It's a sure relief from this kind of living. I can't call it running away from a fight because it's asking for permission to go to a fight. The only credit I might get is for enduring the refusals that I've received to every one of such requests. I feel very close to my Irish-Catholic buddy I spoke of, the German-American, the Greek-American and the others. We'll have fun wherever we get together and I can tell them about the future that they left. Maybe we'll get to know a lot of Russians. But the reactionaries are afraid even to risk letting me join those buddies that way. Their superstitions make them worry even about their "other world." They want it pure and rid of the virus of mongrelization and the "slums of the world's great cities" as we were called and are treated like now.

Yes, they've already started acting cagey here. One doesn't need a thermometer to know when a chill sets in. They're doing it in an "obscure" fashion. "Intangible" "inscrutable," "wispy." But, you know who'd be sensitive to it first. I know something of how you must have felt and thought about me during the first month after I came into the army and once afterward, I will go through with it, Darling, because you understood and went through those experiences with me. Because I believe that my going through it will result in some way or another to some added happiness for you. I have promised it to you because it is yours. All the best that I can do belongs to your happiness. I want you to know and be convinced of that, Hon. Each crisis that I go through is a pearl for an anniversary necklace for you. I want you to wear it proudly for me some day. I want it to be the thing of beauty and endurance that you deserve for all the things that you've given me.

But I'll be seeing you next week, Honey and I can tell you about all of this first hand. That phone call was nice. You were so close to me. It seemed that when we paused I was running my hand through your hair. Like the time on 62nd St. when I brushed that one wisp out of your face. That time! I felt very close to you then after being so far for so many years and generations. But last night I was even closer than that. There were all the many unbreakable ties that we've drawn between us making us closer at 2500 miles than we were sitting side by side in the same classroom or watching you dance at Bob's or watching you go down the subway steps. Or trying to write you a note with an excuse in it for seeing you again, or dodging you at the big meeting, etc. Distance, time, the elements, events can never break our ties nor separate us. We've been together a long, long time and we'll be together forever.

I love you Baby, with all my heart.

Bunny

FROM JAMES BERNARD (BUNNY) RUCKER

June 6, 1944

D-Day

The Second Front is jumping, and here we are, at the farthest point in the world from the war. Very strategically placed reserves in Arizona. The "Charging Buffaloes"! who are trained to seek out the enemy and defeat him in battle. What's going on, on the other side of these mountains around us? I hear there's a war going on somewhere. We're doing a good job of lying around camp. Plenty beer in the PX. Roller-skating, books in the library, tennis courts, baseball games. Typical Army camp life you civilians have ordered for us.

I am carrying out your specific order to FIGHT. We are all holding the Huachuca Front, just in case Geronimo's ghost or Pancho Villa's start an attack on our democracy. The bitterness rises with each new bulletin that comes over the radio. Many things come to mind as one contemplates an immobilized mass of trained soldiers. Immobilized by Jim Crow. Behind the formidable barriers of the Huachuca mountains. We are in an impregnable position from which to "seek out and defeat the enemy in battle."

Love,
Bunny

But how in the world can I hope for a picture you presented of the American people openly denouncing Jim Crow as fascist. [. . .]

The other night in a newsreel, an Oklahoma white soldier, recently released from Hitler's prisons, was interviewed. He related how he told the Nazis that we have equality in America. The whole theatre rocked with boos for 15 minutes. Does this soldier call Oklahoma Jim Crow—equality? Is that the support which Negroes will expect from a Postwar America? Will a returned army tell us that we have equality in America? Oklahoma "equality" is certainly not a war aim of the Negro people, but that is what we have. Our general was booed something terrific the other day at a ball game. I was at the game but the booing could be heard all over the Post for a long time. The 92nd song was played and no one sang. The general stepped to the middle of the field insisting that everyone sing. It sounded like a Brooklyn-Cincinnati ball game. The general can't be blamed. He was assigned to this job and is under his orders[. . . .]

FROM JAMES BERNARD (BUNNY) RUCKER

July 14, [1944]

Darling [Helen Rucker]:

Soon, I'll be turning my back on the Jim Crow United States and with not a single regret. It won't be goodbye to Jim Crow because the Army seems to have pledged that it will carry Jim Crow to the far corners of the Earth. At least I'll be away from the main source and fountain of Jim Crow. That's a great relief under any circumstances. That relief and I know you are willing to grant it to me, overshadows any possible feeling of regret at leaving you. I won't be nearly as separated from you away from Jim Crow United States as I have been while I was here. You couldn't see me in North Carolina when we were only a few hours of a weekend apart, when you might have spent a vacation with me. For more than a year we were that close and yet separated as much by Jim Crow as we could possibly be by miles of ocean. Then for no other reason than Jim Crow, I was stationed in the most isolated camp in the country just as distant from you as any of the war theaters.

If our hearts could span Jim Crow, they can span any separation. So I have not the tiniest bit of maudlinism about adding a new kind of separation to that which has always been in effect in America. I hope to return to an America that is not Jim Crow. I've been hoping that for as long as I can remember, so I don't bank too much on my hopes, I just wear them like my dog tags. Just the experiences on the ride to and from N.Y. demonstrated that it makes Goddamned little difference to me if I return at all. Any American who can live comfortably in such a regime is someone whom I will never understand. So I could never be very content among them anyway. So I take the coming trip and subsequent events as just another part of the separation that we've already known.

If I am well when the time comes for returning, I'll come if I feel like it. It won't make much difference either way. If I decide not to come back, I'll see if you would want to join me and make arrangements in case you should.

I'm sure you don't feel about Jim Crow United States the way I feel and that you feel capable of finding some satisfaction within its limitations. I never did and never will. I have never been satisfied with all the limitations that we've put up with. I will never look back on those times with any satisfaction. For every pleasure there was an insult. For every embrace there was a kick in the ass, for every kiss I was spit on. For every step toward your house there was a step back to Hell. My worst regret is that I was not allowed to leave Jim Crow U.S. sooner.

The first thing I will do will be to piss in the waters that wash the shores of the Jim Crow South. It will be a great day for me to absent myself from it. Here I have endured and seen as much of fascism as I'd ever expect to see in Germany or Spain. I've seen abuses of an entire people perpetuated in the most cynical fashion that lied and lied to the world. That presumed to impose liberty on people all over the world. God help such peoples if it's the liberty of the South and of Negroes. Promise an Italian or a Frenchman that his liberty will be that of American Negroes. Won't he rejoice at that! But aren't Negroes expected to rejoice at their own liberty! Liberty to ride the back of the bus. Liberty to be last class citizens in the life of the country.

Farewell Jim Crow America. Don't promise me that you will rid it of Jim Crow. Promise yourself. It won't be long before we know all the answers to these questions, Hon, and I'll be perfectly satisfied to know that I played some part in settling them. Whatever I'm leaving has been nothing but the hard lot of a Negro last class American and that is certainly nothing to cry over leaving. I still can't rejoice fully at leaving because I've seen tears of suffering in a Negro woman's eyes as late as the bus ride on Tuesday. It's not joyful to have that as a picture of the country you are serving. But that is the picture.

To you I'll leave all the love in my heart and a hope that my energies will produce happiness for you.

Your husband for always,
Bunny

FROM BURT JACKSON

May 17–43

Dear Comerada

I am happy to say I have left the "sunny south" and am now stationed at Selfridge Field just outside of Detroit. I'd appreciate it if you'd send me the address of some of our guys that might be here or in Cleveland.

Well it looks like this time I'll really make it. The units that my former unit (before it was disbanded) was attached to are now over seas. So I think it won't be long now.

I sure was glad to hear of the African victory; maybe now I'll be able to be with yanks when we march again through the olive fields and streets of a free Spain.

Incidentally I have changed my "profession," I am not on maps anymore. I am now an armament specialist. So when we get over where things are happening I will have a personal hand in arranging "gifts" for the enemy.

Well say hello to the guys for

T/Sgt Burt Jackson

FROM VAUGHN LOVE

Aug. 29, 1943;

Dear Elsie—

[. . .] It is all straight now and I am getting in touch with my friends so that I can get some mail. I came out of Lee as a 1st Sgt., but when I arrived here I found that the situation did [not] call for a 1st Sgt so I am still a buck Sgt., we should be headed across before long. I am with a service company and you know what that means. I wanted something better than that but that is how it stands today.

I don't worry too much about those things anymore. I just feel like getting it over with whatever I have to do as my share.

I don't like Mississippi on principle but I like the camp alright as camps go. I don't go into the town which is Hattiesburg, Miss. It is a famous town for its favorite sports. I hope we clear out of here soon. Write me all the news about the boys. It seems like I won't be able to come home before I go across. It will be pretty tough but I just won't think about it. I would like to visit my wife and see all the folks before leaving. I won't tell Elsie that I can't come in before I go away. She will just get a letter one day that I am overseas.

Salud

Vaughn Love

FROM WALTER GARLAND
----

26 Mar. 44

Dear Anne [Brier]—

[. . .] This place is interesting. The entire cantonment is devoted to giving elementary education to new draftees. All the men, excluding the cadre are either illiterates or men of foreign nationality who do not have a functional understanding of English.

Here they are taught reading writing and arithmetic. Their stay here is from 2 to 16 weeks depending on either their ability to learn or past education. Half of every day is spent in academic instruction and the other half in basic infantry instruction.

If a man fails to meet the required basic IQ in 16 weeks he is discharged honorably from the service.

The above causes some additional problems. Since all Negroes come into the service with a very sharp and bitter feeling to Jim Crow in our army there is a definite movement to refuse to show the necessary understanding to graduate from the school and thus "buck" for a discharge.

Naturally from the view of developing the mighty anti-fascist army needed this is one of the key jobs here. How to instill that understanding is not yet fully realized. I've been talking to some of the men I already know. Others who I smoke out I'll try and do the same.

The instructor staff is made up of Negro and white teachers. They are attached to the same company. They likewise sleep and eat together.

The EM seems to like the negro teachers better. The men feel they learn more from them.

Gosh writing to you about these things makes me think harder about "what is to be done." Tomorrow I'll report this to the C.O. and see what he thinks about getting negro instructors.

The place has little to offer socially. There are hardly 10 negro families in a radius of 100 miles. Watertown is in between the two main routes of the Underground railroad (the one up the Hudson valley thru Lake Placid and Plattsburg is 70 miles east of here. The second thru Ohio is 200 miles west.)

The nearest town, Watertown has none living there, and the townsfolk while not discriminating as to servicing them in restaurants and hotels does not make a move toward the problem otherwise.

There is nothing else that I can think of at the moment. I'll let you know more as I go along.

Regards to Harold [Smith] and everyone that you see.

Salud

W.

4. WHITES TAKE A STAND

From Samuel Waitzman

4/5/42

Dear Hy and Vets:

[. . .] I was shocked by news of Diaz's[11] untimely death. I've always thought of him as the Spanish Earl Browder[12] and felt something twitch my heart when I read the news.

Another shock was the death of John Kozar, we used to call Topsy in Spain. I worked with him for months and learned to respect his earthiness, fancifulness and devotion to the struggle. His career though shortlived is a kind of legend—Briefly he came over on the torpedoed City of Barcelona, May 1937—wore a black tie for a year thereafter because when he crawled up on the Barcelona Beach after the boat went down he had no shirt on but this thin black tie around his neck. He was reputed one of the best "organizers" in Spain. He could rig up a dinner in the wilderness as among the scrub and brush of barren wasteland when food couldn't come up and "the famine was on." His ambulance, which he drove for 14 months throughout almost every important action of the 35th Div., was a wonder wagon. It had hidden chests of reserve & emergency provender, stove, and a few cigarettes. More than all this—nobody ever met Topsy but remembered him and became attached to him. His death brings the war to my personal doorstep even more than my early induction and is a spur to increase my efforts to become a more useful soldier. His fearlessness under fire is an inspiration. [. . .]

Of the South I might add this after one year in its confines: It could stand a lot of afl & cio goin' over—We in the North are apt to think of the Negro question in academic terms—Down here you'd be alarmed at the deep-rooted prejudices, smugness and hatred of the Negro—and the Negro is incited against another minority: the Jews—These two questions appropriately tie up down here—Have been having regular conversations with local people on these questions—Their own mean lives drive them as much as the insecurity ever, at their backs, to support their prejudices. Most of these people are tired, exhausted and hounded daily by their struggle for existence: yet they are the first to attack unionism, small business and the minorities.

USO's are beginning to operate here and though they are of the tea & crumpet variety, they reflect best the level of politicalization of the broadest sections of the army—many questions soldiers have on their lips go unanswered—But the rumblings made by the repetitions of such questions as Why did Japan attack? What is our stake in concrete terms? Define four freedoms brought down to ham & eggs language. As against these questions I'm hearing more frequently: "Lucky brother there's a Red Army." "What about another Front?" "Will we have to fight Russia next?" "When do we haul ass outa' here?" Which shows that no attempt is being made to deepen political understanding in the army. Our boys will have to learn as usual, the hard way. Tonight Mrs. FDR in a good 15 minute cast on the air talked asking gov't agencies to reassure youth in the army and at the workbench of economic security after the war. She also talked of giving youth entering the front line forces, a better grounding of his position, stake and role in the war. I can only hope her suggestions are carried down. So much for now. Regards and affection to the Vets & yourself—

Samuel Waitzman

From Milton Wolff[13]

August 23rd, 1942

Love [Ann Wolff]—

[. . .] A negro soldier killed a cop and wounded an M.P. in Macon the other night. The lynch spirit flared up in a minute. The news got around quicker than you can possibly imagine. Had we won the war on that day nobody would have known it. Each and every Negro citizen disappeared from sight well aware of the fact that they could easily become victims. We revolt in horror at the thought of hostages shot by the Nazis. The degenerate white southerners hunting, as though in sport, Negro victims are no better—in fact I feel they are <u>worse</u>. These decaying, poisoned people of the south are Nazis in spirit.

Of course I do not mean all the people. You have your workers, and poor whites who just don't understand the question though most have been contaminated with the poison of race hatred. For them there must be some hope. But for the lynchers—<u>none</u>.

They are the type that sit in front of hotels, or hang around the warehouses, barber shops and whore houses. So as you say—"nothin from nothing."

Well, I am still sailing along here—pretty evenly. Being approached by all and sundry on my experiences in Spain—though quite disappointingly no official request to speak to the company. I am most anxious to do this in order to counteract some of the shallow crap that has already been slung around[. . . .]

When we go on the range and talk of nothing but women and the "nigger situation." They are akin to the Castilian's of Royal Spain. Pure and rotten to the core.

They have sown a field of poisonous hatred in the South that can only end in a violent blood letting of the kind the world has yet to witness. The small local flareups—unparalleled in their minute violence—are the warning flags of what's to come. . . .

All my love, darling

Milton

FROM JACK SHAFRAN

June 17, 1942

Dear Jack [Bjoze]—

I'm in the hospital now—But expect to be out on Friday or Saturday—I'm in since last Thursday—I had piles (from Spain yet) so I had them cut out—

The point of this letter though is this—Here in the hospital there are both Negro and white patients in the same wards—And to boot—the staff, the orderlies and men who do bandaging, etc., are also mixed—so far I haven't heard one patient say a thing about being treated by a colored ward boy—

The staff also gets on fine—some of the colored boys are non-coms too—none of the white fellows resent taking orders from them either—

If Negro and whites can get along in the medics, why not in combat units also? [. . .]

Well, that's about all there is to say so I'll knock off now—

Salud—

Jack S.

P.S. The hospital is the Mitchell Field one—

From Julius Deutsch

10-18-42

Dear Jack [Bjoze]:

I'm in my third week of O.C.S. now; brother it really tough. None of the laxity of the IB'S. Rules and Regulations are exact and must be followed to the letter or else. The only free time we get is Saturday night and Sunday, and those days must be spent catching up on the week's work. [. . .]

I stay in a room with two Negro candidates and 3 other Whites. The "mixed business" we were made to understand, was purely accidental, and when the situation was going to be changed, the 6 of us made it plain we weren't in favor of a change, so things remained as they were. As a result, open association between Negro and white (there are four Negroes in our class) is truly complete. There has been no Jim Crow in our class as a result; the only place in Ft. Knox where it doesn't exist.

Good luck to all the guys.

Your friend Julie[. . . .]

From Harry Fisher

Nov 26 (Friday) [1943]

My Dear Ruthie [Fisher]:

[. . .] One of the most popular discussions that go on down here is the Negro question. The prejudices are deep, very deep.

There are always about ten fellows on guard who are extras for relieving those on posts. Every night there's always a discussion started in the tent by these fellows. Most of the fellows are from the North and never knew any negroes, but they've been prejudiced by the papers they read. There's one fellow who always argues for the Negroes, and intelligently too. One day a sgt was lecturing to a large group—one side whites and the other negroes. In spite of the fact that he was lecturing to Negroes, he made some derogatory remarks about them. This young fellow, 19 years old, stood up and told the sgt off. The sgt said, "if you love niggers so much, go sit with them." This fellow got up and went right in the center of the group and sat there throughout the rest of the lecture. As he went he said, "They're as good as anybody else."

The remarkable thing of all this is the fact that this young soldier is a German and not a citizen of the U.S. He has relatives in Germany, including an uncle in the Gestapo. He's been here for almost a year now. When questioned, he said he wouldn't like to bomb Germany, which I suppose explains why he's still here.

He's strongly anti-nazi, but a bit confused. He'd like to see the German people kick out the nazis. He's worried about all Germans being hated after the war. He certainly isn't a coward. Otherwise how can you explain his action in regard to Negroes, which certainly are courageous.

Then there's a good union man from the West coast who's the most violent anti-negro here. This guys always talking for unions and the working man, but he hates Negroes. What a mix-up.

I've been taking part in these discussions lately. Sometimes my blood boils, but I'm always calm in my discussions. I tell the fellows about [George Washington] Carver, [Paul] Robeson, Richard Wright, Joe Louis, Oliver Law from Spain and others. I think and hope that I do a little to change their opinions.

There's always a fellow who'll ask, "Would you let a nigger marry your sister"? What can I say? All I can say is that no Negro has ever asked my sister to marry her. There used to be a musician in our group, an intellectual. It was hard for him to adjust himself to the life and surroundings here. His friends at home were professors, writers & other musicians and intellectuals. He was a bit snobbish here, so many of the boys always picked on him.

One day, while taking a shower, one of the Southern boys asked him, "Would you rather have your daughter marry the best colored man in the world or the worst white man." Without thinking, he answered, "The best negro."

The Southern fellow ran through the barracks shouting, "Kubner wants his daughter to marry a nigger." Poor Kubner, all he could do was shrug his shoulders.

There's a discussion going on about movies which I'm taking part in now. So that's all for now, except that I love you madly & calmly and all kinds of ways.

Harry

FROM STEVE "LOUIS" LEVINE

Dec. 18-43

Dear Jack [Bjoze].

[. . .] Am not attending school here. Think my school days in the army
are over. Have been in 15 and a half months and finished my school
training months ago. My job here is to break in green avia[tion]
engineers. Am attached to a Maint[enance] unit here. Am in charge of a
B-17 take care of it on the ground. Also fly with the green crews on their
first few flights. Sorta to give the new engineers a hand. Surely thought I
would be sent over a long time ago. Guess I'll just have to wait until the
army makes up its mind to send me over. Have volunteered for so many
overseas shipments that now I have reached a state of mind where I just
relax and hope for my break. In any case I know the score and know I'll get
my chance either now or later on. A big job still lies ahead both during the
war and after it.

Here's some good news. Saw some Negro soldiers working as radio men.
The first Negro G.I.'s I have seen given the chance to do skilled work. Made
me happy to see this. I hope this is a sign of letdown of Negro
discrimination in the army.

Regards to the boys and best of luck with the dance. Have a drink
for me.

Salud

Steve Louis Levine

FROM STEVE "LOUIS" LEVINE

Jan-26-44

Dear Jack [Bjoze].

[. . .] Enclosed is an article from our camp paper. I thought you would
find interesting. The Negro troops on the field just had a service club
opened for them. Of course "white" soldiers are not allowed to visit it or
are Negro soldiers allowed in at the "white" service club. This discrimination business is rough to take in silence. I feel that one day in a more
enlightened world all this slime of discrimination will be done away with.
As you know I have been at a lot of posts during my 17 months in the army.

Vaughn Love, 1944

At my present base I find anti-Semitism to be the strongest, then at any of the others. It is really very bad here. Seems to me that a lot of the gentile boys and officers have fallen for Coughlin's[14] fascist propaganda. That the Jews are the cause of the war. Have heard plenty of remarks to this effect. Have had a few fights, which I really couldn't avoid. Without losing the respect of my buddies. It's hard to keep the old temper down when you hear some of the things I do. Well I guess enough of that, "some day" perhaps not far off, a man will be measured by his worth and not by his color or nationality.

Regards to Al Prago, Ken Bridenthal, Al Koslow and all the boys.

Yours for Victory in '44.

Salud

Steve Levine

FROM HARRY HAKAM

Feb 20, 1945

Hello there

I meant to write to you before but just never got around to it. We had a party here in Berkeley last week and did not think that I would be able to make it for my outfit was to ship out a week earlier. But with (as Freddy Keller says) with one foot already on the gangplank I get what they call in the Navy "deleted" and I found myself back in "replacement" again waiting for a new assignment. So that is how I managed to make the party. However I have been assigned to another overseas unit to leave in a couple of weeks. It looks like I'll make it this time if I keep my fingers crossed— It's almost two years since I enlisted and have not been able to make it up the gang plank yet [?] due to some flukey circumstances. As it is I have already had <u>five</u> embarkation dates with always the same story when I got back. "<u>Deleted</u>."

The party was not as successful as the last one they had here although the set up was almost perfect. It sure did lack that old New York spirit. Felix gave a short talk on Spain after which the hat was passed. I haven't found out what the take was as I did not stay for the end of the party. Steve Nelson was there with a few other vets. I brought a few sailors up from Camp and for a while they were confounded as the number of negroes who were there too, three of them in Naval uniforms. You know we don't mix in the Navy and it really gave them something to talk about to see them treated [as] human beings the negro problem is much alive out here and they are really making great progress out here. I've attended a number of dances given by progressive organizations out here and the number of Negroes who come to these affairs is wonderful. I can't say the same for New York. Also this Frisco Bay are[a] is sure a melting pot. I worked in a shipyard during one of my leaves and for the first time I saw Negro journeymen electricians, with white women helpers both carrying cards in the same AFofL local. In my gang, all electricians, we had two Negroes, one Chinese, an "Oakie" and an "Arkie," Filipino, Mexican, a German refugee woman, one "native son" and myself. Later I met a Negro electrician who was one of the for[e]man and was doing a swell job for us. Steve told me about him and I found him O.K. They will have a big job on their hands trying to maintain their membership in the postwar period for the AFofL local has them all classified as Victory members—that is all the women and Negroes and do not take any initiation fee from them on the grounds that they will be employed for the duration only. That's going to be one tough nut for them to crack and I hope they can make it.

Well so long for now and hope to send you a letter from Iwo Jima pretty soon.

Salud,

Harry. [. . .]

From Dr. Julius Hene

December 13, 1944

Another day closer to final victory and unconditional surrender . . . I think I'll have to sit down and write a battle hymn some day.

[. . .] Last night we had a big bull-session about the Negro problem. It was quite interesting. Some of the guys thought that after the war they would have to go back and put these —— in their places! I pointed out that the colored soldiers were going through the same suffering over here as anyone else and all that had the chance were doing well in combat. They might not want to be pushed in the gutter back home after taking the worse the Wehrmacht has to offer. One of the Southern boys said they ought to take several of the Southern states and turn them over to the colored population and let them run the show and see what they could produce. . . .

At any rate, despite all the prejudice, people are starting to think of these things. One thing is sure, if we had 10 colored divisions like the 92nd instead of just one, the whole army would be that much stronger. Everyone is agreed on that.

December 14, 1944
I guess you will be surprised to learn I am now somewhere in Germany and I sure feel damn good about it. . . . It certainly was a long wait after being in the Army for so long—but now it's like walking on air—hard to believe it's true. Hope it won't be too long before all the Nazi beasts are put back in their cages. . . . I am in the best of health and have a swell time.

TELEGRAM FROM THE WAR DEPARTMENT

We regret to inform you that Captain Julius Hene was killed in action on December 23 while a prisoner of war of the German Government.

NOTES

1. Quoted in James Yates, *Mississippi to Madrid: Memoir of a Black American in the Abraham Lincoln Brigade* (Seattle: Open Hand Publishing, 1989), 206.
2. Testimony before the Subversive Activities Control Board, 1954, quoted in Danny Duncan Collum and Victor A. Berch (eds.), *"This Ain't Ethiopia, But It'll Do": African Americans in the Spanish Civil War* (New York: G. K. Hall, 1992), 175.
3. Oral History with Peter N. Carroll, 1978, Tape 5A, ALBA.
4. See biographical index of African American volunteers: http://www.alba-valb.org/curriculum/index.php?module=2&page=P018.
5. Bunny Rucker to Helen Rucker, August 2, 1943, ALBA.
6. Bunny Rucker to Helen Rucker, July 3, 1942, ALBA.
7. Archie Brown to Esther Brown, November 12, 1944, ALBA.
8. Vaughn Love, Oral History, August 2, 1943, ALBA.
9. In the rear guard it is better for you.
10. Max Werner, *The Great Offensive: The Strategy of Coalition Warfare* (New York: Viking, 1942).
11. José Diaz was a leader of the Spanish Communist party during the civil war.
12. Browder was head of the U.S. Communist party.
13. Milton Wolff Papers, University of Illinois Library.
14. Father Charles Coughlin's popular radio broadcasts often expressed antisemitic bias.

CHAPTER FOUR

IN THE COMBAT THEATERS

Although most Spanish Civil War veterans who entered the armed services after Pearl Harbor encountered considerable difficulty trying to transfer from stateside assignments, a significant number did eventually reach the war zones. In fact, a minority of those who were dispatched overseas slipped through the relatively loose and often ad-hoc screening as early as 1942, even before the 1943 Pearson exposé.

Veterans served in all theaters: in the west from North Africa to Italy to France; in Asia, in the South Pacific and the subcontinent; and in the air and on the seas. Several, including Vincent Lossowski, Milton Wolff, Irving Fajans, and Irving Goff, were attached to the Office of Strategic Services (OSS) to work with the underground in Italy. William J. ("Wild Bill") Donovan, the conservative chief of wartime intelligence, had no compunction about using politically progressive brigaders to complement military operations during the Italian campaign. In a recommendation for promotion of Lossowski, who successfully ran agents behind enemy lines in Italy, the commanding officer called attention to "his ability, diligence, his understanding of the guerilla situation, his seriousness, his willingness to work and his ability to produce results."

Many veterans served with distinction on the battlefield. Most famous was Herman "Butch" Bottcher, the "one man army of Buna," who earned a Distinguished Service Cross for his exploits in the South Pacific. Among others who received impressive decorations were Robert Thompson and Edward A. Carter, who also won Distinguished Service Crosses (Carter won a Medal of Honor as well, awarded posthumously in 1997); Lawrence Cane, who won a Silver Star; and Anthony Toney and Gerald Weinberg, both of whom won the Distinguished Flying Cross.

The brigaders' letters from the war zones are rich with descriptions of combat, military tactics, the nature of the enemy, the local political and cultural scene, and, especially, sophisticated commentary on the politics of war and the postwar international system. Older than the average GI, generally better educated, and certainly more politically involved, they filled their letters with serious discussions of the events of the day, often reflecting back on their experiences in Spain.

In this chapter, we will follow them through their letters chronologically and by theater of operations, beginning in North Africa in 1942 and ending in Germany in the spring of 1945, when the war in Europe came to an end. Many of the main themes that emerge in this chapter appear in letters from all theaters of operations and during all periods.

Not every veteran who made it abroad saw combat. Many, like Nathan Gross, chafed at the bit, writing from New Guinea in January 1944, "But hell, like all the rest of the boys, I've been wanting to get in to close grips with fascist bastards too. . . . Every application I've sent in for transfer was rejected." Burt Jackson in Italy in December 1944 was "more of a 'rear line general' than a fighting 'soldato.' When I hear of the good jobs our guys are doing up front, I feel more than a little chagrined." Along with many other African Americans, Jackson had been relegated to rear-line duty. As for the white vets, in some cases, their inability to get to the front lines had to do with their training and branches of service. After all, the majority of U.S. troops who went overseas during WWII never saw combat. In other cases, however, the discrimination the veterans encountered stateside carried over to the war zones.

Those like David Altman, who did see combat, described their action vividly. Altman, who was in the Pacific theater, explained, in August 1944, what it was like to be protecting a perimeter in a dense jungle where "you peer into black shadows. If you look long enough you can see practically anything from elephants to dancing fairies. . . . Birds of all kinds are squawking and whistling, crabs crawl, twigs snap, trees fall and crash and to blend it all harmoniously, your buddy is snoring sonorously." On another front, Harry Schoenberg wrote during the same month about how his "battalion destroyed in one afternoon (no artillery support either) a nazi S.S. battalion; in the process captured about 200 of the bastards, destroyed four or five artillery pieces and a tank, captured about 12 of their jeeps, a number of trucks." He was especially proud to be an officer attached to the famed all-Japanese-American unit in Italy.

Many vets who served in what we would call the Third World today were distressed with what they witnessed. Irving Weissman in North Africa in April 1943 explained that he was "in a French colonial possession, where our main contact is with the Arabs, who have suffered from generations of imperialist oppression, as well as feudal oppression of their own sheiks and sultans. . . . [T]he Americans don't understand the language and look upon the Arabs as inferior people, despite the fact that the country abounds with proofs to the contrary." Stationed in India in February 1944, Milton Wolff described "an annoying sight . . . the town's upper crust indulging in a round of golf" while he and his comrades were "engaged in the earnest task of fighting a war." Later that year in India, Nick Demas was appalled to discover that "India's millions don't live, they merely exist. About 99.9 percent of the people I have seen were hungry looking, bare-footed, badly 'dressed,' undernourished, undersized."

Wherever they were, the vets recalled their experiences in Spain. In Italy in January 1944, Sam Nahman was gleeful after he "went on my first raid already + dropped the first installments in payment for Spain. I marked the bombs + we gave them the whole load. In fact I even kissed one." In France one month after D-Day, Gerald Cook was "constantly surprised at similarities between the men and conditions here and those we knew in Spain. . . . [N]o matter what a man was—his religion, politics or nationality—a soldier is very like another in any army." Saul Birnbaum, in Germany in November 1944, was proud that "what we owed them [Nazis] for Spain has been partially liquidated. However the only final payment is the complete freedom of Spain. Think quite a few of us would like to fight in that one again if we live thru this one." Writing in 1945 from the South Pacific, Robert Klonsky acknowledged that "we were temporarily defeated [in Spain], we were confident—we knew that we had contributed to a greater, clearer understanding on the part of millions throughout the world."

Several brigaders threw themselves into political and informational activities in their units. Bill Gandall, in England in February 1944, was "lecturing all over the countryside" to numerous Army groups. Reactions have been tops and it's sure swell to hear the rank and file speak up with some darn good progressive ideas." But he was concerned, as were many vets, about racism. He asked, "Any reactions from other vets on the way we're handling the colored troops over here? Frankly it stinks and it's about time some hell was raised about it."

Of preeminent concern was the shape of the postwar world. In Italy in November 1943, Irving Weissman was encouraged by the Allies' Moscow Conference, a "guarantee that our blood is not being squandered. It's the guarantee of a new period of democratic advances in which the people, educated and organized in the bitter years since the last war, will reject the weaknesses which hobbled democracy in the past." Yet others like Jack Lucid worried when he learned in December 1944 that "British forces and the Greek regular army have joined in an all out effort to destroy the democratic military and political organizations in Greece," thus posing "a threat to allied unity." For his part, Lawrence Cane, writing from Germany in November 1944, wondered about de-Nazification plans: "Up at the front, we're all full of hate, and our first reaction is pretty much summarized by the phrase, 'Kill the bastards!'" But in order to win the peace, "You can't practically destroy 43,000,000 million Germans and expect it to stick. And it doesn't seem to jibe with the picture of the democratic world of tomorrow."

Many veterans were optimistic about the role of the Soviet Union in the postwar world. Milton Wolff, writing from India in February 1944, was not alone in thinking that "history has proven in the span of our lives that the existence of the Soviet Union has been a godsend to the peoples of all countries . . . in the past as an inspiration—as a bright light lighting the treacherous path of Munich diplomacy and exposing it before the whole world . . . in the present as the unquestionable savior of millions of American lives that would have been lost on the futile fields of battle" had it not been for the sacrifices of the Red Army. Although most Americans would not have gone as far as Wolff in his praise of the Soviet Union, because of the Red Army's heroic efforts on the Eastern Front and cooperative attitude at wartime conferences, Russia's image in the United States had improved immeasurably. President Franklin D. Roosevelt contributed to this sea change in attitudes with his frequent paeans to "Ivan's" bravery and sacrifice.

Several brigaders wrote quite movingly about their experiences at war's end in France and Belgium. Archie Brown, in Germany in March 1945, reported that "everything you have heard about the Germans having slaves is true. The boys in the company and I have run into Russians + Poles who were 'leased out' to the farmers. They worked in the fields all day, and then had their hands tied and were locked in a barn all night." In Belgium just after VE day, Harry Fisher expressed similar sentiments after watching POWs alighting from a train, "people who were worked to death, beaten, starved, looked down on by the super race, always facing death, seeing comrade after comrade die, and now they were free men again, among their own people. . . . It was like going from hell to heaven, a new life."

The overseas letters from GI veterans of the Spanish Civil War are remarkable. Ducking artillery shells, scribbling notes from foxholes, and in transit, they found time to write thoughtful, literate, and politically sophisticated letters that continually displayed their commitment to the values that first sent them into combat against the fascists in Spain. Above all, they took great pride in their participation, often in leadership roles, in the U.S. armed forces in their struggle against fascism and Japanese imperialism. This pride can be seen in the first letter in this chapter, an unpublished letter to the editor of *Time* magazine sent by Irving Fajans in November 1943.

FROM IRVING FAJANS

Nov. 21, 1943

Editor, "Time" Magazine
Rockefeller Center
New York City

Dear Sir:

"Time," Nov.22, carries a review of Professor John Dollard's "Fear in Battle," a study based on the experiences of the veterans of the Abraham Lincoln Brigade in the Spanish Civil War.

In the course of the review, your writer parenthetically observes, "the study concerned their military experience, not their political views."

Where the hell does "Time" get the nerve at this late date, to continue to pacify Franco lovers in this country with this kind of "aside"?

What in hell is wrong with our political views? I am damned proud of being one of the 3000 odd Americans who went to Spain to fight Hitler and Mussolini when "spit and fascism" were horrible words to "nice" people in this country.

"Time" may not know it, but about 1800 of the Americans who fought in Spain were killed and over half the remaining 1200 were wounded.

Yet today, you will find 900 Lincoln Veterans serving in the Armed Forces and the Merchant Marine. Five that I know of personally have been decorated, and many others commended. The records of Capt. [Herman]

Bottcher, Lt. [Irving] Goff, and Sgt. [Robert] Thompson and others rank with the very best of our fighting men.

"Time" is certainly in a position to know, though you would never get it from reading its pages, that veterans of the International Brigade are in the leadership and forefront of the guerrilla bands fighting Germans in Yugoslavia, Italy, Greece, and Poland, and in practically every one of the conquered countries. What in hell is wrong with their political views?

The last five years have shown stupidity enough in our relations with Franco and in the inexcusably bad treatment of International Brigade veterans and Spanish refugees without "Time" adding its bit to the pile.

Irving Fajans

I. NORTH AFRICA AND THE MIDDLE EAST

FROM DAN FITZGERALD

Somewhere in North Africa
Nov. 12, 1942

Dear Jack [Bjoze]:

Well, kiddo, here I am in Africa where you can guess away at. Everything has gone great with us. The troops opposing us contained a lot of Spanish refugees, Republicans who were forced into the [Foreign] Legion. I was talking this morning with some of them—their battalion with the exception of 100 non coms mostly German, deserted en masse: they walked 80 kilometers to our lines, traveling by day and night a circuitous route so they would miss any Pro-axis forces. They ask only one thing— that they be allowed to fight the axis—. What plans the army has for them I do not know. The people here are damn glad we came, the only opposition was based on a misguided idea of military honor. It is a screwy angle to me. The town has quite a few political refugees, all who see the downfall of Franco a near-event as a result of our blow. In the words of one of them— "it is the day of liberation." The French around here are nearly all O.K. The Germans have been draining the region of foodstuffs, bringing misery into a region where food abounds. The usual story of fascism. [. . .]

Fraternally
Dan

FROM ALEXANDER SCHWARTZMAN

Somewhere in North Africa

Feb. 2, 1943

Dear Vets,

Greetings from North Africa. We've been in North Africa for just three months now, and the way things are moving along, we should be finished soon.

Our coming to this zone meant the liberation of almost all of the Spanish Loyalists who were in concentration camps since the fall of France. These Spanish Loyalists, along with members of the International Brigades were doing forced labor for Nazi military construction.

I've met hundreds of Loyalists everywhere we've traveled. The reception they gave me, an American who fought with them is beyond description. The other American soldiers who were there were swept away by their love, their respect, their warmth "por el Americano quien ha lucado con los Republicanos en Espana." [for the Americans who fought with the Republicans in Spain]

I've met many who fought in the International Brigades, many who were with us in the Fifteenth. All of them wanted to volunteer with the American Armed Forces. "Esta tiempo, no pocos Americanos van a luchar pero muchos." [This time not a few Americans are going to fight but many].

At one place where we were stationed there were many Loyalists working in common on a rancho. Among them was a Captain of the Engineers assigned to the Fifteenth Brigade. He had been thrown into a concentration camp in France. Finding out he was due to be shipped back to be shot, he made his escape in a fishing boat, and made his way to the rancho. The Nazis and the Vichy officials never caught up with him or the others. Every time a searching party of Nazis were sent out to the rancho, they were warned, and would take to the hills. They were never prisoners of the Nazis in Africa.

Every time, generally on Sunday, myself and a group of American soldiers would spend the day at the Rancho. They would bring all of the Loyalists around, and what a fiesta we would have. We'd talk over old times.

After the war is over I'm certainly going to visit Spain again. Got many invites to revisit a strong Republican Spain. Invites to Madrid, Barcelona, Murcia, Seville, Valencia; each one warmly extended an invitation for a stay.

Not a day has gone by that is not full of interest. I'm writing from our front positions. Our outfit has played a marvelous role in destroying the Nazis. We've given them the same medicine they gave us in Spain. Plenty of TNT from the air, a language they can well understand.

I wouldn't miss this present experience for anything in the world. It's a continuation of our former experiences. True, its damned important to be working in war industry turning out the stuff. But for me, I'd rather fight up in the lines dealing it out, to be in there on the kill.

In this part of the world, events move fast. And we've just been part of those fast moving events. I'm proud and happy to be part of the American forces pushing the Nazis into the Sea.

Right now I'm sweating out a bombardier's assignment. Trained and ready to take off. Just imagine dropping those high [?] on the Nazis. For me it's a dream coming true. To be able to retaliate for the bombings in Spain, with your own hands. Can't describe the feeling it gives a guy. Not only that but also a heavy machine gun for straffing. Nothing could be sweeter.

In between am acting as an interpreter in French, Spanish + German. Spanish certainly came in handy when we arrived. Keeping up with the news by getting the French papers every day.

My sister wrote me that she attended the dance the Lincoln Vets gave Christmas Eve. It made me think back to what we did that particular night. We worked all thru a bitter bitter cold night loading bombs onto planes. Don't think for a minute its warm out here. Hell its been damn cold ever since we arrived. It made a guy feel good to load all of that TNT onto the planes. The next day it was dropped successfully. I joined and fused a good portion of them. Checked and rechecked to make damned sure they were O.K., and they were. [. . .]

> Regards to all of you
> Alex

FROM IRVING WEISSMAN

> Somewhere in North Africa
> April 6, 1943

Dear Jack [Bjoze],

I'm writing you from North Africa. Quite near our old stamping grounds. Maybe I'll see them again. Spain is bound to be sucked into the vortex of belligerency.

I understand quite a few of the boys are around here. Please let me know their addresses.

There are lots of refugees, both Spaniards and Internationals. There are still plenty of them in the concentration camps and, with increasing democratization of the North African government, sizeable numbers of them are being released. I don't have statistics. I've been here only two weeks, and means of information are limited. I'd like to locate a good census, with statistics; then I'd know more about this country in general. What I know so far I've learned from conversations in broken French and Spanish, from observation of the local life and from perusal of the French press. What stares one in the face of course is that this is a colony— and how!

Well, the longer one stays in this army, the more one learns to admire its organization. The transportation of a vast body of troops was carried out with efficiency that clicked like clock work at times. It's something to sit up and take notice of. I've talked with some of the troops who participated in the November invasion and from them too one gleans the same sense of efficiency. What we did when we crossed the Ebro was fine: but when some of these engineers told me of their equipment and how it had been used, well, it made me envious. I hope to hell I'll be able to see this whole vast organization in action in the invasion of Europe.

It's a shame of course that the coefficient of effectiveness isn't increased by political education. The army still shies clear of that. Morale here depends above all on team work, on the individual's pride in himself as a fighter and as a soldier, on his pride in his unit, and on his respect for and confidence in his officers and non coms. Of course, there are such things as food and other material comforts, but they are so well taken care of that they don't pop up as a problem. (Do you remember how we had one kitchen for a whole battalion? Here they have one kitchen per battery! And what a variety of food!)

Do you remember how preoccupied the Yale questionnaire was with fear? There is open acknowledgment of fear, and of homesickness as well, and homesickness particularly is exploited to aggravate the soldier's ire and to make him feel, 'Come on—let's get this over with.'

It's hard headed and realistic and it works and has worked for generations, but it has its negative sides, negatives which contain within themselves the danger of befuddling and obscuring the whole character of this war as one of national liberation. Thus the negative side of homesickness is the failure of the soldier to achieve the fullest possible integration with his allies in this foreign land. Result: chauvinism; fruitful soil for the Germans to exploit.

To give you some concrete examples: We are in a French colonial possession where our main contact is with the Arabs, who have suffered from generations of imperialist oppression, as well as the feudal oppression of their own sheiks and sultans. Chauvinistic moods arise and express themselves—the Americans don't understand the language and look upon the Arabs as an inferior people, despite the fact that the country abounds with proofs to the contrary (an agricultural region rendered rich by centuries of irrigation; a stony country transformed) and by the history of the Arab peoples (their conquests in the Middle Ages and their development of mathematics, medicine and architecture). Vichy agents— that is to say German agents—of course, profit from this.

That is not to say that nothing is done to bring home to the population our liberating character. Food and clothing and employment have been given to the Arabs, but all this work is done from the top amongst the generals and the sultans. The soldiers don't even know what is going on. Consequently, despite the inherent democracy of our soldiers and their humaneness, a lot of viciousness comes to the surface. The main thing is that among the soldiers themselves there is no sharp combatting of these tendencies. A corollary of this is the resultant failure of the soldiers to integrate themselves with the life and struggles of these peoples.

North Africa is also the arena of sharp struggle between the de Gaullists in alliance with all anti-Axis Frenchmen and the Vichyites, some of whom, like [General Auguste] Nogues still retain power. Certainly, clarification about these matters amongst the American army would hasten the removal of obstructions in the path of victory. Yet here too knowledge about the current situation percolates into the Army from sources other than the command. And yet were the command to tell us our role here, how it would arouse the American troops, infused as they are with faith in democracy!

It is too bad. It is really too bad. Political education could act as a catalyst, and also it would integrate us all into this magnificent and critical struggle. It is not only our experience in Spain which proves this—three

years of war against superior armament, three years in which we were
sustained above all by faith and knowledge, which in their turn were
cultivated constantly by political education. It is also the experience of the
American Revolution, the great work of Thomas Paine at that time, which
prove the power of such education. More instances still can be cited from
history—the delegates from the National Assembly of the French Revolution, the political comissars of the Russian and Spanish armies, the party
leaders of the Nazi armies. Faith in the justice of one's cause evokes
unpremeditated self-sacrifice and devotion. Orientation on the part of
the soldiers would increase their devotion a thousand times over. For
you and me, these are old truisms.

What's happening back in the States? We read hints of a big program
projected by Roosevelt for post-war employment. But Congress must be
fucking him proper. What about the drive against labor? Has labor's
leadership become clearer in the last few months? It would seem to me
that, especially after the elections, not only does such leadership become
more desirable, but it becomes the more necessary from the point of view
of labor's preservation of its hard-earned gains. [. . .]

    Salud y victoria,

    Irving

From Dan Fitzgerald

                Somewhere in North Africa

                April 19, 1943

Dear Jack [Bjoze]:

    [. . .] Since I last wrote we have been tangling assholes with Axis
bastards, "Jerries" and "Ities" the British call them. It is rugged as hell
"far more intensive than the other affair" the mortars in this war are
devilishly cruel. I had the joy of seeing a lot of German planes go down,
Stukas + M E 109's and one afternoon 14 out of 14 Junkers 88's. [. . .]

    Could write a book about the case of our friends but I guess you know
the story now. Hitler has the Germans all jerked up—"the pricks across
the way"—all of whom came from the Russian front think that Hitler is
mopping up in Russia; in two weeks it will be all over and then the whole
army will come to Africa to clean us up. They are nutty as fruit cakes.

We have some colored soldiers who work a large caliber artillery gun. Every time they fire they kiss the shell and yell "Rommell count your men" or "Mr. Rommell you sure done fucked up" Boom!! They have a lot of guts, no Luftwaffe can phase them. Boom! "Mr. Rommell count your men!" [. . .]

    Best Wishes
    Dan Fitzgerald

FROM JERRY WEINBERG

                Somewhere in the Middle East
                July 20th, 1943

Dear Saully [Saul Wellman],

After the soft life of Merrie England you might call this "roughing it." It's a lot like camping on the old hillside. We have our swimming, plenty of fresh air, even tho it is saturated by sand when the wind is brisk and we sleep on cots under a canvas top. True, we have movies every other night and a quiet camp to return to after a day's activity but after the pubs of England and the "Liberty runs" to town we consider this "tough."

As for our activities, a little imagination plus reading the papers will give you a good idea of what we are doing. The news of yesterdays "little" job should prove interesting. From what I saw I'd say it was Mussolini's time to fiddle.

From the observations I can make I cannot see how our forces can be prevented from completely occupying Sicily and eventually all of Italy. Unless the Nazis decide to make it the decisive Theatre of operations I don't think it will prove too difficult a job. Though I don't believe Italy is the key to the defeat of Germany, I do think it is the key to the Balkans and that it will have a tremendous effect on the Yugoslav and Greek partisan movements. If the Germans should move many troops into Italy they will leave themselves wide open on other fronts. Apparently they are afraid to withdraw many men from the Russian front. All in All, there is every reason to be optimistic. The liberation of Europe has begun.

Well, Saully we are veterans now. As a matter of fact we are "heroes." We've earned the Air Medal and will probably receive it when we get back to England. Funny part about it all is that I've felt more like a passenger on all our trips. And if that is deserving of medals the boys on Sicily should get them by the car loads. The Air force is very generous.

The best award we have received to date was a bottle of Scotch from our Squadron C.O. We've made as merry as 10 men can on one bottle. We are on a short vacation but will probably be back to work shortly.

Yours,
Jerry Weinberg

FROM JERRY WEINBERG

[Turkey][1]
August 8, 1943

Dear Abe and Rose [Smorodin],

There is no end to surprises as you probably said when it was triplets. My present military status is "interned in a neutral country." I can't divulge the name of the country. But you can guess and if you have been reading the papers the past week I can't see how you can miss.

Our host is gracious and sympathetic to our cause. We eat the best foods and are very comfortable. However this is an unfortunate condition to be in. We may be here a long time, possibly for the duration. It all depends on International Relations. There is always the possibility of an exchange, tho, at present, it is remote. There is another possibility which I cannot discuss.[2] It's tough but we had little choice. It was this or ——.

So here I am with nothing to do but read, eat, sleep and go to town when we receive parole. Ordinarily we would not accept parole, but our representative in this country has authorized and advised us to take advantage of it. We walk around the city, which has been built up from a small town to a modern city in the last 15 years. People who can talk English, aside from those at the Axis Embassies, stop us and congratulate us on the job we did. The people are really very friendly.

This country is lot more beautiful than I had imagined. This is the first time I've been on this continent and I'd like to see more of it. Prices are very high, a shirt that would cost a dollar when I was home draws about six or seven here. The confectionery here is swell. Had a nice piece of [censored] yesterday. Beer is very good. Whiskey very expensive. ($12 for a Scotch and soda—yes, one glass)

Our greatest difficulty is the language. It is very hard to learn. I get along on French, which is the secondary language. If I can get a good grammar I think I'll make a stab at learning the native tongue. [. . .]

Love + kisses to all,

Jerry

FROM HARLAND GERALD QUIGGLE

Somewhere in North Africa

June 21, 1944

Amigos:

For the past four months I have been receiving copies of the "Volunteer." I am grateful to you for your kindness in sending the paper to me. I have discovered from it the locations and activities of many of my former comrades.

Some of them have indeed made history and have put to good use the education they received in Spain. Many, I noticed, had been sent to England, and are now, no doubt, in the forefront of the invasion. One paper said that Bill Aalto had been sent home, but did not mention why.[3] I surely hope he had not been injured because he was not a bad sort of a fellow.

For over a year now I have been stationed in North Africa. I cant say exactly where. During my time here I have met many of the Spaniards in exile. They all still have their old fire. They maintain political and self-help organizations where-ever there are more than two of them in any one place. The FAI, the CNT, the UGT, and the UHP have a net-work of offices in the larger towns.[4] It gives a fellow a thrill to see the familiar old signs posted above the doors of these offices. The Union Nacional Espanol is the leading self-help organization. Members wear the tricolor of the Republic in their lapels. Some of the refugees have secured fairly satisfactory jobs but the greater part still are ostracized because they chose to fight against the fascists before the rest of the World was ready to do so. One and all are eagerly awaiting the day when they can return to Espana to finish the War. One of them explained the situation to me as follows: "During the war one part of Spain was white, the other part red—The whites won so now both parts are red." That puts it in a nut-shell.

Mark Billings, Wade Rollins, Don McLeod, and Dick Cloke are all in the
San Francisco area, in war plants.[5] [. . .]
  Hasta Luego
  El Conejo

2. ENGLAND

From Sam Gibons

England
November 19th, 1942.

[. . .] Two weeks ago I was in London and attended the commemoration
meeting for the International Brigades. It was excellent—the only bad
feature was that I had to leave early in order to get back to camp in time.
Among the speakers was a British M.P., the Polish Minister of Labor and
Public Welfare, The Czech Minister of Public Welfare, and a woman, whose
name I can't remember, but who's done a hell of a lot for us. And of course
lots more. Mike Feller was there, myself, and a number of Czech, Yugoslav,
and German Vets, and of course Jack Brent and the English, and Irish Vets
of the I.B. Almost all of us vets were in uniform of the Forces. We had the
seats of honor. The audience numbered about 500. There were quite a few
of our Spanish brothers there and mujeres too. I bumped into one of the
Fighting Irish name of Sean Dowling who seems to know me and our guys
and says he was in the original Lincolns. He was telling me that he bumped
into Bob Masters in Hyde Park. If that's so, and Bob is the guy I'm thinking he is, then we have three of us American Vets in merrie England.
  The operations in North Africa are cheering and promising. At last we
have begun to go on the offensive and even though this is no second front,
it brings the prospect of operations on the continent that much closer and
has the axis buggers worried. Our administration's attitude on [Admiral
Jean-Francois] Darlan[6] and the Four World Freedoms are cheering. Now
to save our Internationals in the concentration camps.
  As for me, I'm corporal now, batting my brains out trying to speed up
my code. Us guys are becoming philosophical, discussing politics, war,
women and sex. And my wife who is in New York now sets the pace as
usual, bless her, as a sheet metal worker in aircraft production so she can

get the boys back home that much sooner. I think she is a sterling example of what can be done by our women folk to prosecute the war. So till next time, Salud—

Just a minute—the meeting mentioned above sent a resolution of congrats etc. to [Colonel Aleksandr] General Rodimtsev, commanding the Stalingrad Front, who is an International Brigadier too and helped carry out the Defense of Madrid. And of course I know you know that, so so long.

Sam Gibons

FROM MILTON (MICHAEL) FELLER

"Somewhere in England"
September 28, 1942

Dear Vets,

[. . .] England is a beautiful country. The people are becoming increasingly aware of the invaluable aid the Red Army and the Soviet people have rendered to the peace-loving peoples of the world. They are clamoring for more effective aid on their own part and are willing to make any sacrifice that is necessary to speed the day of final victory. When the Soviet Premier or other Soviet leaders appear on the screen in the cinemas the audience goes wild with applause—thus demonstrating their appreciation and realization of the enormous sacrifices the Soviet people have already made in this sacred war against the greatest enemy of mankind.

It is a healthy sign; it indicates that the British people are becoming more and more alert to political events and are beginning to realize that liberty and freedom can be secured only when ALL the people themselves participate in formulating policies—both foreign and domestic. [. . .]

Salud,
Michael

FROM JERRY WEINBERG

England
Oct. 23, 1943[7]

Dear Abe and Rose [Smorodin],

Arrived in England in tropical outfit and now I know how a member of the "Polar Bears" feels when he takes the plunge. Coming out of warm Africa to Cold and damp England is sudden change. But in spite of it all, including the nuisance raids on London, I am glad to be back. I didn't care for the "land of the Pyramids and the Stinx" at all.

I met one of the boys in Algiers, Joe Rehill, of the N.M.U. [National Maritime Union]. He had been in Port some time and was able to give me some of low down on the situation there. It is still very bad. The feeling that exists is one of confusion. Most of the people look upon the Americans and British armies as armies of Occupation and not Liberation. Joe attended a youth conference while there and he tells me that they look to our country to clean up the confusion that does exist. Another important point is an almost complete absence of stress on the United Nations. Though there are many British and American flags and posters proclaiming the Anglo-Saxon Alliance, there is little evidence of the Soviet Union being in the Coalition. I don't think I saw a Soviet Flag in the entire city. I am not confused but I must admit I was hurt by the state of affairs.

I also notice that one of our Congressmen told the press that we couldn't hold a bridgehead in Western Europe for 48 hours. The dirty—no I take it back. I can't say anything disrespectful about any member of Congress (Military Regulations.) Watch Hitler spread that around occupied Europe. I recently spoke to a young man just out of France. People have been waiting expectantly and hopeful for invasion.[8] He says Morale sunk greatly when it did not come during the good weather. Whoever the Congressman was he will most probably get the Iron Cross. [Joseph] Goebels [sic] couldn't make the French believe it. Now he can quote "a U.S. Congressman."

Have to Close. Write Soon.

Love + Kisses.

Jerry.

FROM WILLIAM (BILL) GANDALL

England
Feb.12, 1944

Dear Jack [Bjoze],

[...] I've been in a whirlwind of work, mainly Public Relations, then Special Services and Plans and Training. I've been lecturing on "Anglo-

American Understanding" and "the United Nations" etc. etc. all over the countryside (limited) and to numerous Army groups. Reactions have been tops and it's sure swell to hear the rank and file speak up with some darn good progressive ideas. Among other groups I have talked to on the outside have been rural groups like the Women's Institute, Women's Land Army, Farm Groups, Methodist and Church of England groups. I am scheduled to speak to quite a number of youth groups in the next few weeks. I have formed a small staff of competent progressive speakers in my camp and we are really going to town in our area. [. . .] The chow is swell except that we all had a run of the drizzles lately and holy hell has been raised by the command. If there's one investigation there's a dozen. I have to laugh, it's just a minor thing, and we used to poop our very guts out at different times.

Any reactions from other vets on the way we're handling the colored troops over here? Frankly it stinks and it's about time some hell was raised about it. Chauvinism runs rampant and little is done to check it. In fact, most of the time by poor handling it's encouraged. The new training film "Welcome to Britain" handles the problem good but not enough. Probably a whole film or series of lectures plus stern measures against the "baiters" would help. What do you think?

 Yours
 Bill Gandall

FROM WILLIAM (BILL) GANDALL

England
July 27, 1944

Dear Harry,

Sure lucky to be attending a short session (extra-mural dept.) given by one of the leading Universities. Our Captain has given both Sgt. Paul Lomasney and myself a break so off we go this Saturday. Our discussion groups are showing signs of definite progress, our classes becoming better organized and our Education Directors on the various posts hitting the ball. In addition to and supplementing the discussion groups we have brought in outside speakers of merit. We had people like Madame Cathala, of the French Underground, tell the boys just what they could expect in

Season's Greetings from Jerry and Ethel Weinberg, 1944

France and what the French people had suffered under the Nazi Terror. A British Army Officer, veteran of Burma, spoke on that theatre (The fellows disagreed with his ideas of "the white man's burden" and other "old school tie" angles he harbored. However the good point about him, was to knock false complacency and optimism in the head.) Then we had a Mr. Richards another Britisher who made a tremendous hit with the boys. He spoke on South America, mainly Brazil. He's traveled all over the world and has lived a very adventurous and exciting life which included 7x (seven) long years in the State of Texas. Oh Lord! He knew Luis Carlos Prestes, the "White Knight of Brazil," or was it "White Hope"?[9] Aren't they ever going to let that guy out of the brig, now that we are all fighting the Hitler gang? Is anyone in the States or elsewhere squaking [sic] about it?

We've had a few other French speakers, combat pilots, and others on our schedule and all of them were good. Lately, we had a real top-notcher, one Major Buck, British 1st Army, 23 years old, Honor Man Cambridge, rounded vet of Tunisia, and the best British speaker I've ever heard. He had one of our audiences of 500 [?] and Officers rolling in the aisles. We've booked him for a solid week starting Monday, after that session. At the office we've had a lot of fun with him. He struts in with the inevitable swagger stick most British Officers affect. I pick it up, examine it, hand it back with a rude remark and we'll all have a good laugh. While waiting for the escort to take him to the meeting, we show him around the place and leave him back in the art dept. with Bill Turner, our artist (does all the orientation posters) and Sgt. Charles Hare who though he is now in our army used to be Capt. of the British Davis Cup Team in 1937 and is married to another British Tennis Star, Mary Hardwick. The escort finally arrives. The Major is unwilling to leave as "a real cup of tea is being prepared by ONE WHO KNOWS HOW TO MAKE IT!" meaning Charlie Hare (who is still a British subject), and obviously a dig at the Yanks' method of making tea. It was with great delight, then, that I found our dear Charlie round the corner doing the most dreadful thing. Really it was! He was dipping a tea ball into some hot water! I rushed back grabbed the major, called the entire staff to witness this horrible incident and we roared and razzed. Poor Major Buck could hardly get a word in, but he sure was a good sport. [. . .]

I have never seen such enthusiasm in the Army since working with the Cadets. After a long day or long night (we have afternoon talks and films right in the Wards, are thinking of developing them in the Guard House) of hard work, these Jimmy Higgenses[10] come to this office, oft times a matter of walking and hitching some miles, to organize and lead discussions and give their buddies a real down-to-earth orientation of the war, current events, and problems of the peace. [. . .]

Talking about democratic development did I ever tell you of the Enlisted Men's Councils? They are organized by Special Service and elected by the men to give volunteer leadership to their entertainment, recreational and other off-duty needs. We have a good young Lieutenant on this, Geo. Washburn, and I'm working in cooperation with him. To my mind, this is one of the great new steps in making a People's Army. Just to keep the record straight all the steps aren't taken by the right people. [. . .]

Yours

Bill

3. ITALY

FROM JOHN PERRONE

Sicily

July 29, 1943

Dear Jack [Bjoze]

How's tricks? I can imagine how surprised you looked to hear that I'm somewhere in "Sicily." I feel the same way.

It's Spain all over again, only this time the Germans are on the run and the Italians are only too glad to surrender.

I miss the old gang and would appreciate hearing from any that know me personally.

So far everything is not too tough, or comparable with Spain. We get plenty of cigarettes, feed, etc. so please don't send me anything.

I received the "order of the purple heart" for receiving a slight shoulder wound in action. Outside of this I'm in pretty good condition.

What I do lack is a knowledge of what the hell is going on in this world & home. You can do me this favor and clarify me a little bit on this subject. You know what I mean.

Yours for a better world,

Johnny

FROM SIDNEY VOGEL

Pantelleria, Italy

Sunday

Aug.1, 1943

Dear Pussey-cat [Lise Vogel]:

You have no idea how anxious I am to hear from you. You can't write about these things because you feel it so deeply. All soldiers feel that way because they are away from their families and those they love—& in this case it is you & Mommie, and that's why I write you so often, & feel disappointed when I don't hear from you.

I wish I were in a new place so I could write you about it because those are the things you want to hear about.

I'd like to tell you about the houses on this island. They are like bunga-
lows made of stone. The walls "of stone" are thick, and every room looks
about the same. The walls being so thick they keep the rooms cool in the
hot weather of which there is so much, and warm when it gets cold. Some
of the rooms have only a door, and no windows, so that air only comes thru
the door, which makes it very stuffy at times. Some of these houses have
toilets but very few. In most the little boys and girls use a pot in the house
and then go out and dump it in a hole in the ground and cover it with dirt.
What I am trying to tell you pussey-cat is that all over the world, most
people do not have all the wonderful conveniences that you do. Now these
people here they are Italians—are peasants, and live off the land—they are
farmers and grow grapes, tomatoes, some onions and wheat. As I told you
before they are not as poor looking as the Arabs or Italians I saw in Africa.
The little children have (some of them) very nice dresses. All the children
either go barefoot or wear shoes like slippers with wooden soles. Like all
children all over the world they love candy & keep asking us for it all the
time (& we give it), because there is no candy on the island & no stores.
All the children swim & love it, just like you. Maybe you ought to live
here—I wish you could as long as I was here, and that's because I love you,
& want you near me.

Love, hugs & kisses from
Daddy

FROM SIDNEY VOGEL

Italy
Oct. 18, 1943

Dear Ethel [Vogel]:

[. . .] I think I have told you that on my last stay in Africa, before coming
here we were at a place where for the first time I felt the tempo of war by all
the activity that was going around. Not actual war activity (danger) there
was none of that as Africa is ours, but everything around us seemed to [be]
so active, so alive, so full of the rash, systematized, yet chaotic, fast, life of
war. This was so in spite of the fact that we were waiting to come here. I
think the whole picture was accentuated by the fact that we had been so
long on Pantelleria,[11] which after the first few weeks seemed to be in a
minor sense a sort of forgotten place. It became so as we invaded Sicily,

and more so as we got into Italy. Well, when we came here, after a very short wait, we were rather excited especially since the spot was rather desirable and seems more so all the time. I think I've told you the type of buildings we are living in, the furniture and all the comforts of home (except for you and Lise). One thing I noticed tho, which I mention lest I forget, was that tempers were shorter than they've ever been, and everyone more irritable, in spite of the fact that we are living better than we ever have. But this too is not strange to me, as I have been expecting it, and seeing it develop, as we all get more homesick, etc., and at times, sometimes a long time, seem so divorced from the war and what is actually going on. I'm sure this would not happen if we were a front line outfit, or were more in the midst of things. Sometimes its really amazing how little we think of the war, as contrasted with the time we think of griping, mail, personal comforts etc. I really am learning a lot. But back to my story.

As I see it, Sicily is going the same way as Pantelleria. By that I mean that as we advance in Italy, the importance of this place becomes less and less. True, Sicily is much larger and more important, but from a military point of view its importance must diminish—that is as this armchair general sees it. Anyhow, we as station hospital, are here, and will set up taking the place of a different kind of hospital. By our very nature, as you know, we are not in the thick of things, which all corroborates my appraisal. Well, temporarily on arriving, we were placed to live for a few days, when we arrived, with another hospital, and when they learned that I am a "psychiatrist" (I'm modest) they asked me to see a case, as they were without one. From this it was just one step for Hall to praise me to the sky, and as they were setting all of us to work, till we set up or take over one of these hospitals. I was assigned to this hospital as a psychiatrist. And it sure has been a pleasure. Some of us were assigned to this hospital and others elsewhere, this I imagine to keep us out of trouble (Halls approach) etc. At any rate, most of the boys have been spending their time sightseeing and a few of us have been working. What you are interested in naturally is me and my work and I will adhere to that.

Naturally, as I started I explained to the regular army colonel in charge what kind of "psychiatrist" I am, and he of course thought I was modest. Actually, I know the work as the most important thing is not so much categorizing the cases, as knowing how to dispose of them, and that I know from experience. That I explained to him which was far from modest. Anyhow I do know the stuff not so much in a formal (tho I know that better

than the average doctor) as in an intelligent way based on experience. I
hope I make myself clear. So since then, which is about a week I have been
working all day and it has been swell. In the first place, it is like a breath of
fresh air to be away from my inbred, petty gang all day. When I get back I
am so tired that most nights I have been falling asleep after my censoring
job at 9 o'clock, and maximum at 10. (Did I tell you that I tried in Africa to
get out of my censor job but received "you have done it so well" which is
true—and it ties up so well with our other duties etc.—that I had to
continue.) The men at this hospital are from a big western university, are
young, intelligent fair haired boys, and since I am a stranger and we don't
know each others foibles such as irritability at breakfast etc. everything is
really wonderful. Pleasant, calm, polite, no crap or exhibition of medical
knowledge, no sycophancy, and a really swell atmosphere. I feel like a new
man. What is more important is the volume of work for me, with everyone
coming up to me to see cases, and the leisurely decent air about it all.
Of greatest importance is the type of case. These are really war cases,
altho these will taper off. By war, the men and type of reactions that one
associates with war, and not Osh kosh. At that dam island I did straight
medicine which consisted of G.Is (diarrhea) and malaria, with occasional
N.P. (neuropsychiatric) cases thrown in. Here I have only that and as I
said above cases that really have their roots in the war such as "shell-
shock" etc.

And since in psychiatry you listen, direct the conversation by innuendo,
and since these cases are oriented, and not whacky in a lay term, I have
been getting a real close up of some of the horrors, difficulties, reactions,
behavior problems of front line stuff. And for the first time medically I
feel really close to the war. I have examined a paratrooper etc. who has
been jittery, and various others who have had reactions to rough going,
and have really learned a lot, and realize for the first time what real heroes
we have. Naturally many of the cases are more mundane and less dramatic
such as chronic alcoholism reacting etc. But what I am trying to tell you is
that I have really learned from some of these boys what rough going
Salerno etc. was, which of course you know from the papers. To talk to
these boys warmly, and give them a feeling of closeness, intimacy, interest
in their problems, and care, is a swell feeling both for me, and as I hope
for them. When I get home I eat, then censor, and reading a bit fall asleep.
Recently I have been awakening at 5 or 6 which must be sex, or is it shell
shock? At any rate I know it is connected with you. Unfortunately my work

there will end soon as we take over the place, and I will go back to GIs etc., and if I have time the psychiatric cases, with Spiv in his office and all the things I hate there. But that too is war, and even tho I would like to get with this other outfit, and there may be a chance, I am waiting and mulling it over as to whether I should try as my position here is so settled and you know how I hate change. But I'll talk to you in another letter about that. Naturally, I am no fool, and know that they too must have their internecine troubles, but ours have been getting worse and worse as we travel, and our feelings are at a pretty low ebb, and don't even show the occasional recoveries we used to show. But that too is another story, and one of little interest as that too is war.

No mail yet here from you, and naturally I await it expectantly, and expect a bunch. All the other boys play poker every night, and a few to the movies. I have not been to one—so I must be tired! I'll get them in later. Much to see here, but that too must wait. I love you both terribly, am feeling O.K. working hard and smoothly, think the news is swell, and would like to put my arms around you right now, after kissing Lisa a few times. All my love.

Sid

From Irving Weissman

Italy
Nov. 15, 1943

Dear Jack [Bjoze],

I am writing from Italy. [. . .] I wasn't able to find out anything about [John] Gates—is he overseas yet? [Robert]Thompson, I know, got the Distinguished Service Medal, as did [Herman] Bottcher, but is it true that Bob got a Medical Discharge? I remember how sick he was in Spain too. Did Johnny Perrone get the Silver Star? You know, these things continue to interest me. It isn't the usual practice for organisations to keep out of contact with their members. You should see the links that are maintained between the other men in the outfit and their organizations and towns. (My outfit is mostly Mid Western—Wisconsin and Illinois). It is not at all typical of their connections to have them severed.

The news we get is very good. I mean the Moscow Conference.[12] It's the guarantee that our blood is not being squandered. It's the guarantee of a new period for humanity, a period of democratic advances in which the people, educated and organized in the bitter years since the last war, will reject all the weakness which hobbled democracy in the past and in which they will practice in all consistency, and in its most logical conclusions. Great forces are at work which will not be gainsaid. All the reactionary connivings will not prevent this people's victory. At the most they can put obstacles in its way, impede and delay it, but they cannot prevent it. These obstacles are all being overcome—witness [Henri] Giraud and [Pietro] Badoglio—by forces which are aroused and on the ascendant.[13] The years of defeat, the black years of fascism, are behind us.

Don't misunderstand my references to Giraud and Badoglio. I see nothing wrong in making deals with fascism, especially if they want to surrender. The error is only when we hand them the power. It was not wrong to take Dakar from [Admiral Jean Francois] Darlan, but it was wrong to give him French North Africa. It was not wrong to accept Italy from Badoglio, but it would be wrong to exclude the anti-fascists from the governership of Italy. This purism, this raising of the hands in horror at dealings with these people, that I gather from the pages of PM, and also from the Nation—there is a fellow here who gets that too—strike me as childish, and as the protests of sterile people without an organized following, people who do not have the power to participate in the alterations of history and who can therefore only protest in fear and timidity.

[. . .] You may have read the War Dept's little pamphlet 'Fighting on Guadalcanal.' It consisted of the first hand accounts of NCO's and officers of the fighting, and of the lessons they drew. I had to smile—they were all the lessons that we had learned so many years before in Spain—of the importance of the group, and the squad, of the importance of sergeants and platoon leaders, of the importance of individual initiative and resourcefulness. It took them that bitter fighting to learn these axioms of modern infantry battle. That is the best case in point, beyond individual experience, of which I know. [. . .]

Salud y victoria,

Irving Weissman

PS—My outfit has seen some action—it has been shelled and has shot down planes—but nothing like the things we were thru. The infantry is still the queen of them all.

Irv

FROM SAM NAHMAN

"Billet Doux"
Somewhere in Italy
Jan. 1, 1944

Dear Fellows,

Well, I finally got here it took time but it was worth it. I've been here over a month now and everything is O.K. Its almost like Spain all over again although not as rough. In many ways, the towns + people resemble those in Spain altho not their spirit or the kind of friendships that existed then.

Went on my first raid already + dropped the first installment in payment for Spain. I marked the bombs + we gave them the whole load. In fact I even kissed one. We got one hole in the nose from flak but no fighters to bother us. I didn't go with my crew but as an extra with another ship. They needed a cameraman so I became a cameraman. I wouldn't miss that first installment for anything. [. . .]

Salud + Victoria
Sam Nahman

FROM DAVID HYMAN "HY" WALLACH

Italy
May 31, 1944

Dear Nils [Berg]:

[. . .] Just received the May issue [of The Volunteer] and am especially pleased to learn of Milt's [Wolff] transfer to [General Joseph] Stilwell where he should certainly be able to contribute a great deal.[14] Incidentally, congrats to Milt for the sergeants rating. That, too, is about time. And while I'm at it, I would like to take this opportunity to congratulate the most recent commissions, [Irving] Fajans and [Moshe] Brier—(and on the wife, too, Toots)—and [Irving] Goff, [Herman] Bottcher, [Robert] Thompson, [Kenneth] Shaker et al for their wonderful work. Of course, reading George Watt's citation in this issue is a genuine thrill.

The kick that The Volunteer is for us, personally, is very obvious but what makes it exciting reading for everyone else is the grand job you're doing covering vets' activities and their amazing contributions to the annihilation of fascism all over the world. Particularly interesting was the issue which dealt with the part played by the vets in the eviction of the Nazis from Corsica. Really, Nils, copies are grabbed up and if you can possibly lay your hands on some back issues, would appreciate them. Liked the British issue you sent and would be nice to receive more of them.

Good to see that a lot of vets are getting into action. Been trying myself but here I am well over 2 years in the Army and more than a year overseas and still in a service group. But, as Milt says this war is taking a long time and now it looks as if I might finally get into something. There's a call for volunteers for the Paratroops. Have already passed the physical and my application has already been endorsed by my C.O. Hope for fast action. Did have to request waiving the age limit as I'm slightly over (30) but think that's a small technicality. [. . .]

Yet Nils, although I haven't contributed anything, I've still gotten something out of my travels. In my first days in North Africa, it was my pleasure to meet some Spanish Republican fighters in the Corps France D'Afrique. Was a completely volunteer unit composed of Free French, Socialists, Republicans, Communists, Jews, (who could not be in regular French forces) and chock full of IBs who had just been released from the prisons. Yep, the same element as the IB in Spain and Tito's Partisans. The Corps Franc offered one inducement: volunteers would see action against the Nazis within 4 weeks. That promise was kept. And they were put in the hottest spots. The Corps Franc came through gloriously despite the fact that unfortunately, they had the same thing to contend with of peoples' armies everywhere; notably an almost complete lack of arms and equipment. Armed themselves just as the Yugoslav Partisans by capturing German equipment. Same old story but things have finally changed in this respect. But you can bet your life on one thing, that change sure is appreciated in a way that would never have been possible otherwise!

Another pleasant thing for me was to see the surprising antifascist sentiment in North Africa. Incidentally, not the least important element in the Corps Franc is the much maligned Arab. Of course, the Arab population, in general, is not as politically advanced as the European. Naturally, the justifiable resentment of Moslems toward French imperialism was cunningly utilized by the fascist powers. In view of that, the genuine antifascist sentiment of the people of North Africa is, indeed, inspiring! Met some wonderful people with whom I felt completely at home. Many of them has spent a lot of time in fascist prisons before the liberation of North Africa and were then intensely active in purging the fascist elements in their own antifascist committees and governments. That was the issue of the day!

It was therefore hardly surprising when I went on to Italy to find more extensive, more highly developed antifascist sentiment and activities. Really does corroborate our theories! Could imagine what France is like. Had some indication. Firstly, I met some people from France. Secondly, met some Italian workers who had escaped from the north of Italy and got some first hand accounts of the people's resistance there. And you couldn't ask for more militancy and greater sacrifices! That's what north Italy is like and that, I know, is what France is like. Here again, I've met the same kind of people as in North Africa and am consequently pretty well informed.

But the best thing of all is the fact that there are so many of Tito's Partisans here, who, of course, are extremely popular with the Italian people. Heard some thrilling firsthand accounts. Made me feel especially proud because, as you know, the vets have formed the nucleus of the leadership of the Partisan army.

Became pretty much acquainted with a Partisan major, in particular, because of our mutual love of the chess game. Plays the way the Partisans fight. Its attack, attack, attack, is exceedingly resourceful and is fighting all the time—like a true officer of Tito's army!

Haven't got much to say but, as usual, take a hell of a long time saying it. [. . .]

    Salud & Victoria
    Hy Wallach

From John Perrone

Rome

June 25, 1944

Dear Harold [Smith]

Yes its me again, but this time a trifle late althou I received your most welcomed letter quite a while ago. Anyway better late than never.

I guess you've already read the highlights on the capture of Rome. Theirs very little for me to add outside of the fact right on the heels of the Jerries a few buddies & I had the time of our life on entering Rome. The people went crazy with joy on seeing us come in. We happened to bump into a bunch of anti-fascists and guerilla fighters and did we celebrate. Wine, Women & song, and we danced with the Signorinas in the streets. Madrid did not compare with Rome in any respect and will stand in my memory for years to come. Many of our anti-fascist friends had a lot to tell us. They still face many difficulties and fears but they are growing strong and where ever we go theirs evidence of their activity. Some of the big shot fascists may have been done away with but they still have many friends.

The first night in Rome while celebrating etc. only one block away 7 Germans were eating in one of the homes of the Italians. This was told us by some of Italians next day. If we would have known about it on time the results would have been very obvious.

Rome is a very beautiful city and its buildings etc. very modernistic, and people very proud. I seen it all in the 7 or 8 times while there. Its ruins, the Vatican City. Their all something to see! I'm sure you envy me Harold and I don't blame you. I've painted a pretty picture so far by letting out the struggle for Rome itself. From the moment we attacked at Anzio it was a blazing inferno or as someone else put it a "tornado of lead & steel." It was a bloody path to Rome. Some here said Rome captured according to plan. Lots of the boys fell by the wayside, but not according to their plan. Lots of them who survived still ask "was it all in vain"? They have many questions to ask on returning home. As we Lincoln Vets know only too well, patronizing remarks about their glorious deeds will not satisfy them. They want a stake in the future they help to defend.

Salud

Johnny

From Burt Jackson

Italy

12.VII.44

Hi Comaradas,

I am very pleased to be getting the "Volunteer" so regularly. As an ex-soldier you know well the political stagnation that soldiers are subject to.

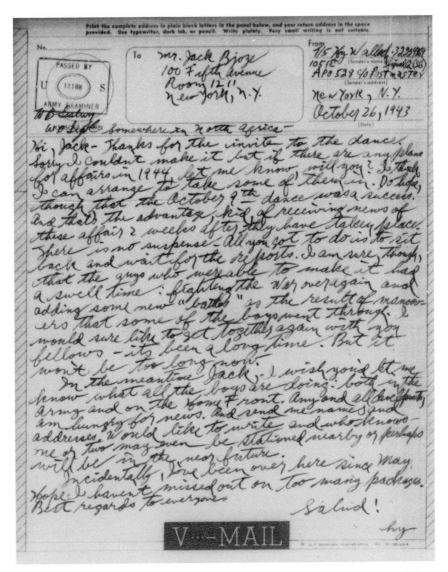

V-letter sent by Hy Wallach to Jack Bjoze at the Veterans of the Lincoln Brigade Office, Oct. 26, 1943.

The longer one is over seas, the greater the ideological gap between home and the theater of operations becomes.

In this war my job is more that of a "rear line general", then a fighting "soldato". When I hear of the good job our guys are doing up front, I feel more than a little chagrin. I consol[e] myself however with the knowledge that the last time I was too far up front (sometime behind it) and consequently will carry scars of that fray to my grave.

Another compensation is the amount of traveling I am able to do. I am confident, we will never again come to fear, or fight against a fascist Italy.

All over Italy like bill boards back home are fading and crossed out fascist slogans "The role of the fascist is the role of the hero!" and similar garbage.

Now we see in its stead the usual "vivas" and "Long Live Roosevelt; Long Live Churchill, Long Live Stalin!" There are more red hammer and sickle signs to the square kilometer than there were throughout the whole of Spain.

Burt Jackson

From Harry Schoenberg

Italy

Aug. 24, 1944

Hello Harold [Smith],

[. . .] As far as the outfit I'm in is concerned, it's tops. We're one of the few outfits that has gotten a war department citation. The citation is given to a unit which executes a mission which, if performed by an individual, would rate a D.S.C [Distinguished Service Cross]. In our case, our batallion destroyed in one afternoon (no artillery support either) a nazi S.S. batallion; in the process captured about 200 of the bastards, destroyed four or five artillery pieces and a tank, captured about 12 of their jeeps, a number a trucks. Also a complete Regimental headquarters, with everything intact, including radios, maps, etc. Previously, we were the first outfit to successfully cross the Rapido River in the battle for Cassino (January). I could go on for the rest of the letter. What I want to bring out, though, is that these boys are all of Japanese descent. In fact the parents of some of them are still in concentration camps back home. [. . .]

Salud y Victoria

Harry Schoenberg

FROM JAMES BERNARD (BUNNY) RUCKER

Italy

Sept. 4, 1944

Darling [Helen Rucker]:

There's not much change in life here, except for whatever you might read about in the papers.

I'm learning a lot of things about people. This is a very enlightening experience for all of us. It should go a long way toward bringing about a fundamental and much needed understanding between America's two largest minority groups. And deeply fundamental! No American of Italian descent could ever consider the Negro question as a problem for philanthropy and charity if he could witness some of the scenes here. Our troops are often (innumerable times) faced with situations where they might be the "charitable" ones. That is if you call sharing your food and saving scraps for the hungry people who come out of the hills when a village is liberated from the Tedeschi [Germans]—Charity! These can't be the people who cheered exultantly when Mussolini flattered them for their heroic Ethiopian conquests. These are the young men from Harlem who demonstrated against the Ethiopian massacres. It is they who are most human in sharing rations with the liberated people. Will these people's kinsmen at home give assistance back home in the same spirit to the fight against Jim Crow which is a liberation struggle. What an impetus that liberation struggle would receive, if it were supported whole-heartedly by Americans of Italian descent! There is one basis for fundamental unity between America's two largest minorities and there is no need for any difference of religion to inject itself as an obstacle to that unity. (It has been done). Reflecting on that angle and thinking through the question a lot, I believe it's very significant that this Italian Front is the first one in which Negro combat troops have been used on a large scale and in an excellently well-integrated fashion. More even than if it were on the more spectacular and decisive French Front. That is, if the use of Negro combat troops in liberating oppressed peoples is to have any bearing on liberating their own peoples from the status of second-class American citizens, then the unity between them and the next largest American minority must be a unity that's fundamentally based on mutual common experiences and respect. This is more important in this sense than if it were the American

French minority. The French Spirit has was always been a positive factor in the Negro people's aspirations for Freedom. The Italian Spirit of Freedom has been obscure at best in its reflections cast on the Negro people's struggles at home. Only the bravest individual Italian Americans have projected this spirit. So that not always does it show up to be present in Negro and Italian-American relationships. For Negroes, the very words "France" and "French" have long denoted Freedom. Now Negro combat troops themselves are helping Italian-Americans to find a way to use to the heights the French spirit of national Freedom. And the new Italian spirit has a much more direct object and broader means of expression right in America than does the French. The most important instruments of carrying this spirit, human, individuals and collective groups of Italian Ameicans are present in America, which is not true of French to such an extent. If I can use these people's gratitude as they come to the hospital for treatment a stream of them all day, after having spent months in the mountains hiding from the Germans. As an example, then I have a right to expect great improvements in Negro-Italian relationships (based on common struggles) back home without ever considering religion as having any bearing whatsoever. [. . .]

All my love Darling. Keep writing.

Bunny

FROM MILTON WOLFF[15]

Italy

Nov. 3, 1944

Hello my lovely [Ann Wolff],

[. . .] What is now exciting us in an unofficial way is the news from Spain and the news about Spain. I was wondering if our papers to home were carrying much on it. The "Stars and Stripes" and the "Union Jack," American and British Army dailies, are now carrying a story a day on the subject. The wonderful part of it is that the stories are tremendously favorable to the Republican side. And since it is fair to assume that both of these Army newspapers are somehow officially controlled it would seem that we are lending some amount of moral support to the cause of the loyalists.

V-letter sent by Hy Wallach, March 19, 1944.

Besides that, I think I already told you about the Spanish Maquis that I met in France. Well, the point is that something big should be happening in Spain right now. The guerrilla movements are stronger than ever in the favorite guerrilla sections; Estremadura, Guadarrama, Asturia and in the foothills of the Pyrenees. Also there probably exists strong underground

movements in all the large cities and it is clear that there is an underground body or junta in Madrid itself directing the activities of all the
resistance groups inside of Spain. Now if that guy Charles de Gaulle
doesn't get squeamish in the le [Leon] Blum manner the thing will be
over with in a hurry.[16]

The thing is that the decision now approaching in Spain is even more
important than the business with Germany and the remaining terri-
tories to be conquered. And that is just it, Germany must be defeated—
conquered by the might of the Allied Armies and that shall come to pass—
by next Spring at least, but Spain is a horse of another color. It is a nation
to be recaptured by its own people. There is where we stand the test. Do we
want the people of a country to destroy their own fascists or do we reserve
that right for ourselves. You see, we are committed to the destruction of
German fascism but are we committed to the destruction of Spanish
fascism or Polish fascism or Argentinian Fascism ad infinitum????
So you see the importance?

Now what I want to know, is what are we doing about it? The Vets and
the other bunch? Seems to me an excellent time to get on the job and see
whether some of that old Espana spirit is still around. Find out for me,
won't you?

How do you like the news about General Stilwell? That is part of the story
that I couldn't tell you from CBI. But you can well imagine the rest if so
much had to be made public. At the time all of this was happening I wrote
a letter on it and it bounced right back on me with a stern warning that
such stuff could not be sent through the mails. So you missed out on it.
However, I trust it didn't shock you too much, my emotional lamb. Looks
as though my old friend, Chiang Kai-shek, is determined to precipitate a
civil war. And when it becomes clear to the Chinese forces in Northern
China that an internal struggle will be of less aid to the Japanese than the
present Koumintang government . . . well the Generalissimo [Chiang Kai-
shek] shall have his wish. And that might happen any day now unless the
pressure we can bring to bear makes a radical change in Chungking.[17]
But that, as I have said before, is very unlikely . . . we have much less
influence with the Chinese rulers than most people think.

We were also thinking that the Soviet Union should be taking a hand to
the East. . . ? [. . .]

and all my love to you always and especially now
Milton

Milton Wolff, 1942

FROM JAMES BERNARD (BUNNY) RUCKER

Italy

April 22 45

Darling [Helen Rucker]:

Isn't it a wonderful feeling to look around you and know that everyone you see, everyone you are acquainted with or have any contact with has played and is playing an important part in winning the big victories that come so often these days.

The capture of Massa was a long accumulation of small victories. It's a classic example of qualitative changes turning into quantitative changes. The liberation of Bologna and the opening up of the Po Valley is the result of an accumulation of Massas. It's the high point of the Stalin campaign and in that action are fused all the factors which have characterized the whole history of the war in Italy. You can see the development and growth of a man like Gen. [Mark] Clark. And I don't put any American military leader above him. He has really handled his difficult complicated job well. If you ever get to know about this past winter in Italy you'll find that it's no less "spectacular" than any other theater. That is if you can consider grimness as spectacular.

What is spectacular now is the skillful way in which the Allies are cooperating to deny the Nazis any of this "mountain retreat" business and how many lives are being saved by their present methods of closing in on the enemy.

Hon, I want to put in a big boost for one of the best of the Services. They are really under-rated. You seldom hear or read about campaigns to bring them home. You don't hear them gripe, (They seem to be denied that inherent right of a soldier) and you don't hear spiritual songs about them and their work. Whenever they are portrayed on the screen it's usually pretty "inaccurate." But here I'm going to put in my nomination for the heroines of this war and it's the Army Nurse Corps. How they do it is a miracle. A 12 hour day and no break. Never in bad temper and always helpful. Talk about spoiling a guy! Well, they make you want to get well and help them. And as soon as patient is well enough he does all he can to help them. And the average soldier doesn't realize until he's in the hospital, how much of a comrade he has in the nurse. At least I didn't. I never ever thought about them even when I was in the "Medics." But now and forevermore if anyone ever makes a thoughtless remark about any nurse in front of me I'm going to let him have it. The same thing is generally true of the whole hospital personnel. But you'd never know from any publicity that nurses get homesick, or tired of war, or need furloughs or special considerations. They are taken much too much for granted by the general public.

My leg is doing fine. It's just a routine case of a broken femur now, which takes time, patience and good humor. Your cablegram came today with two letters of the 10th and 12th. Thanks a million, Hon, I'm glad you know about it. You'll be up-to-date on the whole case long before you get this letter.

I bet you were the prettiest girl in the Easter Parade with your new coat. I hate missing being with you and don't be surprised if you find us enjoying some mid-summer days together. [. . .]

Here's a big kiss and all my love,

Bunny

4. ASIA AND THE SOUTH PACIFIC

FROM NATHAN GROSS

Somewhere in New Guinea

January 16, 1944

Dear Jack [Bjoze]

[. . .] I've been away almost 2 years + I can't say I've done very much more than they have. Oh, I suppose indirectly I've done a little to help. But hell, like all the rest of the boys, I've been wanting to get in to close grips with the fascist bastards too. If I'd been in the infantry I'd probably have gotten the breaks + gone into action. Every application I've sent in for transfer was rejected. Luck has been stacked against me. About 3 or 4 months ago I was helping on the supply lines for the offensive which is now history. The closest I got was one night bringing supplies in on the beach. Quite safe, I could only hear our own artillery going off, but that's all. I got caught in air raids at various times but hell they weren't any of them bad or close enough to make me worry. The ones I went through in Spain were worse + you know how much more intense some of these present raids can be. I've seen wounded + prisoners but only as a spectator in comparatively quiet + safe areas. The best chances I had, were 4 months ago too, but again lady luck disappointed me. I managed to get friendly with some navy officers + sailors. On two occasions I managed to unofficially sneak out on night patrol with them on their PT boats. It was lots of fun + I was full of expectation. Those boys really get into some tough spots + do a hell of a lot of damage. But here is where the bad luck comes in. On both occasions, they were dark, rainy nights + we didn't contact an enemy barge or vessel at sea, nor did we see a light, installation or Japan shore. Every night but those + the boys got their boats in, sunk many barges, with men and supplies sinking in the briny. It's all been quite frustrating. You don't know how jealous + curious I've been of the boys fighting on the other side. Even though one is surrounded by thousands of soldiers, + comparatively, as comfortable as possible as the army can make it, it's hell. One day is so much like another. To me, it's a slow death. Hell, I could be doing more, I feel as a civilian in war work. [. . .] It makes me feel pretty good everytime I run across some belated recognition of what we did in Spain. Most of the men + officers recognize this too + can't understand our present appeasement of Franco. Excuse is given of having been blind before. But there can't be any such reason now. It's still the same old fascist reactionary clique who even yet hold important powerful positions. I'm sure the American soldier won't be as easily hoodwinked after this war. Though he sometimes has an apathy toward political matters, this is only slightly superficial. Underneath, and not too dormant is a feeling + understanding for better things. He knows that this time he really is making the world safe for democracy. And when this war is over I doubt if he will submit to such a state of affairs as succeeded the last one. The American army is really the best clothed, the best fed, the best equipped + best paid army. So you see, things are really very comfortable, except when one is in battle. Even with all the talk of jungle diseases, malaria, etc, its not too bad. I haven't been sick yet since I've been here. And my spirits are really quite excellent. As for entertainment, there's reading such as it is (Thanks for the book—that is one of the few needs I have), the radio with its rather skimpy news, the movies about 3 times a week. [. . .]

As ever,
Salud Nat

FROM: HILDA BELL

Australia

January 26, 1944

Dear Sid [Sidney Vogel],

I just received the card you wrote on November 15. It is a long time getting here. But it seems as if my letters take longer to get to you. I answered the letter you wrote from Pantelleria, and wrote another one after that.

I am glad you met Lizzy Liss. I hope you like her as well as I do. She is such a healthy young thing. Your mentioning of her is the first I heard of her since I left home.

We, the nurses of our Outfit, are back in Australia. They decided that almost a year of New Guinea was enough for us. Frankly, most of the girls thought that it was enough for them also. Even if the work wasn't tiring, the climate itself is. Then too, the food was far from adequate for that climate. Though I wasn't anxious to go back, I felt that the girls were perfectly justified in wanting to return to the mainland. There are plenty of nurses in Australia and there is no need for any nurse to stay in the tropics until she feels worn out. If nurses weren't so plentiful the situation would be entirely different.

We were quite busy when we left. I would have liked to have stayed until the rush was over. It isn't too often that I have felt that I too am doing my lot for Victory. (Have you used any Pencillium? We have used it here, but from what I understand, without miracle results.) But one doesn't have any choice in the matter. We all came down together. Ten more in number than those who left, took our place. We won't be missed—which is as it should be.

At present, we are sitting around—waiting. It doesn't seem as if we shall be working for awhile. So I started enough needle-work to keep me busy for several months. In addition to that I am trying my hand at some wood carving.

We are stationed at a General Hospital. It is equipped as well as any general hospital at home. Help is plentiful, both civilian and Army, the food is delicious, and though I have little use for the liquor, it can be had here, and best of all coco-colas can be had by the case. But the cry down here is "everything is going North."

I went ice-skating this week in an ice-rink. The most delightful thing about it was the hospitality of the patrons. You know everybody at home ignores everyone else in a rink. Not here!—women, children, and soldiers befriended you and skated with you. I hardly had a chance to skate with the friends I came with. But it was a lot of fun.

There was a piece in one of the papers here about Churchill and Stalin. They were discussing the Peace. Churchill suggested that the Pope should participate in the Peace negotiations. Stalin's answer was "and how many divisions does the Pope have fighting"? I thought it was a good answer.

Give my regards to Ethel and that child of yours. And write a little more.

Love,

Hilda

FROM MILTON WOLFF[18]

India
February 23rd, 1944
Wednesday Morning

Dearest Ann [Wolff],

Usually I have some provocation for writing—but this is merely for
the feeling of remote communion. Unique, it will be, and somewhat
incoherent. I have a strong desire to write direct to Susan but at the same
time there is that fear that I will miss the mark. What should the level of
my approach be to a child who thinks the sandman is "a jerk?"

An annoying sight is the town's uppercrust indulging in a round of golf.
Bright and clean are their costumes against the brilliant green of the
course. . . . And we hurry past, dirt begrimed, in the earnest task of
fighting a war. The contrast jars one—and it is a test of understanding to
realize that you and your sacrifices stand between their morning pastime
and the Japanese invader.

One gentle woman—oh! so typical—inquired of one of the boys, "when
are you going to repair the road?"

"Why us"? he replied, "Its your town, when will you repair it?"

"Oh! of all the nerve," chirped the lady, "Didn't your trucks tear it up?"

See—they won't even realize the discomfits that war brings. We owe it to
her ladyship to repair the roads we used so her ladyship might have her
afternoon tea undisturbed. Is it any wonder then that certain groups of
Indians find it difficult to realize this as a war of National Liberation?
Why they still label it an "Imperialistic" War? Of course they are wrong—
and yet I would not be too harsh with them. After all one needs the
foresight of a prophet and the patience of a saint to understand—and
understanding—to act. It is very, very difficult.

And so I picture the confusion and wavering of those members and
followers of the C.P. when confronted by the accomplished fact of
co-operation with the "J.P. Morgan's." I say "accomplished fact"—what
I mean is that is what we have been doing since 1941. Now that it is
incorporated in Party theory—there can no longer be the question of lip
service on the part of the hot blooded ones. Now it becomes obvious that
we mean what we say. And so they will waver. These romantics, these
emotion-ridden people—"what is left of the struggle?", they will demand.

And scorn them not. Listen to them and reason with them. Do not reject them too hastily. This is a deep question that requires detailed education. And the contradiction of apparent "selfishness" on the part of the J.P.'s and the "sacrifices" of labor must be a delicate subject—treated in that manner. We must realize that the giant capitalist who supports in his way this war against the Axis—who realizes the need for coalition war and coalition peace—with the U.S.S.R. as an equal partner—is making the greatest ideological sacrifice. For the entrenchment of socialism on ⅛ the surface of this old sphere remains the victorious achievement of the best efforts of the more advanced peoples the world over.

Here we run into the danger of appearing to be putting the interests of the U.S.S.R before those of our own people. How facile—and yet how untrue! For history has proven in the span of our own lives that the existence of the Soviet Union has been a godsend to the peoples of all countries . . . in the past as an inspiration—as a bright light lighting the treacherous Munich diplomacy and exposing it before the whole world— in the present as the unquestionable saviors of millions of American lives that would have been lost on futile fields of battle—had not the Red Army and its supporters raised the spectre of defeat before the eyes of the terrible and once unconquerable hordes of Hitlerism! And what a beacon of inspiration in the future of this better world we shall try to create!

(Not that you require all this verbiage—but I needs must talk once in a great while—this is such a barren group of men . . . almost) [. . . .]

All my love, always
Milton

From Milton Wolff[19]

Burma
May 1st 1944

Dearest Ann [Wolff],

There is a tavern in the town—and I'm it. Namely a Red Cross tent with boxes for tables and canvas cushions for seats. Movies three times a week (again!) and toasted sandwiches + coffee at night, hard candies and a good loud radio. The canvas cushions are stuffed with coconut matting, the reading material is indifferent; a brilliant "old glory" on the tent ceiling;

a pin up girl or two on the uprights and, a few bulletin boards with clippings from U.S. papers on the doings of General Stilwell's outfit; here and
there a damaged parachute, white and attractive, curvingly ornaments a
wall or a corner—and this very free running ink!

So you see, so far my latest adventure has led to nothing exciting—and I
must say I'm giving it plenty of time to develop. More time than I would
have given it in my youth. Five years ago I would have been pushing and
finding ways and means to anticipate things. But here the trend is so
hostile to that attitude that I can't seem to get started.

The main inconvenience here are the flies. They are more numerous
than the sands of the desert. And no matter where you go—once you've
settled down for a bit they are swarming all over you. One can keep out of
the rain and one can frustrate the night flying mosquitoes—but you simply
can't avoid the flies.

The weather is much cooler than it was in India. The days are tolerable
and the nights are refreshingly cool. This may be in part due to the
constant rain—but even so—the rain where I was before hadn't that effect.

The food is well prepared and last night we had chocolate cake. Truly a
wondrous Army. However I don't expect these ideal conditions to last
overlong for me. Soon, I suppose, I'll be shuffling along again and then it
will be "C" + "K" rations—dished out to suit your need—cold or hot—as you
manage it.

We bathe and wash our clothes down at the river. The water runs swiftly
over a rocky bottom and is very clear—though fishy smelling. You should
have seen me doing the wash "Dhobi" fashion. That is smashing the
clothes down on a rock repeatedly. The theory being that the dirt is thus
bashed out. "Dhobis" are Indian laundrymen. Its tough on the garment
but it works.

The Chinese are always down there in large numbers either washing
themselves or their clothes. They impress me as being a very clean people.
It is true, though, that as yet I have not had close contact with them so that
any impressions I have may seem superficial. I hope soon that that will be
remedied. As it is they seem to be of boundless cheer, ever ready to laugh,
to share a friendly word, to look at pictures or show them to you; to trade
for cigarettes and exchange money. Also they are impressed with
American-Chinese friendship—treating it as something sacred—while
their hatred of the Jap seems to be the only one thing they [?] They drill
with real precision and discipline that withstands the acid test (not

counting combat) [?] the chow line. Chow is rice which they eat in huge
quantities. Sometimes they add a bit of meat. They use chopsticks—some
merely to shovel the food from the cup to the mouth—others, more
skilled—the way we always imagine they should be used. When I get to live
with them I shall try to master the art. It, somehow, makes eating more
dignified and graceful. The food at the remote end of two slender, white,
ivory sticks.

As I say—this is all superficial—as I do not understand the language—
aside from "Ding-how"—meaning o.k.—so take it for what it's worth.

As far as the Americans are concerned I think I've already demonstrated
that they rate higher in many respects than those I've hither to associated
with. The reason is obvious and one I've argued countless times before.
Give a man a real task; give him activity and he improves. Only the sad lack
of real education keeps us from hitting the high spots as we did in Spain.
But then Burma is a rather far fetched idea. . . .

Well, I received the clippings of B.M. (5 of them) you sent and now I'm
rather ashamed that I asked you to slap him. You comments on his stuff
are very stimulating—enough so to cause me to read him carefully. I doubt,
however, if you're really as naive as you make out to be. The things you say
you never knew—til now always existed. It merely was hidden, obscured
and confused by incompetent minor instructors. How often have I
bemoaned the gap between the top rank and the rank and file? How often
have I complained about the lack of true leadership—the type that brings
it's followers along with it—on every idea, every development? Too often
we hollered "education" without going about it properly—or leaving it
unsupervised. And you, my darling, scoffed too readily at source materials
while lapping up half digested theories from Sam's and such other idols
you choose to follow. Of course it was the easier way—but it hardly paid—
did it?

And don't forget this—certain things are true—certain contradictions
exist—certain crises are inevitable—certain problems remain—And these
things may smite us again as they have before. Only now the Teheran
business offers a solution to change all this.[20] It is working in the war
period—and it should work in the period of peace—But so should have
"collective security" in the 10 years of 1929–1939—It didn't with the result
we live in. The period of "collective security," of Popular Fronts could have
averted war and economic crisis in peacetime. It was sabotaged by the
Fascists aided + abetted by their friends and by the unthinking. How a war

has forced both Popular Fronts and Collective Security upon us. After the war the Fascist powers will be destroyed. Fascism as such will have no base in a State. And the Socialist State has proven it's value as a friend and it's strength as a power. These two differences and others domestic, would seem to assure the success of Teheran. The rest depends on our work and other conditions impossible to foretell at this moment. This is the change—can you understand that! (Further discussion could more fully develop this—do you care?)

(I hope the censor doesn't mind the length of this letter—after all I write so very few.) Still, I'd best desist at this point—before I start telling you how sauerkraut and weenies reminded me of you at lunch time—and started a day dream.

How are my two darling children? God! Peter must be all of seven months old by now and Susan 3! Gosh—they are getting away from me aren't they? [. . .]

    All my love
    Milton

FROM NATHAN GROSS

New Guinea
May 17, 1944

Dear David [McKelvy White]—

It's 2 months since I last wrote to you, + more than that since I've had a letter from you. I'm sure your answer is on the way + should catch up with me after a while. For the past month the mail's been quite screwed up + hasn't been straightened up yet. I think it will be a while yet before it even gets to be normal. I received mail one day from my family about 2 weeks ago, in all this time. You'll soon see why. From the newspapers you prob- ably know of our activities in this area. Well, I finally got into action. We were attached to the 41st. Division. It was an easy + successful campaign. If all the war were to go as easily + as well, it would all be over very soon. But, being a realist, that's mostly wishful thinking. I was one of the first to see the show. It was all one sided. I never fired a shot, not being an infan- try man. The only Japs I encountered were dead, except for those who were taken prisoner. I didn't see them until after they were captured. Needless to say, I never received a scratch. My spirits were high + health generally good. The first night I was pretty wet from sweat + rain. Sleeping in my wet clothes gave me a slight cold, which lasted several days. Having little to do these past weeks but sleep + eat + take it easy, I got better quickly + am O.K. except for an occasional diarrhea, which isn't exceptional. I found these hills + climate a strain + when I finished my first day I was quite exhausted. I believe that the 5 ½ years since Spain have taken their toll, somewhat. Since the first day, its been rather easy + quiet for me. At first, where I was bivouacked, had few comforts. But now, there are many improvements. I've camped near a stream + can keep fairly clean now. A group of 10 of us camp together. We eat, cook + sleep fairly close together. We've built ourselves a fairly comfortable little encampment. Many of our utensils + other improvements are at the expense of the former Jap residents. We work together fairly well. It would give you quite a kick to see me help out at mealtimes. I'm quite a hand at cleaning dishes + our table (almost all came from the Japs.) Also, with the light cooking. I don't burn the rice, overdo the bacon, nor make the coffee too weak. I'm enclosing a Jap invasion bill, which I picked up here. They probably prepared them for their expected conquest of Australia + her mandates. I thought you might like to have one as a souvenir. I'm getting restless again + would like another chance, though most of the men think I'm crazy + say I'm "action happy" because of my feelings. I was glad to find my courage is still with me. I believe I'm still as war calloused as I was in Spain. Too, I'm glad to see I'm still cool + exercise the necessary calm + care in action. [. . .]

As Ever,

Nat

From David Altman[21]

Somewhere in the Pacific

Aug., 2, 1944

Dear Charles:

[. . .] Speaking of words and actions I hope I can live up to my ideals. So far I have been in only a little, and that of a secondary role. I was with a group on detached service that brought in supplies to the beach. We followed right after the assault wave and were under a little mortar fire. You probably read about that island invasion. Life in the infantry is a lot more rugged than yours. I'll guarantee that any guy spending three days with an infantry outfit in a combat area would never again utter a bitch in an outfit like the 49th. That is anyone who thinks life is hard back there. As for myself I have no regrets as I knew I was not coming to a picnic.

Boatloading details, holding perimeters, packing up and moving about are some of the things we do. Holding a perimeter is something a guy has to experience to appreciate. You live in a muddy pillbox on the alert for any sneaky Japs who might try breaking through. Perimeter defense is what is used in holding a line in the jungle where the advance stops temporarily. If you are not on patrol or KP during the day you're free to improve your pillbox, clean your rifle, etc. Patrols anywhere from five men to a platoon or a company go out beyond the perimeter. The distance may vary from 1000 yards to 14 miles. Often they stay over night depending on their mission. The theme song of the perimeter is "I Hate to see that Evening Sun go down". With a mass of jungle ahead of you you peer into the black shadows. If you look long enough you can see practically anything from elephants to dancing fairies. So when your eyes prove not too dependable you try using your ears, and you really get an earful. Birds of all kinds are squawking and whistling, crabs crawl, twigs snap, trees fall and crash and to blend it all harmoniously, your buddy is snoring sonorously. But the usual rain downpour at night simplifies the problem. You neither see, feel nor hear anything—but the rain. If your imagination is not too vivid you may get a few hours sleep during the night when you're off watch.

There's plenty of waiting, long preparations, etc. The army is pretty much the same everywhere in those respects. While you see a lot more activity, Old Man Monotony still plays his part. Naturally, recreation, lights at night, libraries, etc. are practically nil. We'll make up for that after the war.

Haven't had the opportunity to kill any Japs yet tho I've seen prisoners come and have seen and smelt the stinky Jap dead.

I'm not giving you a bitch session, just trying to give you a picture of the job of the infantry. A guy gets a good perspective of the working of the whole army. [. . .]

Hope your morale is raising as much as mine as that Russian offensive sweeps on toward Berlin as well as the second front.

Thanks for writing.

As ever,

Dave Altman

FROM LESTER "LES" ROWLSON

Marshall Islands
4 September '44

Dear Harold [Smith],

[. . .] Perhaps you'd like reading something of our place—here goes. Conditions here are so much different than I had imagined they would be that I was staggered. In our outfit, we have really exceptional accommodations. Four men are assigned to each tent. Each tent has a floor, screened in sides and door and we have extended the tent walls to act as awnings and to give extra roof surface to keep our thirsty rain barrels filled with fresh water. Our tents are all equipped with electricity, which was a luxury in Spain. And these palm trees are really something, furnishing both food and drink when an extra snack is desired.

Our unit is kept busy, maintaining ourselves and the base. Our usual work day is about 8 hours about 6 days per week. When there is extra work to be done, we work overtime. Doing laundry is a problem, as are the other phases of sanitation. This salt water just simply doesn't work either for washing clothes or for washing the body. The stills, or water purification units are pretty good but can't turn out enough water to keep us supplied with more than the necessities.

The climate here is pretty warm, but we go about in cut off pants and no shirts. If there were women here, we'd have to dress up. I'm glad we're just poor homeless critters with no petticoats around. Swimming in the raw is so much simpler and more invigorating than having to hide in the bushes while putting on trunks.

About three weeks ago, I found I had a double hernia. I was really tickled because I thought I'd sit on the sidelines back in the States. I'm still out here, and sporting a couple of nice scars. They form a sort of "V." I'm still convalescing but next week expect to be back in harness again in our carpenter shop.

The news from here sounds very encouraging. Hope this letter reaches you in about 10 days and—maybe Germany has capitulated by that time. Hope to see everyone again in the not distant future.

Salud

Lester Rowlson

FROM NICHOLAS JOHN "NICK" DEMAS

Somewhere in Assam, India

December 8, 1944

Hello Harold [Smith], Hello Everybody,

I find myself—as to date—well, in health if not in spirits.

It is a long time since I last wrote to you or seen you and it is many thousands of miles where I am writing you from.

I have crossed more than one Ocean, and traveled over land for many but many hundreds of miles and by practically all conceivable means of transportation.

After a long and uneventful journey by sea I (we) arrived at an "unnamed" port of this ancient and mythical land, this much oppressed and exploited land of 380,000,000 people and my impressions so far are humiliating.

India's millions don't live, they merely exist. About 99 $^9/_{10}$ percent of the people I have seen were hungry looking, bare footed, badly "dressed," under-nourished, undersized. You could not stop anywhere in a railroad siding or station without seeing swarms of people coming to you for "Baksheesh" that is, for begging.

It is conspicuous everywhere that nothing has been done—for many generations—to improve the conditions of these people or. . . .

I had an opportunity to visit a big city and the sights I have seen, I'll never forget.

One thing that surprised me is seemingly, the freedom of expression of some of the nationalist papers. They do not mince words about imperialism, tho how wide is the appeal of the papers is a question. The literate class must be minute. The various papers seem to be organs of various personalities more than anything else. The situation is much as in France before the war. In Calcutta alone there are about 119 different newspapers. Where I am now stationed is far from any center of civilization and social life and therefore I lead a rather lonely life.

I was separated from all my buddies that came over on the [?] with me and haven't had time as yet to cultivate new friendships.

The only news we get of what is going on in the world is the Army station broadcast and hardly any thing else. I would appreciate if you send me the "Volunteer" and any clippings of "important" happenings through first class mail because second class takes more than 3 months to get here—[. . .]

Give my regards to all and take good care of things until we get back—
As ever Nick.

FROM ROBERT KLONSKY

The Marianas

3/26/45

Dear Mom + Pop—

Out here in the islands, where one day isn't very different from another,
you're bound to lose track of time—Well, I just realized, only a few
moments ago, that this coming Wednesday nite is the first seder nite of
Passover, and that realization provoked me into writing these few lines to
you both—

I recall another first seder nite, eight years ago, when just as today, I was
many thousands of miles from home—then as now participating in a
struggle against the enemies of the people—against those who sought—
and still seek—to destroy all that, which the people—the common, decent
people, have fought for + won through hard, bitter struggles over a period
of centuries.—.

And I recall receiving a letter from you in Spain at that time.—

It wasn't a pleasant letter to read. The letter written by one of the boys,—
actually was meant to describe your own sorrow—the sorrow of one family
—my family—sorrow at a time traditionally meant for joy + rejoicing.
Looking backward, it seems to me that it wasn't merely a question of a
chair, my chair, being vacant at the seder table that night, eight years ago.
More than that, the joy was being taken away from the seder tables
throughout the world. Not alone the Jewish people, but all peoples,—all
peace-loving, democratic peoples were in retreat. They still lacked the
necessary understanding , organization + unity to stop + drive back the
advancing plague of fascism.—Those of us who knew and understand +
tried to stop them, were still too few. But, although we were temporarily
defeated, we were confident—we knew, that we had contributed to a
greater, clearer understanding on the part of millions throughout the
world.—

Now eight years later, there may be another empty chair—many
thousands of empty chairs in thousands of Jewish homes—Millions of
empty chairs in homes that are not Jewish—The young Catholic + Prot-

estant son or husband is not there to join his family in their Easter church services either. But today—today we can at least begin to rejoice—today we are not in retreat—today there are countless millions, where then we were so few—today those millions are armed, not alone with powerful fascist-killing weapons—But also armed with understanding,—with organization—with unity. And as we continue to deal the last death blows to the last German Nazis and Japanese fascist-militarists—that understanding will deepen + grow clearer; that organization will be strengthened + and more stable; that unity will become deeply rooted, more unbreakable.—

So let's really rejoice this Passover—not that the fight is over + won—but rather that the end is in sight. Certainly, there's no room for any breast beating or pessimism. Best of all, let's balance it off—rejoicing at the advances made—(and they've truly been great—) and a sober realization that there's a task that is still to be completed + finished off right!

Well, Mom and Pop—Perhaps, as the boys say it here—I've been "beating my gums"—you know me—popping off into a speech at the first oppor-tunity—But I've tried to express a few of the thoughts buzzin around in my head.—And because I feel we've really got the answers to "Ma Nishtanah Haleilo Hazeh," etc.—[22]

That's all for now—give me love to Mac + Gloria + Danny—to the Wainers + the Barons + a special kiss to my darlings Helen + Mike.

All my love to you both.

<u>Bob</u>

P.S. I will attend a special seder here on the island, Wednesday nite, arranged by the Jewish chaplain.—

5. WESTERN EUROPE

FROM GERALD COOK

France
July 9, 1944

Dear Harold [Smith],

Many thanks for the copies of the Volunteer both American and British, as well as for the copy of Dollard's study—all of which I've just received.

I've intended writing you ever since the invasion but it's been too active a month for me to find the time. Work and sleep have occupied me almost exclusively. I haven't seen nor heard from any of the boys since I left England but I suppose some are here and I may run into them.

I had a fine letter from the office of the British vets sent to all I.B.ers in the Allied forces in this theater on the occasion of the opening of the 2nd front. Although I saved it to send you I've since misplaced it but I suppose you've had a copy from one of the other guys.

I've heard that the invasion was the most thoroughly covered event in journalistic history so there can be little for me to add. From a personal point of view my being a participant in the assault on Hitler's Europe was extremely satisfying. It was the best way possible of returning to the continent we had left at the close of '38. The veterans of the I.B., the boys of Dunkerque, the Fighting French, the Canadians of Dieppe[23] all felt (and still feel—when a thousand of our heavy bombers thunder overhead or when the earth trembles under the weight of our heavy tanks roaring by) a special sort of satisfaction. This time when we leave Europe fascism will have fought its last battle and suffered its final military defeat. Teheran assured us of that and now six months later its decisions are being delivered with a vengeance to the Nazi in the East, West and South. He's reeling and stumbling and perhaps it really isn't premature for me to revive that old favorite "out of the trenches and into the wenches" by Christmas.

I am constantly being surprised at similarities between the men and conditions here and those we knew in Spain. Someone once remarked that no matter what a man was—his religion, politics or nationality—a soldier is very like another in any army. I find a good deal of truth in that. I hear the same beefs and rumors we heard and see the same characters we knew. The old "vino front" has come to life again. We even have a rumor factory—streamlined and run on mass production lines—that would put [Morris "Mickey"] Mickenberg's Non-Intervention Comm. Establishment[24] out of business and its members selling apples. It's very amusing to observe and compare these things.

I've rambled enough for now and must dash for something to eat. Let's hear from you. Regards to everyone.

Salud,

Jerry

FROM LAWRENCE CANE

Germany

5 Oct., 1944

Dear Harold [Smith];

We finally got the O.K. on being able to announce that we're in the home of sauerkraut, wiener schnitzel, and paranoic Nazis.

My outfit was among the first to hit the Siegfried Line about 3 weeks ago. Right now, we're doing what we usually do when we're not building bridges, clearing mines, or blowing up pillboxes—we're fighting as infantry.

By the time you get this letter I believe we'll be on the move again toward Berlin. We've been out in front since H-hour D-Day, and hope to stay that way on into the Wilhelmstrasse. The only thing that seems to be holding things up is the weather—which stinks over here these days.

We've all decided that one of Corporal Schickelgruber's [Hitler] V-weapons is a rain-generating machine. But, weather or not, I believe we'll break Jerry's back before the winter is over.

About my Silver Star—it's been officially confirmed. Now, I can wear a pretty red, white and blue ribbon. Ducky, eh?

You probably are wondering about the details, so briefly here they are.

I was attached, with a platoon of combat engineers, to the advance guard of an armored division which punched through at St. Lo a couple of months back, and led the big breakthrough.

We went into that action riding the tanks—you know the way the Russians do it in the movies. If you were at Fuentes del Ebro, you saw the 24th Battalion try to pull the same stunt.

Anyway, it was one mad dash allright. Talk about your Wild West shows.

At one point, we got out too far and got cut off by a large force of Krauts who were trying desperately to get out of our trap. It was night and pitch black and we had to get the tanks and vehicles back to establish contact with our main body.

The enemy situation was not clear. Which means in G.I. language that we were up the creek and the oars were leaking.

After a hasty consultation with the Colonel in command I hopped into a jeep and went on reconnaissance to find a way out. The jeep got shot full of holes, but I found an opening and led the column out under fire.

P.S. the Krauts did not get out.

But, enough of this. The thing I'm really busting my britches about is the fact that my wife has presented me with a son. Yessir, a seven and three-quarter pound boy named David Earl Cane.

Yeah, the Earl[25] after you-know-who.

Too bad you're not here. I'm handing out cigars these days.

I'm sure hoping now that I'll be able to get my fanny back home in one piece pretty soon. After all a guy likes to at least see his progeny.

Well, take it easy Smitty. Hasta la vista.

Salud,

Larry Cane

FROM DAN FITZGERALD

Germany

October 24 1944

Dear Harold [Smith]:

A number of times since June 10th I have wanted to write to the organization and to express my thanks for sending the Volunteer and other items of news. However we have been in the thick of things and have never been out of the sound of artillery even during our light days of rest since landing. The Ninth Division has been giving a good account of itself I believe; my own battalion has been cited for its drive on Cherbourgh and I believe we will get another for our work here in Germany.

Naturally the election is of great importance. Jerry seems to think so and has shot over propaganda leaflets bearing a caricature of Roosevelt and a text holding him responsible for the war and all casualties and urging the soldiers to vote—rather subtle or what?

Right now am in mud and all its miseries—very much like Jarama, only the intensity is such that one is unable to express it adequately. How would you phrase it when the Kraut has put in five weeks of sniping with an eight inch railroad gun—rather monotonously irritating? The general tempo of the news seems encouraging however. Inspite of all the resistance the Krauts have been putting up—they have too many fronts to hold and in turn they must go under when the pressure builds up. The good news of Belgrade and the Phillipines is mighty encouraging.

However it is discouraging to observe the Krauts as a Nation, passively allowing their worst elements to plunge the whole country over the abyss. The easy fat living they enjoyed from the plundering of a continent and their seduction of Pan Germanic Chauvinism has corrupted the people. I see no hope for German redemption by the present generation. Boy the one real fear they have is of the Russians, not a bad conscience operating, just the shakiness of a bungling, unsuccessful hoodlum who has to face the music.

While passing thru Liege and vicinity I met a leader of the local Socialists who knew Luis Companys[26] well—had a desk set gift from him and this fellow showed me how he and others had forged identity papers for the Belgian underground. He went into the garden and dug up a cleverly designed counterfeit rubber stamp that "authenticated" their documents. However he felt pessimistic about many things—rather sectarian I'd say. It was good to see the first "free press" in Liege—a paper published by the local trade union center.

Hope all is going well with you.

Salud y surete

Dan Fitzgerald

From Lawrence Cane[27]

Somewhere in Germany

15 Nov.1944

Hello Darling;

Just received your letter of Nov. 4th.

So you participated in the election campaign for Roosevelt? I should have known you'd get in on it. Can't keep you down, eh? . . .

And you've even got David starting in his political education?

I'm glad to hear you're in there punching again, hon. But, one thing I'm going to insist on—Take it easy. Don't get into things over your ears. I want you to take good care of yourself. And don't get starry eyed about any job or campaign that comes your way, so that the next thing you know you're limp as a rag physically and mentally.

No kidding, now—I'm expecting you to take care of yourself. You do so much and absolutely no more. And I don't care how important anyone tries to tell you it is.

Talking about politics, I want you to do me a great big favor. I want you to sit down and write me a long letter telling me what we are going to do with Germany after the War—No fooling.

All we get here is the Stars and Stripes, and back issues of Life, Time, Newsweek, etc.

But what's the real dope?

Up at the front, we're all full of hate, and our first reaction is pretty much summarized by the phrase, "Kill the bastards!"

But we're not fighting for today and tomorrow alone. I hope to God that David Earl never has to go through the things I and so many millions of others have had to experience the past few years.

Solutions that sound good on the spur of the moment, just won't work out for five or ten or twenty years.

You just can't practically destroy 43,000,000 million Germans and expect it to stick. And it doesn't seem to jibe with the picture of the democratic world of tomorrow.

Sure, destroy the Nazi state and all its organs, execute all the war criminals (hundreds of thousands, a couple of million, if necessary) establish a military government, take away the estates of the Prussian generals, revamp the educational system, establish an international organization that will stop aggression—based on the closest collaboration between the Soviet Union, the U.S., Britain, and China.

But what about German industry, should it be destroyed? That doesn't smell so good to me. Should Germany lose her national independence permanently? I'm also suspicious of that—nothing takes root of a people so much as a war for national liberation.

And I'll tell you another thing—much as I hate the no good Nazi sonsabitches—I still have faith in people. I believe that Germans can be like you and I, some day. I believe that they can take their place in Humanity's march to progress. And, by god, for Humanity's sake the necessary preconditions should be established.

But what are those preconditions? That's what's bothering the hell out of me. I think I know some. But the others are not quite clear.

Help me out, will you?

If anything is being said about it in Church [the Communist party] these days, give me the dope—clippings, articles, etc.

Help me out, will you darling? . . . Be good darling. I love you terribly.

Well, we've had a delightful change in the weather the past few days. In addition to the rain, we've been getting snow and sleet. It's just ducky, and we make the loveliest little mud pies.

Some day the sun's coming out over here. When it does, I'm going to fall on my knees and yell "Allah be praised."

Your own, Larry

FROM SAUL BIRNBAUM

Germany
11/27/44

Dear Harold [Smith],

In the past you mentioned some subscription being made for the Vets. Enclosed you will find 10.00 to cover that subscription and reading matter for the amount left over.

We have been destroying Superman, their tanks, their guns, etc. What we owe them for Spain being partially liquidated.

However the only final payment is the complete freedom of Spain. Think quite a few of us would like to fight in that one again if we live thru this one.

The Heinies look like Sing Sing graduates. It seems their political philosophy shows in their face.

Salud.

Saul Birnbaum

FROM JOHN "JACK" LUCID

Eastern France
Dec, 12, 1944

Dear Harold [Smith]—

[. . .] This last week has brought news from Greece which is far from pleasant. Our service paper has space only for the barest facts, and thus the information available here is little enough. But such as it is—that the British and the Greek regular army have joined in an all out effort to destroy the democratic military and political organizations in Greece[28]— would indicate that a threat to allied unity is in the making. I hope it will be cleared up promptly and satisfactorily. Sweating out the Kraut leavies is a lot easier when there is no such deplorable threat to the democratic objectives of the war.

With the Red Army closely investing Budapest and threatening Austria it looks like there is a chance that the Italian front might be "relieved by the tactical situation" as the old bromide has it. Although the Krauts are still very much a functioning army their zeal to do and die for Der Fuhrer is not what it once was. For example some time ago a big mortar shoot by this company caused a Kraut major and over fifty officers & enlisted men to surrender before they even came under small arms fire.

So long and all of the best.

    Hasta la Victoria

    Jack Lucid

From Gerald Cook

                    Belgium

                    13 Dec. 1944

Dear Harold [Smith],

Sorry I've not written sooner but something always intervenes to keep letter writing to a minimum.

It's been some time since I received your letter, the last Volunteer and the excerpt of the remarks of that so-called representative of the people of Nebraska ([Rep. Carl T.] Curtis?)[29] He fails to annoy me and I've been too busy trying to rid the world of his type here in Europe to obey my first impulse, which was to reply to his weak sniping with a few well chosen but naughty adjectives. Anyway your letter to him was better than I could do and seemed to settle the matter.

I've been on a regular Cook's Tour (no pun intended) these past months; it has taken me through France, Belgium, Holland and Germany. All of which has been exciting, interesting and most satisfying.

Just now I'm back in Belgium after having returned to France to spend some time in an old familiar port. You'd not recognize the city in which we were held under a somewhat loose arrest in 1938. It has been considerably changed by the events of the intervening years. After an assiduous search I found the site of our "concentration" camp and from it looking out over the city thought of the ease with which it could all have been prevented.

While there I managed a week's leave to Paris. I know the gay town has been painted before but I'd like to think that my daub with the brush will cling for a little while at least. I had time for more than merry making though, and with a little thought—a little remembering—I jumped into the Metro and came out at the station of the Place de Combat, a half a block from which I found # 8 Mathurin Moreau, Le Maison des Syndicats. I was amazed to find that nothing had changed. Not only was the building still there on its hill, surrounded by the same wooden fence (still in need of paint), but the name of the newspaper—l'Humanité was still painted on the wall of the building. I climbed the steps and entered, after passing through the flagged courtyard where we left our luggage (the bags which were to follow us—remember); inside in one of the two halls a meeting was in progress and in the other a neighborhood dance. Of course I had to explain my business and the result was that I spent the evening there with these people whom the Nazis had failed to murder and who had once more taken over their building. That was, by far, the most enjoyable incident of my leave to Paris. [. . .]

Salud,

Jerry Cook

FROM ARCHIE BROWN

Somewhere out at sea

Feb. 16, 1945

My Darling [Esther "Hon" Brown];

We are on our way and the ship is going right along. We are really living under wartime conditions. There is no waste of space. I hope my feet don't smell like the guy's who had his in my face last nite. But you get used to things like that. The chow is tolerable, and that's about all. This A.M. we watched The Girl With a Light [Statue of Liberty]. She stood there just as serene as ever watching us go out. I'm waiting for her to see me come back. I remember the last time I went over. I saw the statue all night and then went down below [?] in one of the boy's stateroom. They would never have known of my being on the ship at all if it hadn't been for that German steward who I knew was a Nazi.[30] He used to come unannounced into our stateroom and we had to be careful. One day we had our hunting knives out comparing them, when he came in. I took the knife I had in my hand and said, "Just what do you want?" After that he knocked.

There was a boy from Boston—I believe Bob was his first name. He died on the hill—[?] the day we retreated. But on the boat he met a handsome German girl who was with her husband. She and her husband broke up conveniently and Bob went with her. She pumped him dry. She found out that we were going to Spain, how many there were and that there were also stowaways. I threatened to leave him behind when I found out. She was supposed to meet him in Paris. Of course we saw to it that he didn't.

But now, there are millions of us who are crossing the ocean to finish the job that was so badly neglected. They are for the most part good soldiers who know their weapons and have the ability to really learn them. The one trouble is that too many only vaguely understand what its all about. I hope they will learn. [. . .]

Archie

From Archie Brown

Somewhere in Germany

March 12, 1945

My Darling [Esther "Hon" Brown];

Everything you have heard about the Germans having slaves is true. The boys in the company I am in have run into Russians & Poles who were "leased out" to the farmers. They worked in the fields all day and then had their hands tied and were locked in a barn at night. One Russian man upon being freed told the boys he didn't intend to work for the Germans any more. He just goes around demanding food + gets it.

Many Germans upon approach of the allies suddenly become Chzechs, French, Poles, anything but Germans. When they can't get away with that stuff they pose as anti-Nazis. They have been just waiting for liberation. Of course most of it is a lie and some of them are Nazis who just wait for a chance to kill our boys. On the whole they accept their lot meekly. It seems they know they are guilty of innumerable crimes and are surprised that nothing worse happens to them.

When I joined up with this company I found some people who not only didn't have use for Heinies as such—but were anti-Fascists. They seem to understand what has happened. I'm going to like being with this company. They share everything between themselves—packages, food, etc. It reminds me so much of the Brigaders.

The scenery here is beautiful—you wonder how such ghouls could have developed in a country like this. That reminds me; the Nazis paint signs in English that they think are very clever. "The scenery is beautiful but deadly" is one of them. Another is "'Die for America and save the Tommy." They must think we are really fools to fall for old stuff like that.

Enclosed you will find some pictures. One appeals to the women to work for Hitler. Another shows a German showing that they have—work— Freedom and bread. They might of had work allright, preparing for their war—and bread that they stole. The freedom part is a big laugh. No nation that enslaves another can be free.

Things look good dear, before long the war should be over and we'll be together—you, the kids and I.

    Archie

P.S. The other pictures are of the Olympics. They must have loved a "lower race" winning from them.[31]

FROM BILL SUSMAN

Germany

27th of March, 1945

Dearest Sweetheart [Helene Susman],

It's been a few days since I've written, but the glorious reason is obvious enough. What a wonderful feeling! It's a long road from from Madrid to Berlin, but most of it is traveled now.

Here in the heart of Hitler's homeland, the whole mask of Nazi life is ripped away. The bastards lived well. What a difference between the life of the French and that of the Germans. Right now I'm sitting in a room (warmed by a very excellent stove) in what was a German middle class housing project. In every room there are the usual marks of the Nazis: pictures of Hitler, textbooks on tank warfare, plane warfare, all sorts of warfare, written for adults, and for children (in verses). In the closets hang uniforms—SS brown shirts—Nazi flags—uniforms for boys—men—women—girls; posters showing the banker Jew—the Negro Frenchman—the "stupid DeGaulle"—and underneath, the slogan, "This was France's guilt." The houses are well furnished, the beds are soft (I slept and slept on a deep mattress with a warm, feather-filled comforter last night.) The kitchens are well equipped—the pantries full of preserves—canned jerries—I mean cherries—etc., the closets are full of the best French wine. In France, the wine was putrid, the saloons here are full of beer, good stuff too. Plenty of everything pilfered from every nation in Europe. Here are the well fed—well clothed, rotund bastards. For them, the war has been an orgy of loot, and so they love Hitler. The sullen expression on the faces of the Germans bespeaks their "love" for us. We for our part reciprocate in kind. No German gets in our way and stays there for long. If we require anything, the fact that we have no German money does not prove an obstacle. For the Germans, there is nothing but the fact that they are conquered—a conquered people—the shoe is on the other foot, and the foot packs a kick. Run, little lice, run. Their would-be rulers of the world have nothing but the gutter for their domain now.

But there is no cure for a Nazi—reeducation is a crock of nonsense. You could cut them into little pieces, and the pieces would still "heil." Organization—why every man—woman—and bastard had a card in some organization. Upstairs in this house, there are some old Spanish papers dating back to the Civil War. There must have been a pilot living there who dropped his load on us a while ago. I wish he were here to see his home now. What a sweet coincidence—the load I dropped will be no sweeter to him than was the load he dropped on us. Oh how wonderful it is to see the Nazi crawl, the superman squirm—the sight of a hungry German child does no more affect me than the sight of an infant rat. Had the child been hungry before we got there, I might conceivably feel different, but knowledge that this child was eating well till we got here while millions of children were starving—their lives and health permanently affected by malnutrition so this little Nazi bastard could eat—well to hell with 'im.

You may disagree and I may change, but hatred is not easily directed. I hate them not just with a mild cold, logical hate, but with every fiber in my being. This world will never be safe until rivers of German blood have wet the soil.

Well, beloved, I've got things to do now, so one small goodnight. Oh
yes—I feel fine, need little, but when you get a chance to send some
foodstuff—socks—handkerchiefs, swell.

I love you with all my heart, sweetheart, and kiss you.

Best to all Moms and Pops.

B.

FROM ARCHIE BROWN

Germany

March 29, 1945

My Darling [Esther "Hon" Brown]:

[Brown begins with a sample of German typewriter letters]. How would
you like those gadgets added on to your typewriter? You would start out
your letters for the firm as follows: Mein Herr: Der Furher says there will
be no bombing of Berlin. I understand that some people in daus Reich
have been disobeying mein orders. They have claimed to see
Americanishe Lufftewaffe over Berlin. Correct this situation immediately.
THE FURHER suggests they be shot.

These damn keys are in the wrong place so bear with me. It isn't always I
can type my letters to you. Everybody is busy pecking away at their letters.
It sounds like the office of the waterfront Employers Assoc. Everybody is
having a fine time.

We have a lad of Mexican descent in our outfit. He is a good guy and a
good fighter. He just came back from the hospital having recovered from
a wound. We don't talk to the Germans except on official business. Sometimes they come up and want to do this and that and have to receive
permission and we guide them to the proper authorities. On this occasion
this dame stopped me and pointed to Poncho and asked if there were
more of them coming. I asked her what the hell she meant. Then it turned
out she thought he was a Negro. I asked her what she wanted to know for.
She saw the expression on my face and said she didn't mean anything, she
just was afraid. I told her they were Americans and not Nazis, the ones to
fear were these German Nazis who wanted to conquer the world. SHE was
one of those who disclaimed being a Nazi and didn't know any one who
was. So I went and produced a Nazi uniform we found in her house. She

said, its not me, its not me—I don't belong. Those yanks who are not on their guard are going to permit themselves to be divided. THEIR own prejudice might creep in and agree with these Nazi bastards that they should fear certain Americans. Thats all the opening these Germans need.

I guess you've been reading about the breakthru across the Rhine. Its great stuff and I hope we can keep it up. I told you that all they needed was me over here. Seriously I don't think we'll be over on this side too long. Not that it won't take every thing we've got. We need all the effort that we have been using and more, particularly at home. I'm just sure that every-body will turn to. I got four of your letters the other day. I'm looking forward to more. I look forward to seeing you real soon. With all my love.

ARCHIE

FROM BILL SUSMAN

Germany
April 9, 1945

Dearest Sweetheart [Helene Susman],

Again there has been a lapse of a day or two between my writing, and again you can understand the reason. I believe my last letter was dated the 10th or 11th—but as you can see by the above, I was wrong. Things are going along wonderfully (according to plan). It appears that we will have completed our job here before too long. The most wonderful part of the local task, aside from pumping hot metal into Nazis, is "liberating" slaves. Late last night, we stopped in a tiny hamlet and in the course of ordering Germans from their homes, I found a few Russian "slaves." They were still working under threat of their "masters" but a little straightening out radically altered the situation. We found some Red Army soldiers who had escaped internment during the fighting and they ate with us and sang songs and smoked, in short, were quite happy.

The country itself here is beautific but the people—the tall, blond, Aryans—are a degenerate lot. There isn't a village that doesn't have "slaves." In a village of about 18 houses, we found 11 slaves. These people know full well their responsibility. When I cite it to them, their arguments about "it was Hitler's fault" evaporate and they docilely agree. After all, these slaves were kept in their houses, not Hitler's. Now they all mumble over and over again, "Alles is kaput" (everything is lost). How right they are.

I feel fine sweetheart, just a bit sleepy right now—so goodbye for now. Oh yes—I've had no mail the last few days, but it probably will catch up with me shortly. I love you very much. Best to all.

    B.

FROM BILL SUSMAN

Germany

22nd of April 1945

Dear Sweetheart [Helene Susman]

Right now I'm sitting in what was formerly the room of some Nazi Flyers. In front of me is the picture of a handsome young Nazi who was unfortunate enough to die on Spain on the 24th of January, 1939. He's so very handsome—many an American maiden's heart would flutter at the look on his face. How is it possible that such a face could represent the destruction of Guernica—the upturned tear tracked face of a Spanish child, the horrible degeneracy of a nation taught to not love but war, to extol the death which he has so appropriately met? So they hung his picture in a room full of pictures of fallen Nazi flyers—under each a different date, a different country. The history of burning cities of looted home, of concentration camps, of slave laborers, was all written in these dates under the handsome faces. Now, that the room would be too small to hang a 20th part of the pictures of fallen co-gangsters and we will make the percentage even less.

You can tell the lassies who exclaimed over the loss of one so handsome not to grieve, for beneath that arrow collar face was a brain full of pus—the baby-faced killer reveled in his job—he was eager to kill even before Germany got into a "large" war. What fun he must have had describing the beauty of the bombs, causing clusters of people to fly like mushrooms. Well he's got his fun now.

Meanwhile, the war goes on apace and a meeting with the Russians is imminent. There's a portable radio in this room, and I just listened to a Red Army broadcast from a German station.

All in all, I feel great despite the dreary cold weather that suddenly hit us, and look forward to victory and you. I love you and miss you very much. Best to all the moms and pops and folks.

B

From Edward A. Carter II

Germany

April 25, 1945

Dearest Mil [Mildred A. Carter II]:

How is every little thing with exotic you? As for myself, well I have never felt better. By the time you get this letter, I should be on my way to Berlin. I have a score to settle with Jerry. Although I was shot up a bit, I feel I can fight any Jerry on two feet.[32] We of the armored Inf. are the first to make the break through in the Jerry lines. And then the regular infantry follows after us. So you see, we go through a lot of hell. Only Jerry catches one hell of a lot more. The American dough boy is one darn good soldier. General [George S.] Patton as you already know is our leader. One thing I like about him is that he has plenty of guts. He is a regular G.I.-Joe.

Your, Eddie

From Edward A. Carter II

Luxemburg

May 4, 1945

Sweets [Mildred A. Carter II],

I have been through hell in the past two months. And baby, I am not kidding. I am on my way back up to my unit. And baby I intend to fight like hell. The boys in my squad are the best bunch of Jerry killers in this outfit. Now don't you go worrying about me. There isn't a Jerry fighting that could kill me. I think I have proved that by taking eight machine gun bullets in the flesh. Well sweets, I must close these two sheets with loads of my undivided love. Kiss the children for me by proxy. Love to one and all of our family. Keep your chin up as I keep mine. And as long as I have you on my side pulling for me, nothing can happen to me. So long Love, until we meet again. Always your devoted husband.

Your, Eddie

From Harry Fisher

Florennes, Belgium

May 13, 1945

Dear Ruthie [Fisher]:

For the past ten days or so, I've been keyed up to a highly emotional state. Now I'm finally down to normal. I wish I had written to you while in Paris, as I'm sure I could have written the things I saw and felt much better than I can now. But I'll do the best I can, hon.

On our anniversary, May 7, we were flying in the afternoon, when the radio announced that the Germans had already signed the agreement to surrender unconditionally. Although it wasn't official, it was obvious it would be official any hour. For me, the European war ended on May 7, which gives even more meaning to us for that day.

The next evening, Boyle, Gibson, myself, and a few others from our squadron, started out for Paris. A truck took us to Charleroi, quite a big town. We arrived there about 9:00 pm, in the midst of a huge V.E. day celebration, and since the Paris train didn't leave until 2 a.m., we still had lots of time.

The first thing we saw was a huge crowd jamming towards the railroad station. A train load of Belgian prisoners, released from Germany after nearly five years, many from the town of Charleroi, were coming into the station. It was a heartbreaking sight to see mothers and fathers, craning their necks, wishing, hoping their sons might be on that train, then walk away disappointed with tears in their eyes. The released prisoners looked tired, dirty, hungry, haggard, but happy. Their eyes almost popped out of their heads as they looked at the friendly people welcoming them back to their native land. Many were openly, unashamedly crying, their heads going from side to side, as though saying to themselves, "It can't be true" "It's too good to be true." I know how they felt, dear. Here were people who were worked to death, beaten, starved, looked down on by the super race, always facing death, seeing comrade after comrade die, and now they were free men again, among their own people, their own families, realizing as they looked into the kindly welcoming faces that decency and goodness and love were not dead in the world. It was like going from hell to heaven, a new life. They were happy men.

Our gang then went down the flag bedecked street, into the huge, laughing, singing, shouting crowd. We stopped off at a place and had a few beers. The whole town was drinking and we wanted to help them celebrate. After all, they were celebrating V.E. day.

Then we continued down one of the jammed streets. I saw an American major, a WAC and a few enlisted men walking down the center of the street, arms around each other's shoulders, singing an American song with these words, "Roll me over, in the clover, roll me over, lay me down and do it again." The tune was catchy. The few Americans marching and singing down the street provided an excuse for another parade, so hundreds of Belgians got behind them shouting, cheering, singing. They sang "Over There," "Three Cheers for Red White and Blue," "Tipperary," and others.

Then down the street a little, we saw another American, drunk as hell, giving a soap box speech to a crowd of laughing, cheering Belgians. And there's Frank and Dozet, also drunk, urging him on. His name is Ted Barrows, and he's been on our crew instead of Van Cleave for our last few missions. (Van Cleave was getting special training to be a lead bombardier.) Barrows is an enlisted man and a toggelier. His job is to release our bombs as soon as the lead plane releases its bombs.

Barrows is making a speech and Frank and Dozet are encouraging him. When they see Boyle, Gibson and me, they throw their arms around us and insist we have some drinks with them. I couldn't see how they could take any more drinks, they had been drinking all that afternoon. Anyway, Barrows is up there making another speech. He has a sign around his neck which says "Ajax." His arms flailing all around him. He shouts, "I want to go home." No one understands him but the crowd gives him a loud "Hurrah." Then he shouts, "Finis la guerre." They all understand this and that calls for an even louder cheer.

Finally our crew ends up in a swanky cocktail lounge, where Frank and Dozet keep ordering expensive drinks for the crew. Dozet is trying to tell the people that Boyle is Frank Sinatra, but the people there never heard of Sinatra. They wanted Boyle to sing, but he didn't have enough drinks in him.

Every time a Belgian soldier came in, Dozet would go over to him and say, "Are you Belgique"? and of course the soldier would proudly answer in the affirmative. Then Dozet would slap him on the back and let him know how good the Belgians were. They loved it. Meanwhile Barrows got hold of a violin. When he tried to play it, the result was some sour squeaks, which brought loud laughter from the people. When Barrows learned that he wasn't a musician, he decided to try his hand at hunting. So he goes over to a very distinguished looking businessman and begins to look for bugs in his hair. Then he decides to make a speech. Meanwhile Dozet is yelling his head off and Frank is telling him he's drunk and Dozet's insisting that Frank is drunk. At this stage, I'm getting happy, but we have to leave. Frank, Dozet and Barrows plan to celebrate all night and go to Brussels the next morning to continue celebrating.

Let me interrupt once again. Do you remember I told you about another crew we used to be friendly with? They were crew number 6 in training and we were number 7. Some of the fellows on that crew were supposed to visit you while I was still in Savannah. Well, Frank and Dozet bunked into one of the fellows from that crew. On their 16th mission, their plane was shot down over Germany, and all six bailed out and were taken prisoner. Now they're on their way home for a 60 day furlough. Lucky boys.

We got our train at 2:00 a.m. It's a special G.I. train taking fellows from all fronts to Paris. It was well-crowded when it reached Charleroi, but we found an empty box car and got in. The trip was only 150 miles, but it took us about 11 hours to get there. Fortunately, I had enough drinks in me to make me very sleepy in spite of an uncomfortable, dirty box car. I had a good night's sleep. We arrived in Paris at about 1:00 p.m.

That's all for today hon. I'll write about my stay in Paris tomorrow. As you know many restrictions were lifted as to what we may write, so I'll be able to tell you about my missions.

All my love,
Harry

FROM HARRY FISHER

Florennes, Belgium
May 14, 1945

Dear Ruthie [Fisher]:

The next weeks or months will be tough on both of us, because they mean weeks or months of waiting. It wouldn't be so bad if we knew what the future prospects were, but as things stand today, we're still in the dark.

So keep as busy as you can, hon, and I'll keep busy here. Time will pass much quicker this way. In the meantime, I'll write as often and as much as I possibly can. I'll certainly have more time for longer letters than during the past active days. I know you'll continue to write the beautiful letters you've been sending me all along.

Now a few words about Paris. The first thing I saw at the station was a large crowd, all excited about something. I learned that a group of women from Paris, who had volunteered to work for the Germans in Germany a few years ago, had just returned. Thousands of people were welcoming them by shaving their heads and tearing off their clothes. A quaint French custom. Most of the welcomers were women but there were plenty of men too.

Next we were taken to one of the big Paris hotels, many of which are used solely for G.I.'s from the fronts. The first thing I did was take a bath, and boy, did that feel good. I stayed in the bathtub for over half an hour. Then we went out in the warm Paris sunshine. It was a holiday in Paris. Everybody was dressed in their best clothes. The streets were crowded. Joy was written on the faces of all. The streets glowed with the color of victory, with every window displaying the flags of the allies. Groups of people sang patriotic songs. Yes, hon, it was a holiday in Paris, a happy glorious party for the people. It was their victory, and their holiday, and they knew it.

After walking the streets, we returned to the hotel for supper. We ate in a fancy, almost gaudy ballroom, with real pre-war service, and real dishes, glasses, but the same G.I. food. But somehow the G.I. food was cooked to make it taste like something expensive. There was no tipping the waiters, but you could leave a cigarette on the table. Cigarettes mean far more than money. After one of my meals, I gave a pack of cigarettes to my waiter. I was afraid he was going to kiss me on both cheeks the way he looked at me, so I hurried away.

During one of the meals, I sat near the orchestra. I noticed one of the musicians looking at the G.I.'s smoking with a hungry look in his eyes. He looked like he was suffering. When I finished eating, I went over to him with a pack of cigarettes. Unfortunately, they were playing at the time, and at that moment, this particular musician was playing a trumpet solo. It didn't occur to me that I should wait till he finished. I wasn't thinking. As soon as he saw the cigarettes, he stopped his solo, grabbed my hand, pressed it and said, "Merci, merci mesieur" (or however you spell it). He was standing near the mike at the time. Imagine the situation. A trumpet solo stops in the middle and a happy voice booms over the mess hall "Merci." So hundreds of eyes turned toward us. Then the musician realized that he had stopped during his solo, so he resumed where he left off. I think he put more feeling into his solo.

That evening Boyle and Gibson wanted to have a good time the way typical G.I.'s do, and I wanted to see Paris. But first I went to a G.I. vaudeville show. At about 10:00 P.M. I walked to the Arc de Triumph. I was drawn to it by surging crowds all going in that direction. It was a parade, not an organized one, but a spontaneous one. I learned that this was the third day that this was going on. In the crowd were many American soldiers, and some British, and even a few Russians, but mostly civilians. I stayed at the Arc till 11:30 p.m. It was a beautiful sight, all lit up with powerful searchlights showering its lite and warmth on it. Tremendous flags of the "big 5" waved proudly under the Arc. Tens of thousands crowded around watching the many more thousands marching by. A band began to play the Marseillaise, and the people began to sing it. Did I say sing? I meant scream. They put their heart and soul in it. Some of the musicians had tears running down their cheeks. Civilians and French soldiers were also crying while singing. These French people love freedom. The hated Boche was defeated. They were free men again. They couldn't hide their emotions and they didn't want to. So they cried, sang, drank, cheered, demonstrated at the Arc de Triumph, and on all the streets of Paris and in all the cities and towns and homes of France. This was a people's victory—a people's holiday. The people were celebrating it— not alone, but all together in the streets. Whole families were in the crowds—mothers, fathers, and children. Yes Ruthie, the people are happy. It was good to see. I went to bed that night dead tired, physically, but wide awake spiritually. I could still hear the people celebrating. But in spite of all dear, I was lonesome, very lonesome. When I saw mothers and fathers with their children, I wanted so badly to be home with you and our son Johnny, especially now that there's peace in this part of the world. My heart ached for you. When I hear that we're going back to the States, I'll be the happiest G.I. in the army. I hope it's soon hon.

So good night hon—till tomorrow. With all my love.

Harry

NOTES

1. Weinberg wrote this letter from an internment camp in neutral Turkey, where he ended up after being shot down during a bombing raid on Ploesti, Rumania. According to international law, he could not reveal his whereabouts to his correspondents.
2. He may be referring here to the possibility of escape. Ultimately, he did escape, making his way to the Allied forces in North Africa from where he rejoined his unit in England.
3. Aalto had his right hand blown off accidentally while instructing recruits in hand grenades. That teaching assignment had followed his transfer from OSS because his Lincoln Brigade comrades identified him as a homosexual and insisted he be removed.
4. These are Spanish Republican political organizations.
5. All four were students at the University of California at Berkeley who, along with Quiggle, left school to fight in Spain.
6. Admiral Darlan was the Vichyite commander of French North Africa with whom the Allies originally collaborated.
7. Shortly after writing this letter, Weinberg was killed in a bombing mission over Germany.
8. The scheduling of the invasion of France, or the Second Front issue, caused conflict between Moscow and Washington and London, with Joseph Stalin, along with many Americans, expressing extreme disappointment when D Day was put off until 1944.
9. Luis Carlos Prestes was the Communist leader of an antifascist front who was imprisoned from 1936 to 1945 by the authoritarian Brazilian government.
10. Jimmy Higgins was a euphemism for hard-working, but anonymous, rank-and-file activists.
11. Pantelleria was an island in the Mediterranean that was captured by the Allies on June 11, 1943.
12. The Moscow foreign ministers' conference in October 1943 appeared to demonstrate Allied unity.
13. Giraud and Badoglio were very conservative French and Italian leaders, respectively, with whom the Allies first worked.
14. Stilwell was in command of the CBI (China, Burma, India) theater.
15. Milton Wolff Papers, University of Illinois Library.
16. Leon Blum was French prime minister during much of the Spanish Civil War.
17. Chunking was the Nationalist Chinese wartime capital.
18. Milton Wolff Papers, University of Illinois Library.
19. Ibid.
20. The Teheran Conference (November 27–December 3, 1943) brought Roosevelt, Churchill, and Stalin together for the first time in what appeared to be another example of close cooperation among the Allies.
21. This is the last letter Altman wrote before he was killed in battle.
22. Klonsky refers to the Four Questions asked at the Passover seder that explain the reasons for the holiday.
23. Canadians made up the bulk of the troops who participated in the disastrous raid on Dieppe on the French Channel coast on August 19, 1942, which resulted in three thousand casualties out of the five thousand men involved.
24. Mickenberg was a volunteer who satirized the ineffectiveness of the European nations' Non-Intervention Committee during the Spanish Civil War.

25. Earl Browder was head of the American Communist party.
26. Companys was a Catalonian political leader.
27. Lawrence Cane, *Fighting Fascism in Europe! The World War Two Letters of an American Veteran of the Spanish Civil War*, David E. Cane, Judith Barrett Litoff, and David C. Smith, eds. (New York: Fordham University Press, 2003), 145–47.
28. In 1944, a civil war broke out between the authoritarian royalist forces that had ruled Greece before the war and the communist-led guerrillas who had been fighting the Germans. The British backed the royalists.
29. Curtis delivered a speech that appeared in the *Congressional Record* on August 11, 1944, that called attention to "Known Communists [who] Receive Army Commissions and Promotions," including veterans Irving Goff, Milton Wolff, Morris Brier, Irving Fajans and "a man named Cook."
30. Brown went to Spain as a stowaway because he could not obtain a passport in 1938.
31. During the 1936 Olympics in Berlin, an African American track star, Jesse Owens, shocked the Germans when he won four gold medals.
32. Carter is referring to the wounds he suffered in March in an engagement that earned him a Distinguished Service Cross, and, posthumously in 1997, a Medal of Honor.

CHAPTER FIVE

PREMATURE ANTIFASCISTS AND THE POSTWAR WORLD

The Lincoln Brigade veterans, like most other Americans, looked forward to the postwar world with considerable optimism. By 1945, their fight against fascism that had begun nearly ten years before appeared to be won, a fact that eased some of the disappointment they had carried since leaving Spain in defeat. On the domestic front, many Lincolns hoped that the progressive movement that had made such great progress in the 1930s would be able to build upon the successes of the New Deal, strengthen the industrial union movement, and perhaps set the stage for socialist reform. Yet 1945 remained a year of uncertainty. Lincoln veterans were unsure about what kind America would greet their return to the home front. Would the country see them as a threat to national security or would it honor their antifascist commitment and heroism? Many worried that conservatives already criticizing the influence of labor unions and Communists would succeed in undermining Franklin Roosevelt's internationalist foreign policy, including the alliance with the Soviet Union.

Members of the Lincoln Brigade, now veterans of two wars, were eager to return to their families, jobs, unions, and political work. Many expected to resume their activities building the industrial union movement and the Popular Front organizations that had engaged them before the war. For the Communist veterans, however, an April 1945 article by a leading French Communist theoretician, Jacques Duclos, that denounced "revisionist tendencies" and warned against compromising Communist ideology by affiliating with non-Communist groups, created an atmosphere of considerable controversy and uncertainty. Interpreted as coming directly from Joseph Stalin, this so-called Duclos letter was followed by the expulsion of U.S. Communist party leader Earl Browder for encouraging wartime cooperation with non-Communist groups. Many years later, veteran Irving Weissman recalled his reaction to this sharp turn to the left in the Communist Party position: "I didn't like the whole tone around the

Browder business. This business of one day you're a god, and the next day you are an enemy, you know, this whole appeal not to reason, but to the most primitive forces of hate."[1]

Most of the Communist veterans, however, did not agree with Weissman. Some, like Archie Brown, were growing restless with the coalition politics and "no strike pledges" that characterized party policy under Browder's wartime leadership. Reflecting upon the economic situation while he was waiting to return from Europe, Brown wrote that "capitalism could not provide a decent living for the majority of the people and that a strong workers movement was the only way to increase wages."[2] Milton Wolff had yet another perspective that was shaped by his wartime experiences. While he had some reservations about abandoning the Popular Front, his disillusionment with the OSS led him to embrace the more militant Communist position. Near the end of the war, Wolff had been in contact with resistance forces in southern France, including anti-Franco Spanish fighters, but when he recommended that the OSS offer cooperation, the military command abruptly canceled his assignment. Wolff was among the first to see the ominous signs of a coming Cold War as the OSS adopted an anti-Communist approach to the partisan movement in southern Europe. "As World War II was winding down," he recalled, "the cold war had already begun. . . . They [the Allies] were undercutting the partisans and the communist and socialist parties and all the resistance fighters wherever they could."[3]

Many Lincoln Brigade veterans understood that the emerging conflict with the Soviet Union would push domestic politics sharply to the right. The origins of the Cold War has been a subject of endless debate among historians, but what is not debatable is the fact that once the anti-Communist campaign began, the Lincolns were among its first victims. The government's suspicion of the veterans' loyalty once again became an issue late in the war when a congressional subcommittee in March 1945 investigated the promotion of fourteen Communist officers, including the Lincolns who served in the OSS. To their surprise, Milton Wolff, Irving Goff, and Vincent Lossowski found that their wartime heroism and William Donovan's testimony about their loyalty provided no defense when a group of conservative congressmen threatened to cut the OSS budget unless the Lincolns were discharged from the service.

Despite these ominous signs and the changes in Communist party policies, after the war most Lincoln vets resumed their trade union and political work with renewed enthusiasm and optimism. Many played prominent roles in the 1946 labor strikes. They were particularly active in the steel, automobile, maritime, fur, and electrical workers unions. However, they quickly realized that the nature of labor unrest, at least in the northern industrial states that had been organized by the CIO, was far different than it had been in the 1930s. The workers were militant, but the new system of contract unionism ensured that the picket lines would remain peaceful, and much of the public battle between labor and management would be waged through "press releases."[4]

The South, which remained steadfastly anti-union, however, provided some opportunities for the Lincolns who were interested in a more radical style of labor organizing. In early 1947 Irving Goff was sent by the National Maritime Union to help organize dockworkers in New Orleans. Many years later he recalled what it was like trying to build a multiracial union in the South:

> I spent five years down there and it was very, very rough. We always
> elected the Black local leadership, but if you put one foot across the line
> to the white local, they had a machine gun, they'd machine gun you.
> Everybody was carrying guns. I even found guns in the [Communist]
> Party office. The white local was extremely reactionary. The Black local
> extremely friendly.[5]

In any case, the 1946–48 period would be the last opportunity that most Lincoln vets would have to work within the industrial union movement. After the passage of the Taft-Hartley Act in 1947, labor leaders who aspired to union office were obliged to sign an affidavit stating that they were not members of the Communist party. Many of the Lincolns preferred to leave the labor movement rather than take this oath. Those who were associated with Communist-led unions, such as the International Fur and Leather Workers, the United Electrical Workers, the Wholesale and Retail Workers union, or the International Longshore-man's and Warehouseman's Union (ILWU), kept their positions, but saw their unions expelled from the CIO and labeled as Communist front organizations.

As opportunities within the union movement rapidly closed, some of the veterans became active in left-wing civil rights organizations that were beginning to fight for racial equality in the South. In 1948 Milton Wolff became campaign director and Pat Roosevelt took the position of general organizer for the Civil Rights Congress. They participated in the 1949–50 campaign to free the Martinsville Seven that Wolff described many years later as "an all too typical incident in Virginia of Blacks being arrested on some kind of a frame up thing."[6] Despite a national campaign in which the Communist party played a prominent role, the seven young men were executed after they confessed under considerable physical pressure. Most progressives believed that the defendants were innocent victims of the southern racist justice system.[7] After this defeat Wolff resigned from the Civil Rights Congress, concluding that it would be impossible to build a field organization in the South capable of advancing a civil rights agenda.[8]

Although the veterans often disagreed about strategy and tactics within the labor and civil rights movements, all believed that Francisco Franco and Spanish fascism represented a major piece of unfinished business. In 1945, David McKelvy White, national chairman of the Friends of the Abraham Lincoln Brigade, lobbied Congress and delegates to the U.N.'s founding conference in San Francisco to keep Spain out of the United Nations. VALB published White's pamphlet, *Franco Spain . . . America's Enemy*, in March 1945 and the veterans joined the American Committee for Spanish Democracy to demand that Franco be brought to trial as a war criminal. The Lincolns organized numerous public demonstrations outside the Spanish consulate in New York. But although the veterans and their allies were able to get a good deal of public support for their position and Spain was not admitted to the new world body, the anti-Communist thrust of American foreign policy meant that Franco was now being seen by many as an important strategic ally in the Cold War. As the years went by the State Department became increasingly reluctant to criticize the Franco dictatorship and its treatment of Spanish political prisoners.

Despite, or perhaps because of these anti-Franco activities, the Lincoln Brigade and its allies found themselves under increasing attack. As early as January 1946, five months after the end of the war, the House Committee on Un-American Activities opened an investigation of the Joint Anti-Fascist Refugee Committee. When the organization refused to turn over membership and donor lists, ten officers, including author Howard Fast and Dr. Edward Barsky (former head of the American Medical Bureau to Aid Spanish Democracy), were convicted of contempt of Congress and sentenced to jail. Barsky served six months and lost his medical license, becoming in many people's eyes the first casualty in the new war against communism. In the fall of 1948, *The Volunteer for Liberty* reported that Communist and non-Communists veterans were receiving "official and unofficial visits from a variety of organizations," a euphemism for the FBI and police.[9] In fact, the FBI had begun to assemble files on the Lincoln Brigade veterans as early as 1940, and many had already been placed on a list of people to be arrested in time of national emergency.[10]

When veteran Robert Colodny wrote in 1947 that "the intellectual night was fast setting in," he was from the perspective of most of the Lincolns accurately describing the political situation in postwar America.[11] In December 1947 Attorney General Tom Clark released a list of subversive organizations that included the Abraham Lincoln Brigade, the Veterans of the Abraham Lincoln Brigade, and the Joint Anti-Fascist Refugee Committee. With the passage of the McCarran Internal Security Act of 1950 the noose tightened even further. VALB was now required to register as an agent of a foreign government. All the officers except Milton Wolff (National Commander) and Moe Fishman (Executive Secretary) resigned. Other Lincolns in the Communist party leadership, including Steve Nelson, John Gates, and Bob Thompson, faced federal charges in widely publicized court trials, while foreign-born veterans were put on trial and faced deportation.

During these years, nearly every Lincoln veteran, particularly those active in the labor and civil rights movements, but even those who were known as non-Communists or even anti-Communists, were targeted for investigation. Federal agents routinely interviewed their employers, neighbors, and landlords. For example, when Archie Brown returned to the ILWU in San Francisco he was followed by the FBI day and night. In a 1980 oral history interview Brown described this experience: "We used to live in a different part of the city [San Francisco], up on the hill also [. . .] 24 hours a day, 3, 8-hour shifts, the FBI parked their car up on the hill and watched our house. If she [his wife Esther] had to go to the grocery store, they followed her to the grocery store."[12] By 1951 Brown felt compelled to join the Communist party underground.

In another case of political discrimination, Sergeant Edward Carter II, a member of a black rifle squad under General George S. Patton, who singlehandedly destroyed an entire squad of German soldiers in March 1945, was not allowed to reenlist in the army in 1949 despite his Distinguished Service Cross and Purple Heart. Carter's FBI file reveals that even though the Bureau knew that he was largely nonpolitical and not a member of the Communist party, his Lincoln Brigade past branded him as a national security threat. For years the American Civil Liberties Union unsuccessfully fought for an explanation of the charges against him.[13] In 1997, thirty-six years after his death, President Bill Clinton apologized for the discriminatory treatment and awarded him a Medal of Honor.[14]

By the early 1950s most of the Lincolns were facing the political inquisition. The campaign culminated in a Subversive Activity Control Board hearing in May 1954. Although several veterans testified that they went to Spain to fight fascism, not to support communism, the government relied on FBI informers and veterans who were disillusioned with the Communist party to establish a direct connection between the Lincoln Brigade and the Communist party. African American veteran Crawford Morgan captivated the hearing room, stating that he had volunteered because as a Negro, who for "43 years has been treated as a second-class citizen," he had a "pretty good idea of what fascism was and I didn't want no part of it." But in the end, the SACB concluded that VALB "throughout its existence has been substantially directed, dominated, and controlled by the Communist Party of the United States."[15]

The Lincolns, like so many other radical organizations, were decimated by the Red Scare and blacklists of the late 1940s and 1950s. But when the long night of the fifties began to lift and the civil rights and antiwar movements began to gather strength, the Lincoln Brigade veterans were still around. During the next quarter-century and beyond, they once again took up the banner of the good fight as part of the peace movements that opposed U.S. wars in Vietnam, Central America, and the Middle East.

The letters in this chapter take the Lincoln veterans from the end of World War II through the mid-1950s, when the postwar Red Scare was at its peak. While they were overjoyed by the defeat of fascism, many soon came to realize that their treatment by the army as suspected subversives during the early days of the war had set the terms of debate and made them targets for the right-wing witch hunters. The first letter in this chapter was written by Bunny Rucker to his wife Helen on June 22, 1945. Rucker is in a hospital in Italy after being severely wounded in the Po Valley campaign. He is wondering if his homecoming is being delayed because of the same kind of "shenanigans" that kept "Spanish Civil War vets and Communists from combat when that policy was in force."

FROM BUNNY RUCKER

June 22 [1945]

Darling [Helen Rucker]:

Here I lie restless, my mind won't stay on anything just a skimming of thoughts. Mental myopia, no power of concentration left. Can't read anymore today, can't listen to the radio, can't plan, can't even rejoice that my leg hasn't hurt for the last four hours, (because it's due to start again just as I get good and sleepy. When will I get a good rest?)

A lot more motion around here in the way of hospital ships in the harbor, rumors flying, records & papers running in and out of the ward office. The rumors sound good. As if this is my last week here. I don't know if I'll be a candidate for the honor of being the last patient to leave Italy, only a very few are left even now. After these two ships leave there'll hardly be any. I could still pin my hopes on returning by plane, otherwise it would be a long wait because I'm sure they wouldn't send a hospital ship back for me alone.

June 23

I gave up last night couldn't make another scratch. Today a letter came from you and one from Paul. He's in an engineer unit near Naples which is too far from this zone for him to get leave to visit me.

Today my leg is worse than ever before. I've taken too many pills already with no relief. They took an x-ray of the area around the pin. I'm hoping they'll be able to relieve it somehow. I wouldn't write now except for something that is very much on my mind in a special sort of way.

Remember the letter I wrote about monkey-business and shenanigans and how I had no suspicion that any were going on, I still don't have any, but in my state of mind, there were possibilities which amounts to a hazard. I hate "post-mortem" politics when everyone rushes frantically to check the barn after the horse is stolen. There was a little item in the paper recently which I didn't pay any more attention to at the time, but its worth some thought. The article was describing the process by which men with their points (85) were prepared for shipment. Among a lot of other interesting things it said that men under observation for political reasons or alien suspects were separated and held back until proper investigation was made of their cases. Those aren't the exact words, but that's the general gist of the remark that was made. It read very much like the excuse that was given for withholding Spanish Civil War vets and Communists from combat during the time when that policy was in force.

When I first mentioned the possibility of shenanigans it was in a letter replying to your early conclusion that I'd be home in a short while. It also was a protest against an attitude which does not take such possibilities into account and taking them into account as the first reactions. It disturbed me more I believe because it was expressed by someone who is directly concerned in this matter. How much less consideration would be shown by persons who are not directly and personally concerned? It is this congress on the part of the people back home that I am forced to depend on whenever any critical question comes up regarding my past military and political activities. There is nothing I can do. And to wait until a crisis did come up I'd be handicapped in the way of corresponding with people, family, and friends at home. As was the case in April '43.[16]

I do depend on their foresight and initiative in respect to the fact that as a member of the Armed Forces with a Communist background, a Negro and a Veteran of the ALB, I am subject to some distributive handling by the Army and that especially people personally concerned with my welfare (at least) they will not take it for granted that the regulations that apply to the rest of the Army apply to me.

I told you how'd I left Huachuca[17] by the skin of my teeth and that because of a clerical error in some office, that I got into the infantry on a similar and much more of an accidental fluke. All in spite of regular procedures and policies. How long do you think my "luck" will hold out? Every time they've waited until the last minute before they pulled a stunt.

Now what is there to keep interested people at home from going directly to congressmen, military officers committees, or War Dept, or civilian aides etc as friends and patriots who have contributed to the war effort and simply ask them what is the War Department policy toward ALB Vets and Communists etc? in regard to post V-E day demobilization? I think that's better than waiting until a lot of inconveniencing and difficulties and extra sacrifice have been placed on these people and their families and they start a whoop and a holler to have it all undone.

As I said before, I say now I have no reason to think that discriminations are being made now. But a recognition of the possibility would warrant the effort it takes to find out. If only out of respect for the men involved. Most of them—(us!) have been annoyed (a mild word) sufficiently by previous adverse policies and practices. I may be wrong but that's the kind of reaction I'd like to see. Of course the idea of returning servicemen is a joyous idea and it must be great for them as they return. But suppose some of them who shared overseas duty and are entitled to return home are denied that pleasure because they fought fascism a few years too soon or because they thought friendship with Russia was a good idea as far back as 1941. Is there an attitude of just writing them off as World War II casualties? Fond hopes of their families and friends of seeing them soon must be buttressed by vigilance in guaranteeing that they will come home. So far these "premature" anti-fascists have shared in no part of the war effort without some activity on the part of the people who were interested in their playing a part. The same will be and is true of all the phases of the "peace efforts" including first demobilizations. To take any part of the post V-E activities for granted would be a mistake that will cause of a lot of unhappiness.

Chances are I will be leaving here next week. But I'll never forget the two day notice I had of my transfer from engineers or the last minute deal when the 370 left Huachuca or the last minute deal when I left the medics. My luck might not hold out this time and I want you to be prepared as you should have prepared yourself for the possibility of luck not holding out and be set or already be in some kind of motion at any rate if luck does not hold out please don't write to me of tears. Write of criticism of why so much was left to luck, and nothing was done to help lady luck.

This is the limit of my physical endurance. All my love. See you in two weeks.

Bunny

I think all of this is something of what Ducks means about giving guidance support and protection to American workers.

Could be.

FROM WILLIAM DONOVAN

Office of Strategic Services
Washington, D.C.
July 1945

2nd Lieut. Milton Wolff
1599 East 18th Street
Brooklyn, N.Y.

My dear Lieutenant Wolff:

I am sorry that, your mission with us having been performed with great credit, you must now return to the Army from which you had originally volunteered to serve with us.

I want you to know that upon the testimony of your immediate commanders, as well as from my own observation of you in action, you have been of the greatest service to our organization.

At all times you have not only shown the discipline and training of a soldier, but a special knowledge in demolition and other skills required in our kind of operation. In addition, you have displayed real ability as an instructor.

More especially, you have been of the greatest assistance to our units fighting with the Partisans in northern Italy, which work won the special commendation of General [Mark] Clark.

More than anything else, I want to tell you that you have always shown the highest conception of loyalty to our common country.

Sincerely,
William J. Donovan
Director

FROM DAVID McKELVY WHITE[18]

[July 1945]

Dear Vet:

The most important happening in many years in the anti-Franco struggle was the public and unanimous branding of Franco Spain as fascist by the San Francisco Conference of the United Nations.

This action is certain to strike a serious blow at Franco's prestige and power. He cannot hope to prevent the Spanish people from knowing what the whole civilized world thinks of him and his government, including those powerful nations without whose approval no nation and no people can hope to prosper. Those Spaniards who "tolerate" Franco and even many of those who actively support him are bound to reconsider whether they have anything to gain from Franco.

I think it can be claimed that the Veterans of the Lincoln Brigade made a modest but useful contribution towards the success of this San Francisco action against Franco.[19] Our activity over the past few months—our news-paper ads, our newsletter, etc. laid part of the base for popular protest against attempts by certain forces in the State Department to block consideration of the question. I do not believe that the week I spent in San Francisco was wasted, nor that our quarter-page advertisement in the San Francisco Chronicle, greeting the Conference delegates and nudging them on the Spanish question, was without its effect.

There is no doubt that the United Nations condemnation of Franco places the anti-Franco struggle in the United Nations on an entirely new level. Much greater possibilities now exist for the building of a broad national mass movement for the breaking of relations with fascist Spain.

Congressman Coffee[20] has amended his resolution (H.R.100) to include reference to the San Francisco action, and it now calls solely for the breaking of relations. We believe that, at the present time, the American Committee for Spanish Freedom should be aided as the main organizer of the campaign for passage of H.R. 100.

The American Committee for Spanish Freedom, whose chairman is Bishop Hartman of Boston and whose Director is now Joe Sweat is situated at 55 W. 42nd St. It has issued a National petition in support of the Coffee Resolution, and we intend to assist in the work of getting signatures and in any other activity the Committee undertakes.

While in San Francisco I spent an hour and a half with Dr. [Juan] Negrin and am glad to transmit his warm regards to the Veterans of the Lincoln Brigade. He spoke in much the same terms he used in his address to the Jan. 2 [Madison Square] Garden meeting, stressing the need for the broadest possible unity for the reconquest of Spain. He has now returned to New York and will leave shortly for Mexico City, there to confer with other exile Spanish Republican leaders.

THEY HAVE SERVED WITH HONOR

Sgt. Bob Thompson
Distinguished Service Cross

Capt. Larry Cane
Silver Star

Capt. Vincent Lossowski
Legion of Merit

Capt. Mike Jimenez
Legion of Merit

Capt. Irving Goff
Legion of Merit

Sgt. Neil Wesson
Legion of Merit

Photograph for VALB publicity flyer, 1945

Agreeing as we do that unity is of the utmost importance and hoping to see the setting up of a responsible and representative government-in-exile at the earliest possible moment, we wish Dr. Negrin all success in his endeavors to achieve a broad coalition of Spanish Republic forces.

Because I was out of New York, I, together with most of you I missed the bang-up party given for a number of guys in on furlough—Milt Felsen, Irv Goff, Milt Wolff, Irv Fajans, and Milt Weiner. Since then Sam Nahman

VALB demonstration, 1945

and Ed Young have been welcome visitors. Sam and Ed, and Milt Felsen
are the three guys we had in Nazi prison camps and we are happy that they
are all present and accounted for. Among other welcome faces, Jack Bjoze,
Danny Fitzgerald, Mike Jimenez—but must stay out of Judy's SDM
department.

    Salud,

    David McK White

FROM HARRY FISHER

Florennes [France]

August 7 [1945]

Hello Hon [Ruth Fisher]:

Late last night I heard the fantastic news of the first atomic bomb dropped on Japan. Its power is staggering to the imagination. The force of that one bomb is equal to the full bomb loads of 10,000 B-26's. That should give you the idea of what the bomb is like.

I once had a talk with Dr. Birhnardt about the atom. He was telling me of its potentialities & I thought he was exaggerating, but he wasn't. It seems to me that with the threat of this dreadful monstrosity hanging over their heads, the Japanese might get wise and surrender. Oh Ruthie, I hope so much that this does mean the end of this war & the end of all wars. The man who wrote that the next war would be won in 24 hours knew what he was talking about.

Think of all the good things that could be done in the world with this knowledge of the atom. I suppose it could be used as the main source of energy—taking the place of fuel, coal, water. But right now I hope it ends the war pronto. . . .

Kiss Johnny for me—all my love—

Harry

FROM ARCHIE BROWN

Le Mans France

Nov. 6, 1945

My Beloved [Esther "Hon" Brown];

Today I received a Reader's Scope, the Volunteer, and the CIO News, but no letters. Yesterday of course was a banner day. Oh yes—I did receive a letter—a sort of an addition of the letter from Celeste. It was a memo— giving a Marxist analysis of the basis for a wage increase and an article by Foster[21] on some key question in building the Party. Bill sure takes out after Browder—for the first time I see Browderism exposed. I'm citing a need to develop mass speakers. He said Browder not only tried to corner the market on theory but tried to be the only interpreter and mass

speaker. As I look back I can think of how true that was. The Party was
Browder or rather—or Browder was the Party or something else. The Party
was an adjutant to Browder Enterprises Inc.

In San Francisco there has been a debate going on regarding the strike
wave. There are two angles to the debate. One is that we shouldn't base our
demands on increased productivity as that leads us to support speed up.
General Motors is claiming that no wage increase can be given unless
productivity increases. Of course we are basing ourselves on the fact that
productivity has increased—way beyond the wage increases granted. And
since the cost of living has gone up the buying power can be maintained
only with a wage increase. Then there seems to be a controversy on
whether we should advocate strikes as a general principle or only as a last
resort. Celeste has asked my opinion. I have not answered her as yet—
I'm still writing the letter. Briefly I'd say that the question is not posed
correctly. The job is to mobilize and activate the workers and their allies
to fight for their immediate needs. In the process to help them realize that
capitalism will always place them in a position where they need must
struggle at all times and to give them an understanding that things could
be done better and without such struggle under a different system. Now
if a mass publicity campaign will do the trick—involve all the people
possible. If an election is taking place—why [not] support the candidate
that is for a full jobs program and wage increase and involve all the
workers possible. Get the people into motion—that's the thing. Sometimes
a strike will not necessarily [be] the last recourse, will be the best method.
If there is a wave developing at present I don't see what we will gain from
trying to stop it—unless it is in those industries that are not converted and
would just as soon welcome a strike now. They could beat it down much
easier. Incidentally, Frank Stout is the proponent against a productivity
argument and Ed Lee says lets strike last resort or no.[22]

The State Dep't and War Dep't have denied that Marines are "involved"
in the fighting in China. Of course they are "involved" in landing the
Nationalist troops and establishing beachheads for them. I prefer to
believe that the Marines are fighting with [Chiang] Kai Shek's[23] troops.
In a few days the real story will come out. Mr. Byrnes[24] has a hot potato to
handle. I hope the folks at home raise so much hell that they force the
withdrawal of the marines.

There is nothing new on the redeployment front but I'm just as anxious as ever to get home to you my love. Oh did I tell you that the 76–79 points left from here and that the 89th Div carrying 65–75 points are scheduled to start sailing Nov. 28? Goodnight my love.

    Archie

FROM BILL SUSMAN

                         Manila
                     November 8, 1945

Dearest Sweetheart [Helene Susman],

    The victory of O'Dwyer[25] certainly made me feel wonderful—not that I expect any miracles from O'Dwyer—it will probably be necessary to fight him as often as not, but the import of the election was not lost here. It's a blow to the most reactionary elements. The criticism of the U.S. policy in China by the Herald Tribune and the inability of the U.S. Seventh Fleet forces to land Chiang Kai-Shek's troops at many points because the Russians have lived up to their promise to depart and Chinese Eighth Route forces were "waiting" for them, is causing a lot of fast backtracking and doubletalk.

    Oh how the "nationalist" (memories of Spain) forces cried—why the dirty Reds left earlier than they were supposed to and didn't cooperate with Shek [to] bring democracy to China. What a laugh! He's so popular that he requires the combined action of a U.S. fleet, transports, equip-ment, air force, and the Red Army to dominate his own country. That proves that he is easily the most popular man in China, or doesn't it? One man here put it aptly when he said, "We're doing in China what Hitler and Mussolini did in Spain."—attempting to foist a govt on the Chinese people suitable to imperialist interests (and perhaps to erect an Asiatic buffer to Russia!). But all is not lost. The black picture of the opposition of the last few days and weeks now has its counterpart in the ever-growing and determined opposition on the part of all progressive forces. The action of the NMU which is as much directed at forcing our ceasing of aid to fascist colonial policy as it is to getting us home, is a clear-cut example, Their "political strike" has the ardent support of the servicemen for all the reasons involved.[26]

    The election of O'Dwyer is another example of the change. Some servicemen here from all parts of the country—Missouri, Arkansas, California, etc—realize the importance of his position as mayor of New York who would express himself on international issues, on cooperation with Russia, on getting us home. I wish you would write to him and tell him just this.

The pressure on getting us home is increasing within the army—on the part of the enlisted man and even some officers. This pressure is bound to bring us together sooner and we will be happy again. This same pressure bodes good for our country on other vital issues. Full steam ahead!

I'm still digging and blasting holes for stumps and latrines, and the physical labor is doing me oodles of good. The only trouble is I find that feeling good physically increases my desire for you.

I kiss you, sweet pussy. And give yourself a caress for me. And give my regards to Moms and Pops.

B

From Martin Krauss

November 3 [1945]

Dearest darling [Evelyn Krauss]!

The big news today is that men with over 85 (!) points are going to disposition centers. The fact that over ½ half of the men with over 80 points have left the base is supposed to be an achievement. At this rate we are running about three months behind the promised schedules.

Perhaps my disgust over demobilization is coloring my reaction to political and world news. But Pres. Truman's speech[27] left a bad taste in my mouth. Protestations of innocent motives fool only those who want to be kidded. We want no territory but besides bases everywhere we evidently are making deals for economic concessions. We ask for "freedom of expression" for reactionary and fascist elements of Poland, Bulgaria, Jugo-Slavia. . . . The shoddy mantle of the "bulwark against Communism" has been inherited from the shoulders of Franco, Hitler, and Mikado. Behind peace mouthings we want to keep the atom bomb our own "big stick" secret.

At home the picture seems no better—the same type of words. No reality is given to hopes by constant reiteration and publicity. Nothing specific has been done about full employment or social problems. The pressure seems to be on from the reactionary side. I wish I would think of the U.S. internationally and our gov't internally as well-intentioned. I am rather enraged by the cynical brass that lies behind the mealy-mouthed confusionism.

Do I go too far? Should I put more weight into Pres. Truman's statement that wages should be raised without relaxing price controls? I only wish I had more information. The little that comes thru you is too late and insufficient for a more clear picture.

I am going to Manila tomorrow that is if the arrangements for the use of a jeep do not fall through.

I need you, honey. To me being with you is the only sweetening agent that could neutralize my sour attitude.

I love you!
Mac

FROM JOE BRANDT[28]

605 East Baker Street
Flint, Michigan
Feb 12, 1946

Dear Milty [Wolff] and Family;

It seems like it never fails with us. We see each other at wars and right after the wars and then off we go each to our own little bailiwick and get so immersed in the daily chords of the class struggle that at times we seem to forget friends, relatives, pals, etc. Of course its realy not that bad. I am realy not forgetting just tied up in work to my neck.

After lots of horse trade and maneuvering I finally landed in the heart of industrial America. Its not that I wanted to come here but couldn't resist the idea of getting into something hot and heavy after being away from my civilian profession for such a long time. Its realy a good idea to get down to earth and into the groove in a hurry so as not to get demoralized and suffer from post war blues.

It didn't take me very long to get down to earth here. I couldn't stay a day here if I wouldn't have chained myself to the daily tasks and proceed to try and solve them as best as possible.

I found Mr. Browder's leadership and line just about wiped out everything we ever had here as far as organization is concerned. The people
here that is our people seem to have lived in a political blackout and they
figured Union Sq.[29] was too far away from here so they couldn't possibly
shake hands with Morgan. If one realy wants to know how anti-working
class that line was they should talk to some of the people from the so called
working class backwoods. If you know any Browder supporter tell them to
come down here and they will soon learn otherwise. Our people here just
couldn't hitch up to something tangible the last few years and became
deteriorated not only politically but also physically. They became tired
and politically lazy. Its realy a pit. Most of them here are the builders and
organizers of the '37 sit down strike and the UAW.[30] Most of them carry
scars and honorable memories of broken ribs and skulls received in the
great struggles of the auto workers and today as a result of a phoney line
are on the out trying to look in. While there are no brakes in the strike and
there wont be any still it would have been a much shorter strike and a
much better struggle qualitatively if we had better leadership and line the
last few years. Of course it is true the strikes and unions today aren't what
they were 5 and 10 years ago and scabs are a forgotten word. Unity on the
picket line reigns supreme and there is a new quality of worker taking part
in these strikes. A UNION MAN but its unfortunate that we are weak because
these strikes could be a means for raising the quality of these workers even
to higher levels.

The union leadership are of the old type. They know how to run a strike
when scabs are trying to break the line, they know how to defy goons,
finks, phoneys, injunctions, and state troopers. But that is not a phenom-
ena in the present situation. The union movement has developed to a
higher level it has greater quality and needs greater qualitative leadership.
Education, politics, national and international etc. It realy needs a few
Communist leaders to give it vision, perspective and greater range of
activities. Looking at the picket line you wouldn't think there was a
struggle going on here. The gates are welded, the great majority of the
workers are sittin home and getting nagged by their females and the union
leaders are sitting in their offices picking their noses and waiting for
pie in the sky. The top leadership is trying to see how many more press
releases they can issue as against those of the corporation. Some of the
guys here call it the greatest battle of the century of press agents.

Well so much for that. The housing situation here is miserable and life here is a series of taverns and 5 movie houses.

I hope to be in the big city in a few months and will take time off to bring you up to date on all other matters. Hoping this letter finds you and your family and old pals in the best of health. I remain as ever Joe.

FROM ALVAH BESSIE[31]

----

21 September 1946

Milt: [Milton Wolff]

You are right. I could not get there. No money. No job. No prospects. Many domestic problems that I will not go into here. I am planning now to fight a delaying action out of this dump. Depends on what happens in the next few weeks.

The factors: 1—can't get a job. In this sense only can it be said that my work for Spain has made it necessary to sacrifice everything. Workers for Spain are automatically Red. 2—A major strike is in the making that will possible break Monday.[32] (This is Saturday). The producers are provoking it, in collusion with the IA[33] group, in an effort to smash the democratic unions in the Conference group.[34] The prods. [producers] want a strike, want to be forced to close down a—they have a big backlog of unreleased films, b—they don't know what to make these days in view of a tremendous falling off at the box office, c—a long shutdown would, they feel, smash the Conference group.

If I can get work and if I can get a grub-stake to write a novel, I will spend the winter doing so, possibly in some small out-of-town place in the desert where it is possible to get a house. You see how contingent it all is. If not, I may have to go to the CIO or someone, and ask for a publicity or editorial job. With my two boys out here [Los Angeles], entering school Monday, and my ex, taking a job, I couldn't very well move to the east. I spent 3 years trying to get the boys out here.

May I say now that I am deeply grateful and quite humble about accepting your award, which is totally undeserved, as the only people working for a free Spain are the boys and girls inside Spain. I said this before, didn't I? But I understand why you are giving it to me, and it makes me very happy, and I thank you and the Vets for the only honor that has come to me since I

had the honor of lending my puny strength to the fight in the lines themselves. I do not need to tell you, I guess, that whatever energies I have will
always be devoted to a free Spain and a free America, and may they come
soon with little loss of blood. I certainly feel much better about a free
Spain than I do about freeing our own country. That is a long time job and
will probably cost all our lives, if we are given the opportunity of spending
them on behalf of our people.

Come to NY? Would I could—if only for a visit. Perhaps you will come
this way this winter. Meantime—our love to you and yours, from us to ours.

Salud!

AB

FROM ROBERT COLODNY

Berkeley, California

March 13, 1947

Dear Mr. [Louis] Adamic:[35]

This is what happened on the first day of World War III. As at every
hour, crowds of students streamed through Sather Gate towards the
drug stores, ice cream parlors etc. It was about 11 O'clock and the first
afternoon papers were out with their Pearl Harbor sized headlines—
TRUMAN ASKS $400,000,000 TO BLOCK SPREAD OF COMMUNISM![36] Feeling somewhat
sick, worse, in fact, than I had felt since the fall of Madrid, I stopped to
watch the reactions of the people as they glanced at the papers. The first
lad, a veteran, carrying a slide rule and a heavy load of books stopped for a
moment, read the streamers, and said to no one in particular, "well, that's
it!" The next two, young girls, who will probably be widows or nothing at
all went by without stopping, and I caught a fragment of conversation
"his mother wants him brought home," and I wondered if "him" was a
corpse somewhere in Europe or Asia. Then two ex flyers with little pins in
their jackets, miniature air medals for some mission well done in the
Pacific or maybe over an oil field in Romania sauntered by. The first said,
"Christ, the cyclotron and the radiation labs make this joint target for
D Day." Then I went down the street to a coffee shop and sat down.
A friend of mine who had been with OSS in southeast Asia and who is
a fellow member of the International Relations Committee of the
University came in and sat down next to me. He was sickly pale, and I am

Edward A. Carter II (Courtesy Allene Carter)

sure that he wanted to cry. Ever since his discharge from the service, he had been interested in international relations and problems of peace. He was convinced that a world state was the only solution, and he had argued cogently and consistently that nationalism was the greatest threat to the survival of the human race. Lately, he had not been so sure that it was worthwhile to fight for anything any more. And this was a common attitude on the campus. The few who thought about things at all had become bleakly despondent. And now, it seemed their attitude was justified. He didn't say anything for a moment. Then he swallowed hard and told me that the International Relations Committee had scheduled a series of ten meetings to be entitled—"a round table on For Whom the Bell Tolls." And I said that I thought it was a good title and that I would be glad to sit on the panel. Then he walked out. Where I live there are two other veterans and one lad who was a 4.-F. The latter, a student of Political Science came into my room and said: "Jesus, what do you do when you hate everybody?" Later, an ex-top kick who went in the first waves on New Guinea and Luzon came in. He sat down and started out of the window, started to say something, then walked out. Hours later I heard him staggering up the stairs, and then vomiting in the John . . . the other vet who fought in some obscure places in the European Theater and who is now studying English and philosophy kept to himself until the six o'clock news cast carried the Washington reaction. As soon as the quotations from Senator Brooks[37] were read, he began to swear quietly, efficiently. Then the radio was turned off, and he too went out.

The last to come in was the mother of the boy who hadn't gone to the wars. Unlike my friend from the OSS, she wasn't ashamed to cry. When she had got herself under control she said, "I feel like I should go outside and walk the streets and warn people, but what's the use, what would I say?" I said that the world wasn't being run from Washington just yet, and to wait and see what replies would be from the people who had learned something during the last ten years. But she said that now she was only interested in the "bleeding fragment of humanity that would be left when it was all over."

Now, it's the next day.

RGC

VALB pamphlets, 1941–1947

FROM ALVAH BESSIE[38]

----

369 South Crescent Drive

Beverly Hills, California

January 12, 1949

Querido Commande [Milton Wolff]:

Never having tried to correspond with that adagio dancer, you remain to all intents and purposes the worst correspondent in my world. However, many thanks for your last and most copious letter.

The current vacuum on the Sp[anish] question extends to the local committee. I've just had a visit from its executive sec'y, and it looks very much as though there were nothing to do but close the office. She has communicated with Helen and if you talk to her you may tell her that Dorothy here consulted all responsible people she could contact. We simply have no support any more and I am in reluctant agreement that there is nothing we can do except operate out of the NY office and supply forces out here for any event or speaker NY wants us to mount or present. It costs some 600 a month to maintain the LA office, which goes entirely into overhead and has for the past year. This is a criminal waste of money, when 600 can be raised it should go into the campaign, and take care of our people abroad.

I have been aware for the past year since the doctor [Edward Barsky] was here that there simply was no support. Our best people have been carrying the progressive movement almost single handed, and the local JARC [Joint Anti-Fascist Refugee Committee] is not the only organization that has been knocked for a loop by the unamericans, the terror, the shrinkage of available funds. We have been taking a beating and I see no immediate end to it. The Progressive Party, the ASP, the Labor School,[39] all are having to cut themselves to the bone to survive. Many fine sponsors of the JARC including big stars began to take a powder with the attack on the nat'l board. They cannot be brought back.

So what kind of a campaign you are creating I would love to know; and how we are going to operate it. Certainly we will do so to the best of our ability. But it is a matter of shame that your humble correspondent is the ONLY speaker available in this town any more. Many attempts were made to form of them a cadre that would service JARC speakers, etc. You were present at one such attempt. Nothing happened. Now they seem to have disbanded as I have had no communication from them in months. We have fallen on parlous times, and in my pessimistic opinion it will be worse before it is better.

On the personal side, I spoke too fast about the job I had. As I had no sooner informed Toots of it than it folded under me. The money to make an independent film in Mexico simply is not forthcoming, as we were confident it would be. Further attempts will be made, but it will be slow accumulating the dough, if at all. So we are jobless and broke as ever, and frantically cooking up a meaningless original story in the fond hope of peddling it under innocuous name. To make the cheese more binding, my older-boy seems to have developed a kidney disorder. He is 16 and this is tougher on him than it is on us, and it is tough enough on us. Don't know the prognosis yet, but it does not look good. The two blonds and I have been afflicted by various viruses that float at large in this salubrious (no freezing) climate, but we are recovering. And to give it all a topper I cannot raise a nickel to eat on, but I have been given a present of five hours free flying time! (Which I accept with thanks, but cannot reconvert it to money.)

Escapism, you might say, but then you confess to similar inclinations. I offer you the following prospects for your future: if we elect HAW [Henry A. Wallace] in 1952, you will handle the reorganization of the Army, and make yourself Chief of Staff. Is that bad? You will then write a book to replace the ancient classic, and call it WOLFF ON WAR, which will certainly be alliterative, if nothing else.

Or—come, the re-establishment of the Sp[anish] Republic you and Cisneros will be in charge the land and in the air. Get me a small job under Ignacio, will you—commandante of liaison aircraft?

Or—if you are hard put, I know a man who can put you in touch with some nice counter-revolutionary movements in China, Greece or Palestine, where your talents would certainly come in handy. Both sides are so hard up that I was offered a job at $1000 a month flying for Israel, even though I cannot handle transport craft. They said they would teach me.

So—the future looks bright for you and me. Do not snoot at your escapist, romantic tendencies. They are normal, human and desirable. And they are not crap. Haven't you done enough to deserve a desert island with palm trees and complaisant hours. Oceanic variety? I would say you have. You would say you haven't.

Or—mayhap we could start a guerrilla movement based on the Mojave Desert? Lead on, my commandante! I will follow as close behind as my

almost 45 years will permit. Read a piece about your ex-hero Heming-
stein[40] in Life. He is a fit subject for their glorification and comes out a
complete drip, which I am sure was not their intention.

Come again. You have a typewriter; use it. And perhaps some day in the
not too distant future I will again be rich enough to take you for a 20
minute ride in a PT-19. Who can tell?

AB

From Edward A. Carter II[41]

Sgt. 1/c Edward A. Carter, Jr.
R.A. #3916 4078
32 Vancouver–Salishan
Tacoma 5, Washington
December 5, 1949

Herbert M. Levy
Staff Counsel
American Civil Liberties Union
170 Fifth Avenue
New York 10, N.Y.

Dear Mr. Levy,

In reply to your letter dated December 1, 1949. Enclosed, I believe you
will find the requested information.

Sir, I was born in Los Angeles, California May 26, 1916. I was reared and
also attended school in Calcutta, India and Shanghai, China. I majored in
Military Science and Tactics at the Shanghai Military Academy. After
graduating, I received my commission in the "Chinese Army." From years
1931 to 1934, I had been in action against the "Imperial Japanese Army."
From years 1936 to 1939 I served in the "Spanish Army" with the "Loyalists." I arrived in the United States of America, the year 1939. I registered
for the draft in the year, 1940. In September 1941 I voluntarily entered the
Army of the United States. I have served a total of seven (7) years and
seven (7) days in the United States Army. In my possession I have two (2)
"Honorable Discharges." My record is without blemish. My character
rating, excellent and my efficiency rating superior.

Sir, overseas, I volunteered for front line combat during the Battle of the

Bulge. I have been wounded five times. I was awarded the "Distinguished Service Cross" GO-580, Hgs 7th Army, October 4, 1945. By the direction of the <u>President</u> "Purple Heart," and four Oakleaf Clusters G.O.#74, Hgs.104, Evac. Hosp., March 25, 1945. Also the "Bronze Star Medal," Combat Infantryman Badge. I also possess other minor service ribbons.

Sir, during my tour of duty I have been constantly questioned by the "Counter-Intelligence Agents." God alone knows how many questionnaires I was ordered to fill out.

Sir, September 30, 1945, I was honorably discharged for the first time. After giving civil life a try for approximately a year, I reenlisted in the U.S. Army. Sir, from my second enlistment until my recent discharge, I was constantly hounded by our "Secret Police." I was questioned about attending a "Welcome Home Joe" dinner given under the auspices of the "American Youth for Democracy."[42] At the time I was definitely ignorant that the above organization was a "Red Front." I was constantly shadowed by two "C.I.C."[43] Agents wherever I went.

Sir in July of 1948, I was ordered to report to Fort Lewis, Washington. My commanding officer and his command fought to keep me in the capacity of instructor to the "California National Guard." Prior to my departure, I was ordered to report to Col. R. L. Boyd, Senior, Ground Instructor. I quote, "Sergeant Carter, It is with regret that I must see you leave my command. I am a very close friend of General Mark Clark. I attempted to get you an interview with the general but he told me he did not care to meet you. Sergeant Carter, General Clark stated, "whenever you are in doubt as to the loyalty of an individual that individual must suffer." Unquote, Sir, I have never belonged or been a member of any organization that advocates the overthrow of our government through force or violence.

Sir, I have letters of commendation from commanding officers that could not have been solicited. I have thirteen years of soldiering behind me. I am a crack soldier because of past experiences as a soldier of fortune. Because of my experience the army has consistently used me as an instructor. Soldiering is my profession.

Sir, two days prior to my discharge a letter arrived from the "Department of the Army," with the signature of Edward F. Witsell, Major General the Adjutant General. One of my very good friends, an officer, called me into his office and I was shown this directive. This directive stated, "Upon discharge of E.A. Carter, Jr., Sgt/ 1/c RA39164078, of your organization is not to be reenlisted. Notation to be included on discharge. Not eligible for reentry into the army unless authorized by the Adjutant General." "No interrogation authorized." Sir, this officer explained that this directive was classified as confidential and that I was not to know about the above orders until my discharge, September 21, 1949, two days later, also, that whatever questions that I asked were to go unanswered.

Sir, I purchased one round trip ticket to Washington, D.C., the same day of my discharge, leaving Tacoma on September 22, 1949. I believed that my personal appearance at the Pentagon Building would dispel all doubt as to my questioned loyalty. Also that I would be well able to answer all questions that could not very well be covered by correspondence. Sir, I begged for a hearing also I requested a trial. Both were refused by the "Inspector General" I quote "Carter, we are sorry, this thing is between you and the Adjutant General," I replied that, "General Witsell is the very person I came to the Pentagon to see and speak with." Army Intelligence, I was handled as though I were a Hot Potatoe. As a last resort I went to the NAACP contacting, Mr. Clarence Mitchell, Labor Secretary.

Sir, after having quite a talk with Mr. Mitchell, he inquired as to why I had not come to him sooner? I explained that I had not wished to cast any undue or unfavorable light upon the Department of the Army. Sir, my record is clean, my conscience is clear. My trip to the Pentagon was in vain.

Mr. Levy, if I were disloyal to my country or a communist, do you not think that I would really be able to get all of the publicity in "Red" and "Radical" papers that I want. I earnestly do not believe that would be the solution to my problem. During World War II, I believed that I was fighting a "Holy War." I believed and fought in defense of the democracy I now find myself denied. According to the laws of our "Democracy," an individual is innocent until proven guilty. According to the powers that be, that law has been interpreted in the opposite. Should that be the case, I ask for the right in the name of "Democracy," that so many profess, to prove my loyalty and establish my innocence. I am not afraid to face any board of inquiry in fact, I invite a hearing or trial.

Mr. Levy, I consider the continued possession of the decorations and awards I have as an insult to ones intelligence. The scars of "Battle" that I must carry to my grave are decorations enough. Scars that were received in defense of the "Democracy" I now find myself denied.

Mr. Levy, do you not think that our great "Democratic" United States of America should cease "exporting democracy and try importing? I suggest that we export only after establishing a sizeable stockpile.

Mr. Levy, please do not consider me a braggard. But, I am continually contacted by officers out of "Fort Lewis" with suggestions and advice. Sir, I believe that the people of our country do not realize how much the United States is gradually becoming a "Police State." The very evils that we fought against in World War II were not destroyed. We have captured and adopted many of these evils. Sir, I shall continually fight for redress. I wish to be charged with whatever charges the Department of the Army has. Once again, I repeat I invite any hearing or trial.

Mr. Levy, I appreciate any and all inquires that you and your offices deem necessary. Sir, I need your help. Please except my grateful; I thank you, for any and all future assistance I receive through you and the "American Civil Liberties Union."

Respectfully yours,

Edward A. Carter, Jr.

FROM EDWARD A. CARTER II[44]

Sgt 1/c Edward A. Carter, Jr.

R.A. # 39164078

Salishan

32 Vancouver

Tacoma 5, Washington

May 2, 1950

Herbert M. Levy

Staff Counsel

American Civil Liberties Union

107 5th Street

New York 10, N.Y.

Dear Mr. Levy,

Please except my thanks for all that you and your organization have done in my behalf.

Sir, after seven months since I was given an "Honorable" Discharge, I find that there is not much hope for redress. I am able to understand the "Stab in the Back" to our country at "Pearl Harbor." I am unable to comprehend my county's "Stab in the Back" to one of her own. I have lost faith, I am disappointed in democracy, "The American Way of Life."

At least I find that government officials are able to get hearings or trials. Myself an ordinary citizen, find that I am unable to do so.

Mr. Levy, I am sending you my "Distinguished Service Cross." Please grant me one last favor and return this cross directly to President Harry Truman, by whose direction I was awarded this decoration. I feel that continued possession of this cross a sacrilege and an insult to ones intelligence. In my country's hour of need I was in the front lines with a sub-machine gun in my fist. My reward? A stab in the back.

Mr. Levy, if at all possible please get some type of receipt for the "D.S.C." At your convenience, Sir, I would appreciate the return of all papers that I have mailed to you so far. Should there be any chance for their further use, return only after they serve their purpose.

Sir, so far I have lost two jobs after word passed around that I had been kicked out of the army because I was a communist. I find it hard to make a living for my wife and four children. The only profession that I am familiar with is that of a soldier. How to kill and not be killed. Perhaps Military Tactics will prove successful against a bank or two.

Respectfully yours,

Edward A. Carter, Jr.

From Moe Fishman

June 5, 1950

Dear Alvah [Bessie]:

Good to hear from you so promptly. Am as confused as you are about the status of the anthology.[45] Will work on it and get it straightened out as quick as I can.

At the moment we are tied up in the mass meeting being run tonite jointly by the Joint Anti-Fascist Refugee Committee for the Arts, Sciences with Professor [John Howard] Lawson and [Dalton] Trumbo speaking for the Hollywood Ten.[46] We are using the meeting to start the campaign for granting of full pardon and for the intensification of the anti-Franco, anti-war drive. The VALB is taking the lead in calling for a picket line in front of the White House on Wed. when the 11 of the Joint [Anti-Fascist Refugee Committee] go down to court and for full mobilization at Penn station to see Jack [John Howard Lawson] and Dalton [Trumbo] off [to prison] on Friday.

With regard to how much help the organization can give financially—it's rough. I am applying for unemployment insurance cause we have no dough to pay me and all we can do for you aside from being able to make an outright contribution from the non-existent treasury we will do. Have already called the gal in charge of raising dough for the two families of the Hollywood Ten that will most need it and we will do anything and everything we can. Have a few ideas such as appeals to special people in the name of VALB and some others. Will keep you informed on developments of this. Originally, Milt Wolff was approached on the matter of bringing your family east—and we raised the fifty bucks without too much effort from the vets. Milt feels we would be in a position to do much more for your family if they were here in the east—but you certainly know best whether they would be better off out on the coast.

If you are discouraged by the reaction of the vets out on the coast, imagine what I should feel, but don't—about the lack of activity on the part of the vets, especially many of our best guys here, who are involved in everything but activity connected with our organization. But we expect to start doing something about it, and soon.

I know how tied up you must be right now—but would suggest that if you can at all find the time, you write or rewrite the introduction to the anthology on the basis you outline in your letter and let me use it as a basis to get a definitive decision next week.

Salud!

FROM THE JOINT ANTI-FASCIST REFUGEE COMMITTEE:
A LETTER TO THE PRESIDENT

----

425 Fourth Avenue
New York, N.Y.
[July 1950]

The Honorable Harry S. Truman
President of the United States
White House
Washington, DC.

Mr. President:

We eleven undersigned leaders of the Joint Anti-Fascist Refugee

Committee, unjustly imprisoned by Federal authorities, call upon you to exercise the executive power you possess to set us free.

Our jailing is intolerable for we have committed no crime.

We assert the right and duty of Americans to aid the victims of the tyranny of Franco, whose fascist regime in Spain has been repeatedly condemned by our Government, by other civilized nations and by the General Assembly of the United Nations.

Four years ago, the House Committee on Un-American Activities demanded that we hand over the books and records of the relief organization represented. This we could not do. The organization's books and records had always been made available to government agencies whose interests were legitimate. But before this openly pro-Franco committee, we could not risk reprisals against the families of relief recipients, still inside Franco Spain. Neither could we allow the many relief contributors to be exposed to the unwarranted harassment to which we had already been subjected.

We undertook to challenge in the courts the constitutionality of this committee of the House of Representatives as well as its conduct. We followed the footsteps of President Franklin D. Roosevelt, and of tens of thousands of American citizens who had publicly condemned the committee as sordid in procedure, lawless in conception and a flagrant violator of the traditional American constitutional safeguards.

The patriotic challenge has not been met, Mr. President, but we are in jail. The Supreme Court, by refusing to review our appeal after a two-year delay, has abdicated its obligations to decide the constitutional issue.

Our imprisonment, therefore, is a grave offense against our persons and a shameful violation of our rights. It has already been interpreted here and abroad as a victory for the enemies of freedom and world peace, as a triumph for Franco.

You have the power to revise this judgment, Mr. President, by issuing a proclamation to set us free. You should immediately exercise this power.

Dr. Jackob Auslander
Federal Correctional Institution
Danbury, Connecticut

Dr. Edward Barsky
Federal Reformatory
Petersburg, Virginia

Dr. Lyman R. Bradley
Federal Prison Camp
Mill Point, West Virginia

Mrs. Majorie Chodorov
Federal Reformatory
Alderson, West Virginia

Howard Fast
Federal Prison Camp
Mill Point, West Virginia

Harry M. Justiz
Federal Detention House
New York, New York

Mrs. Ruth Leider
Federal Reformatory
Alderson, West Virginia

James Lustig
Federal Reformatory
Ashland, Kentucky

Manuel Magana
Federal Detention House
New York, N.Y.

Dr. Louis Miller
Federal Detention House
New York, New York

Mrs. Charlotte Stern
Federal Reformatory
Alderson, West Virginia

EXCERPTS FROM THE TESTIMONY OF CRAWFORD MORGAN
BEFORE THE SUBVERSIVE ACTIVITIES CONTROL BOARD,
SEPTEMBER 15 AND 16, 1954[47]

MR. DALY [U.S. DEPARTMENT OF JUSTICE]: Did you have any understanding, Mr. Morgan, before you went to Spain of what the issues were connected with that were there?

THE WITNESS: I felt that I had a pretty good knowledge—pretty good idea of what Fascism was and most of its ramifications and being aware just what happened in Ethiopia, what the Fascist Italian Government had done to the Ethiopians, the response from the different countries, especially from my country here, of how the people felt about it, and what the people in the streets tried to do about it, and also plus the fact the way that I and all the rest of the Negroes in this country have been treated ever since slavery, then I figured I had a pretty good idea of what Fascism was, because we have quite a few Fascist tendencies in this country. Didn't come to the point of taking up arms and going out and killing a lot of people, but for the last—longest—Negroes have been getting lynched in this country by mobs, and that was Fascism on a small scale in this country.

But over there it was one whole big group against the other. It was the Franco group that didn't like democracy or no parts of it, and they rebelled against the people after the '36 elections and tried to stick their ideas down the freedom-loving people of Spain's throats.

So I, being a Negro and all of the stuff that I have had to take in this country, well, then I had a pretty good idea of Fascism, what Fascism was, and I didn't want no part of it, and I still don't want no part of it. And I got a chance to fight it there with bullets and I went there and fought it with bullets. If I get a chance to fight with bullets again, I will fight with bullets again.

MR. DALY: Mr. Morgan, were those thoughts in your mind before you went to Spain?

THE WITNESS: Ever since I have been big enough to understand things I have rebelled, as a small child of three or four years old would rebel, of inhuman injustice, the way I can understand it at that age. And then as long as I have been able to remember, up until now, the Government, a lot of the people—have treated me as a second-class citizen.

I am 43 years old, and all my life I have been treated as a second-class citizen, and naturally if you always have been treated like one you start feeling it at a very tender age.

With Hitler somewhat on the march, and Fascism starting the fight in Spain, I felt that it could serve two-fold purposes: I felt that if we could lick the Fascists in Spain, I felt that in the trend of things it would offset a blood bath later. I felt that if we didn't lick Franco and didn't stop Fascism there, it would spread over lots of the world; and being a Negro it is bad enough for white people to live under Fascism, they just couldn't live under it. They would be wiped out.

MR. DALY: Were you aware of any time you were a member of the International Brigade receiving any different treatment because of your race?

THE WITNESS: No, from the time I arrived in Spain until the time I left for that period of my life I felt like a human being, like a man. People didn't look at me with hatred in their eyes because I was black, and I wasn't refused this or refused that, because I was black. I was treated, like all the rest of the people were treated, and when you have been in the world for quite a long time and have been treated worse than people treat their dogs, it is quite a nice feeling to go some place and you feel like a human being.

MR. DALY: Can you recall how soon it was after your return that you first had any connection with the Veterans of the Abraham Lincoln Brigade?

THE WITNESS: I don't recall.

MR. DALY: Why did you think it [the recognition of the Franco government] was the most terrible thing the government has ever done?

THE WITNESS: Well, I thought it was terrible because I spent 47 months in defense of my country fighting fascism and I couldn't see—I spent 47 months fighting in the American Army—in the Army during World War II.

MR. DALY: Will you please tell the panel, if you remember sir, who you recall meeting at the Friends of the Abraham Lincoln Brigade office the first time you got there?

THE WITNESS: I feel that I would be incriminating myself naming their names or my name, especially with the hysteria and so where people are guilty by association. I have to use the Fifth Amendment on that.

MR. DALY: The chair requests in the name of the panel that the witness answer.

THE WITNESS: I just stated that the only persons I recognized that were there, when there were other people there, but I recognized Milt [Wolff].

MR. DALY: Were you ever a member of the Communist Party of the United States?

THE WITNESS: I use the Fifth Amendment.

MR. CLAY [ATTORNEY FOR CRAWFORD MORGAN]: If the counsel for the Government would define membership in anything under the law as it now stands, it might enable the witness to answer that question without perjuring himself. But unless we are supplied with some definition of the word membership I insist that the question is incompetent, irrelevant and immaterial, because it is too obscure, too vague, to contain any definition of membership.

DR. McHALE [SUBVERSIVE ACTIVITIES CONTROL BOARD]: Objection overruled.

MR. DALY: Did you ever hear Earl Browder speak in Spain?

THE WITNESS: I don't know.

MR. DALY: Do you know whether or not Earl Browder was ever a member of the Abraham Lincoln Brigade?

THE WITNESS: According to that article I read there I believe he is an honorary member of the Abraham Lincoln Brigade.

MR. DALY: Does the Veterans of the Abraham Lincoln Brigade paper, Volunteer for Liberty, regularly have a column or a section devoted to the happenings or the whereabouts of the doings of its members?

THE WITNESS: The paper don't regularly have the names and addresses and whereabouts—whereabouts of the other Vets for the simple reason that they stand a good chance of losing their job or hounded by the FBI.

Those people that are mentioned mostly to my knowledge is such people that have been persecuted and thrown into jail, like Bob Thompson. That is in the paper.

But, take me for instance, they would not put my name there and address in the paper because it would invite the FBI agents around hounding me or they would be hounding me on my job, and a lot of people are losing their jobs these days because the FBI is hounding them. There are no charges against them but hounding them.

MR. DALY: Now, when you traveled to Spain did you travel by yourself?

THE WITNESS: I use the Fifth Amendment on that.

DR. McHALE: Overruled.

MR. DALY: You testified in your direct examination concerning a person by the name of Bob Thompson. Would you tell the panel what Bob Thompson was convicted of?

THE WITNESS: The way I understand it, that he was convicted under the Smith Act. He wasn't convicted for committing any crime. He was convicted of what somebody thought or somebody else thought that he had in his head.

MR. DALY: Were you ever in the State of California?

THE WITNESS: I was in California. I don't know if it were in '30 or '31. A bunch of us fellows left New York on a freight train and was trying to get to—it was building this dam out there—the I don't know—I forget if it was the Boulder Dam or what it was.

THE WITNESS: So on this train going out, when we crossed on this train, there were several hundreds of people, Negro and white, on the train, whose families, some coming toward Chicago and other going toward the coast, and when we got in, I think it was Fresno, California, every Negro on the train was arrested, and we resented it very much.

It seems that some white man or white women was killed, I believe that is what it was, and somebody had said they saw some Negro around the car or something.

MR. DALY: Sometime before going into the Army you lived at 42 Union Square.

MR. DALY: Did you ever hold Communist Party meetings at that address?

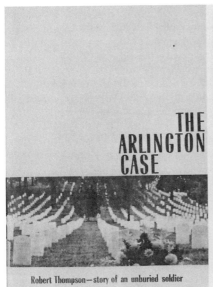

THE ARLINGTON CASE

Robert Thompson—story of an unburied soldier

When celebrated war hero Robert Thompson died in 1965, the army rejected his widow's request to bury his remains in Arlington National Cemetery, citing his conviction as a Communist leader under the Smith Act. A lawsuit supported by the American Civil Liberties Union forced the army to reverse its decision.

THE WITNESS: I refuse to answer.

MR. DALY: Did you ever register as a Communist Party member?

THE WITNESS: I will use the Fifth Amendment on that.

MR. DALY: I ask you whether or not in the year 1936 you registered as a voter for the Communist Party.

THE WITNESS: I refuse to answer on the Fifth Amendment.

NOTES

1. John Gerassi interview with Irving Weissman, June 4, 1981, Gerassi.
2. Archie Brown to Esther Brown, November 29, 1945, ALBA.
3. John Gerassi interview with Milton Wolff, June 6, 1980, Gerassi.
4. Joe Brandt to Milton Wolff, February 12, 1946, Milton Wolff Papers, University of Illinois Library.
5. John Gerassi interview with Irving Goff, August 24, 1980, Gerassi.
6. John Gerassi interview with Milton Wolff, June 6, 1980, Gerassi.
7. Eric W. Rise, *The Martinsville Seven: Race, Rape, and Capital Punishment* (Charlottesville: University of Virginia Press, 1995). The case of the Martinsville

Seven was seen by most civil rights activists and radicals as a classic case of southern "legal lynching." On January 8, 1949, a white woman in Martinsville, Virginia, accused seven young black men of violently raping her. Within two days the police had arrested and obtained confessions from each of the suspects. After brief trials, the defendants were convicted and sentenced to death. Amid nationwide protests they were executed in February 1951. Many in the African American community compared this case to the Scottsboro affair. The Civil Rights Congress, the International Labor Defense, and the National Negro Congress played major roles in the defense effort.

8. George Marshall to Milton Wolff, October 3, 1950, Milton Wolff Papers, University of Illinois Library.
9. *The Volunteer for Liberty* 10 (November 1948): 1.
10. Robert Colodny to Nan Green, March 14, 1947, as quoted in Carroll, *Odyssey* 287.
11. Ibid.
12. John Gerassi interview with Archie Brown, August 14, 1980, Gerassi.
13. Edward Carter Papers, ALBA.
14. Allene Carter and Robert Allen, *Honoring Sergeant Carter: Redeeming a Black World War II Hero's Legacy* (New York: Amistad, 2003); Edward A. Carter case file, American Civil Liberties Union Records, Princeton University Library.
15. Herbert Brownell, Attorney General of the United States v. Veterans of the Abraham Lincoln Brigade, "Official Report of the Proceedings before the Subversive Activities Control Board," May–September 1954, testimony of Crawford Morgan, pp. 3196-3416 and Milton Wolff, pp. 3600–3719.
16. Rucker was inducted into the army in February 1942 and assigned to the 92nd Infantry Division at Fort Bragg, N.C. When most of the inductees that he entered the service with were shipped out to Europe in April 1943, Rucker was left behind since he was identified as a security risk because of his Lincoln Brigade background and Communist party membership.
17. Fort Huachuca, Arizona, was the army base where Rucker was stationed for most of 1944.
18. This letter was published in the *Volunteer for Liberty* 9 (July 1945): 1.
19. At the San Francisco Conference, which established the United Nations, the Lincoln Brigade veterans organized a mass demonstration against admitting Franco's Spain.
20. Representative John M. Coffee was a Democrat from Washington.
21. William Z. Foster (1881–1961) was chairperson of the Communist party, USA from 1945 to 1957.
22. Frank Stout and Ed Lee were prominent CIO leaders in San Francisco.
23. Chiang Kai-shek (1884–1975) was leader of the Chinese Nationalist government.
24. James Byrnes (1882–1972) was the United States secretary of state from 1945 to 1947.
25. William O'Dwyer (1890–1964) was mayor of New York City from 1946 to 1950. He was elected with the endorsement of the American Labor Party. The Communist party backed his candidacy because he supported Henry Wallace's position that the United States should maintain its alliance with the Soviet Union.
26. The National Maritime Union was boycotting French ships carrying soldiers and military supplies to Vietnam. The union was also demanding that the American troops be brought home immediately.
27. On October 23, 1945, President Harry Truman gave a speech to Congress supporting the Universal Military Training bill.
28. Milton Wolff Papers, University of Illinois Library.

29. Communist party headquarters were located near Union Square.
30. In an attempt to gain recognition, the fledgling United Automobile Workers Union launched a sit-in strike at the General Motors complex in Flint, Michigan, in 1937.
31. Milton Wolff Papers, University of Illinois Library.
32. The Associated Actors and Artistes of America held the American Federation of Labor jurisdiction for motion picture actors and screenwriters.
33. The Academy of Motion Picture Arts and Sciences (AMPAS) was considered by many to be a company union.
34. The conference group was the coalition of unions bargaining for actors and screenwriters.
35. Louis Adamic (1899–1951) was a novelist and labor historian. His best-known book is *Dynamite: The Story of Class Violence in America* (New York: Viking, 1934).
36. These funds were for military equipment and advisers to combat communism in Greece and Russian threats to Turkey. This policy to contain communism was known as the Truman Doctrine.
37. Thomas Brooks was a Republican senator from Illinois.
38. Milton Wolff Papers, University of Illinois Library.
39. The Labor School was a Marxist adult education program run by the Communist party of California.
40. This is a reference to Ernest Hemingway.
41. American Civil Liberties Union Archive, Princeton University Library.
42. In late 1945 and early 1946 many progressive groups organized a series of "Welcome Home Joe" dinners to honor returning veterans and build support for a broad-ranging agenda of economic and social reform. The dinner that Edward Carter attended in Los Angeles in January 1946 was organized by Frank Sinatra and Ingrid Bergman. Many Hollywood stars were in attendance.
43. These agents were most likely from military intelligence.
44. American Civil Liberties Union Archive, Princeton University Library.
45. Alvah Bessie (ed.), *The Heart of Spain: Anthology of Fiction, Non-fiction, and Poetry* (New York: Veterans of the Abraham Lincoln Brigade, 1952).
46. The Hollywood Ten—Herbert Biberman, Albert Maltz, Lester Cole, Dalton Trumbo, John Howard Lawson, Alvah Bessie, Samuel Ornitz, Ring Lardner, Jr., Edward Dmytryk, and Adrian Scott—were among the most visible victims of the postwar Red Scare. They were convicted for contempt of Congress in 1948 when they refused to cooperate with the House Committee on Un-American Activities investigation concerning Communist influence in Hollywood. After their appeals were denied in 1950, they all served between six months and a year in jail.
47. Herbert Brownell, Attorney General of the United States v. Veterans of the Abraham Lincoln Brigade, "Official Report of the Proceedings before the Subversive Activities Control Board," May–September 1954, testimony of Crawford Morgan, pp. 3196–3416, ALBA.

APPENDIX:
BIOGRAPHICAL INDEX OF
LETTER WRITERS

AALTO, WILLIAM "BILL" (1915–1958), who had been a guerrilla fighter in Spain, was recruited with other Lincoln veterans to work with the Office of Strategic Services for special military operations. When his associates learned that Aalto was a homosexual, they demanded he be transferred from the group. In a subsequent training accident, he lost his right hand.

ALTMAN, DAVID "DAVE" (1912–1945), born in Milwaukee, was a cabdriver and longshoreman in civilian life before joining the Mackenzie-Papineau battalion in Spain. Fighting with the army's 63rd Infantry Regiment in Luzon in the Philippines, he was killed in action.

BEALE, ELLIS "ELI" (aka BEGELMAN, 1912–1959) was born in Riga, Latvia. He had been active in the industrial union movement before joining the Communist party in 1936. In Spain, he was stationed in Madrid, where he was the Lincoln Brigade's chief of observation and political commissar. He fought in World War II.

BELL, HILDA (aka ROBERTS, 1916–) studied nursing in Philadelphia before she went to Spain to work in a hospital in Murcia. During World War II, she was a lieutenant in the Army Nurse Corps in Australia and New Zealand. After the war, she settled in northern California and was active in various peace movements.

BESSIE, ALVAH (1904–1985) was a celebrated author and screenwriter who fought with the Lincoln Brigade and was an early editor of *The Volunteer for Liberty*. He was blacklisted as one of the "Hollywood Ten" who, in 1947, refused to answer questions about his political affiliations posed by the House Committee on Un-American Activities and was jailed for contempt of Congress.

BIRNBAUM, SAUL (1912–), a New York native, was an office worker and draftsman before he joined the Mackenzie-Papineau battalion. During World War II, he saw action in the European theater with an artillery battalion. After the war, he taught mathematics in New York schools.

BRANDT, JOE (aka SAM BRUSTEIN, 1907–1997), born in Poland, was an organizer for the Communist party in Ohio before joining the Lincoln

Brigade. During World War II, he was a paratrooper for the "Devil's Brigade," a special services force operating in Italy. After the war, he worked as a printer, machinist, and union organizer.

BRIER, MOISHE (MORRIS) (1911–1996), an accountant, was wounded at Jarama, but recovered to fight on other fronts in Spain. He saw action in the Pacific during World War II, rising to the rank of first lieutenant. In later years, he was treasurer of the Abraham Lincoln Brigade Archives.

BROWN, ARCHIE (1911–1990), a prominent labor organizer on the San Francisco waterfront, served as a company commissar during the Ebro offensive. He saw action in Germany in 1945, helping to liberate concentration camps, and remained a political activist until his death.

BRUZZICHESI, AVELINO "AVE" (1913–1999), a nurse with the Medical Bureau to Aid Spanish Democracy, was stationed at hospitals in Teruel and Barcelona.

CALLION, WALTER P. (1919–1974), a mechanic in private life, worked as an auto mechanic in Spain and achieved the rank of sergeant in World War II, where he served as a machine-gun instructor.

CANE, LAWRENCE "LARRY" (aka COHEN, 1912–1976) graduated from the City College of New York and worked as a journalist before going to Spain, where he was an officer in the Mackenzie-Papineau battalion. He rose through the ranks in the army and was commissioned as a second lieutenant in a combat engineering unit. He landed at Normandy on D-Day, fought through the Battle of the Bulge, and won a Silver Star for bravery. Letters to his family were published in *Fighting Fascism in Europe* (2003).

CARTER, EDWARD A., II (1916–1963) was born in Los Angeles of missionary parents who, when he was five, took him to China, where he ended up fighting in the Chinese army. After service in Spain, he won the Distinguished Service Cross for heroic actions on the European front in 1945, and, in 1997, was awarded the Congressional Medal of Honor posthumously. His story is told in *Honoring Sergeant Carter* (2003).

COLODNY, ROBERT GARLAND (1915–1997) was wounded in the battle of Brunete while fighting as a member of the Lincoln Brigade. After the war, he earned a Ph.D. in history from the University of California at Berkeley and taught in the history department of the University of Pittsburgh. Among his many books was *The Struggle for Madrid* (1958).

COOK, GERALD "JERRY" (1912–1980), an office worker, journalist, and union organizer, served in the infantry in Spain. He was arrested in 1940 for blocking traffic in front of the French consulate in Manhattan during a protest about the treatment of Spanish refugees in that nation's detention camps. Such activities led to his appearance before the House Committee on Un-American Activities. During WWII, he saw action on D-Day in naval transport.

CULLINEN, GEORGE "WHITEY" (1914–2003), a native San Franciscan, was a maritime captain. After World War II, he operated an elementary school in New York and founded the Vermont Film Festival.

DALLET, JOSEPH "JOE" (1907–1937), who was born in Cleveland and graduated from Dartmouth College in 1927. He was the commissar of the Mackenzie-Papineau Battalion when he was killed in October 1937 leading a charge on the Aragon front. His widow, Kitty, later married the physicist J. Robert Oppenheimer.

DEMAS, NICHOLAS JOHN "NICK" (ca. 1909–??) was an electrician before he went to Spain, where he served as an interpreter and worked in the Autopark.

DEUTSCH, JULIUS HERMAN (1910–1996) was a physiologist who joined the Brigades in 1937.

DICKS, WALTER (1898–1967), a mechanic born in South Carolina, drove ambulances in Spain.

FAJANS, IRVING ISIDORE "TOOTS" (ca. 1913–1967), a department store union organizer in New York, saw action at Brunete. After World War II, during which he was with the Office of Strategic Services, he served as executive secretary of the VALB.

FELLER, MILTON MICHAEL "MIKE" (1918–194?), a New Yorker, was a student before going to Spain as a topographer/observer. He was killed in action during World War II.

FISHER, HARRY (1911–2003), a lifelong activist from Brooklyn, was a seaman and a busboy before going to Spain, where he worked in communications. He was a turret gunner on a bomber crew in Europe in World War II. He later worked for the Soviet news agency Tass in New York. *Comrades* (1998) is his autobiography.

FISHMAN, MOE (aka MORRIS SIMON, 1913–), born in Russia, worked as a seaman and as a clerk before going to Spain, where he was severely wounded at Brunete. He served in the Merchant Marine during World War II and was executive secretary of the VALB.

FITZGERALD, DANIEL "DAN" (1917–1978) left classes at the University of

New Hampshire to go to Spain. Ultimately attaining the rank of master sergeant, he fought with the infantry in Africa, Italy, and Germany.

FRANKSON, CANUTE OLIVER (1890–194?) came to the United States from Jamaica in 1917. A skilled machinist, he was an automobile mechanic in Spain.

GANDALL, WILLIAM "BILL" (1907–??) drove a taxi in New York City before going to Spain, where he was an ambulance driver and a member of an anti-aircraft unit.

GARLAND, WALTER (1913–1974), a native of Brooklyn, was a musician and Communist party official in Harlem. He was wounded at Brunete and was attached to a military police unit in World War II.

GATES, JOHN "JOHNNY" (aka SOLOMON REGENSTRIET, 1913–1992), a New Yorker who was the last U.S. commissar of the Lincoln Brigade, was a Communist party official when he enlisted in the U.S. Army shortly after Pearl Harbor. He volunteered for the 15th Airborne and served in the Aleutians before coming home to edit the *Daily Worker* after the war was over.

GIBONS, SAM (aka GEBIN, 1915–??), a member of the Painter's Union in Chicago, was wounded at Brunete. Upon his return, he became executive secretary of the Brigade veterans' group in Chicago before shipping off to England with the army in World War II.

GORDON, LOUIS DALTON "LOU" (1915–2006) was born in New York, where he worked as a machinist before serving as a driver in Spain. He was in an engineering unit attached to the Seventh Army in France and was part of the American brigade that liberated the Dachau concentration camp.

GROSS, NATHAN "NAT" (1914–??), born in New York City, was an office worker before going to Spain. He served in the Pacific theater during World War II.

GRUMET, LEONARD (1914–??), a native of Pittsburgh, worked in the American Medical Bureau in Spain.

HAKAM, HARRY (1913–1996) was born in Brooklyn and worked as an electrician before going to Spain. During World War II, he was in a demolition unit of the navy's Seabees in the European theater.

HECHT, JOSEPH "JOE" (1906–1945), a pharmacist born in Brooklyn, participated in the Ebro offensive of 1938 and was chauffeur of the Commissariat. He was killed in action in Germany.

HENE, JULIUS (aka HEENEY, 1908–1944), a Pittsburgh native, graduated from Cornell University and earned his medical degree from the University of Vienna. He organized a pioneering medical unit in Spain and served with the army's Medical Corps until his death during the Battle of the Bulge.

HENRY, DONALD E. (1917–1937) left the University of Kansas to go to Spain, where he was killed in September 1937.

JACKSON, BURT E. (1915–1993), born in New Jersey, was a commercial artist and a National Guardsman in civilian life, a topographer in Spain, and chief of ordnance in the 99th Division of the Army Air Corps. After the war, he and Walter Garland cofounded the United Negro and Allied Veterans Association (UNAVA).

KATZ, HYMAN "CHAIM" (1914–1938) was killed during the retreats in Spain in March 1938.

KAUFFMAN, RUBIN "RUBY" (1915–??), a furrier from New York, was in the original group of Lincoln volunteers who sailed for Spain in December 1936. After World War II, he was a union organizer in Wisconsin and California.

KEE, SALARIA (1913–1991) was born in Georgia and studied nursing at the Harlem Hospital Training School. Kee was the only African American nurse to serve in Spain. During World War II she enlisted in the Army Nurse Corps and later worked in hospitals in New York City.

KIRSCHBAUM, MAX (1910–1994) was a driver in Spain.

KLONSKY, ROBERT MAX (1918–2002), as a Brooklyn teenager, hopped a freighter for Spain in 1937. He later was convicted of violating the Smith Act and served time in prison before the Supreme Court reversed his case. A trade unionist and civil-rights and antiwar activist, he had a bookstore near the UCLA campus that was burned down by arsonists who painted a swastika on its walls.

KORNBLUM, MORRIS "MARTY" (1913–199?), a Brooklyn native who studied chemical engineering at CCNY, served with the medical unit at Villa Paz in Spain. He was attached to chemical warfare units during World War II, achieving the rank of technical sergeant. After the war, he worked for a chemical manufacturing company.

KRAUSS, MARTIN "MAC" (aka MAURICE, ??–1982) was an ambulance driver in Spain. He returned to his original vocation as an arc welder in Cleveland before serving in World War II. After the war, he worked in shipyards in New Jersey.

LENDING, EDWARD ISAAC (1912–2003), a New Yorker, was a journalist and a teacher before he joined the Washington Battalion in Spain. He was among the first brigaders to break with the Communist party after the signing of the German-Soviet Non-Aggression Pact in 1939. He was in an army antiaircraft unit in the European theater during World War II.

LEVINE, STEVEN "LOUIS" (ca. 1912–1975) flew bomber missions in the South Pacific, where he was severely injured by a defective bomb bay door and, consequently, spent most of his postwar life confined to veterans' hospitals or his home.

LOSSOWSKI, VINCENT "VINCE" (1913–1984) was born in Rochester, New York, and worked as a merchant seaman and as a member of the U.S. Army in Panama before serving in Spain as the executive officer in an artillery battalion. He was one of the Lincolns who were recruited to work with the Office of Strategic Services during World War II.

LOVE, VAUGHN (1907–1990) left his native Tennessee for New York in the 1930s, became an officer in Spain, and served in the army's Quarter-master Corps in Europe. His unpublished autobiography and extensive oral history with Peter N. Carroll are in the ALBA collection.

LUCID, JOHN MICHAEL "JACK" (1915–1977) was a student at the University of Washington before going to Spain in 1938. He fought with the Rangers in Italy, earning a Silver Star at Anzio, and participated in the liberation of a concentration camp in Germany. After the war, he was a factory worker and a labor organizer.

LUSTGARTEN, LARRY (1915–1944), a New Yorker employed as a salesman, was killed in action over India while serving with the Army Air Corps.

MITCHELL, IRVING "MITCH" (1911–1991), born in the Bronx, worked in restaurants before going to Spain. He served in the European theater during World War II.

MORGAN, CRAWFORD (1910–1976), a printer from North Carolina, was in the infantry in Spain. He served in the European theater from 1942 to 1946 and later testified in the Subversive Activities Control Board's investigation of the Lincoln Brigade.

MORSE, EUGENE (ca. 1907–1948) was in the original group of Lincoln volunteers, sailing to Spain in December 1936. He was a technical sergeant in the Ninth Army in World War II.

NAGLE, ROBERT (1914–2003) left the College of the City of Detroit (Wayne State University) to join the Lincoln Brigade. During World War II, he

earned two Bronze Stars. Later he taught elementary school and community college classes in the Detroit area. In 1982, Wayne State established a
scholarship fund in honor of Nagle and three other students who left
school to fight in Spain.

NAHMAN, SAM (aka MANNY HARRIMAN, 1919–1997) was born in New York,
where he was a member of the New York National Guard and a construction worker before going to Spain in 1938. He was wounded during the
Ebro offensive. In 1985, he organized an extensive oral history project
with many Lincolns; his videotapes are part of the ALBA collection.

PERRONE, JOHN "JOHNNY" (1911–1998), the oldest of eleven children in
an Italian immigrant family, went to Spain in 1937 and was in the infantry
during World War II. After the war, he worked as a tool and die maker.

QUIGGLE, HARLAND GERALD (1909–??) left the University of California to
join the 2nd Group Artillery of the Washington Battalion in 1937.

REITER, PETER (ca. 1892–??), a native of Hungary, worked in the building
trades before emigrating to the United States. In Spain, he fought with the
Rakosi Battalion of the 13th International Brigade.

ROSS, ADOLPH "BUSTER" (1917–1998), a New Yorker who worked as a
laborer, saw action in the Ebro offensive and served in the Army Air
Corps during World War II. He founded ALBA's biographical dictionary
project.

ROWLSON, LESTER LAVERNE (1916–2001) was a molder in Michigan before
he joined the Albacete Auto Park as a member of a transport company in
Spain. He was a Seabee in the Pacific during World War II and worked as a
building contractor after the war.

RUCKER, JAMES BERNARD "BUNNY" (1912–1992) was responsible for
transporting supplies and visiting dignitaries to the front, among whom
was Langston Hughes. In World War II, he served with the army's Medical
Division in Italy but transferred into an integrated combat unit where he
was severely wounded. He later was a reference librarian in New Jersey.

SCHOENBERG, HARRY (1911–??), who came from Chicago, was in the
National Guard for six years and worked as a photographer and sales-
person before joining the Mackenzie-Papineau Battalion.

SCHWARTZMAN, ALEXANDER (ca. 1911–??) was a letter carrier before he
went to Spain in 1937.

SHAFRAN, JACOB JOSEPH "JACK" (1917–), a New Yorker, was a metal
worker, truck driver, and department store clerk before going to Spain,

where he was among the youngest volunteers. He enlisted in the army in December 1940 and was a staff sergeant in an engineering unit in Europe.

SHEEHAN, ROY J. (1914–??) was a sergeant in the Reserves and a radio operator before going to Spain, where he served as a chief of communications at Brigade Headquarters. During World War II, he was secretary of the VALB's Los Angeles post.

SMITH, HAROLD (1911–1970), who was born in New York, served as an officer and company commissar in the Washington Battalion in Spain. He also was a member of the executive committee of the VALB. Because of hand injuries received at Brunete, he was not fit for military service in World War II, during which time he acted as the private secretary and bodyguard of Earl Browder, head of the U.S. Communist party. After the war, he taught handicapped children in a private school in New York City.

STILLMAN, MILTON (1914–) was a junk dealer from New York who participated in the Ebro offensive with the Mackenzie-Papineau Battalion.

SUSMAN, WILLIAM ROBERT "BILL" (1915–2003), a native of New Haven, was in the New York National Guard, worked as a seaman and labor organizer before the Spanish Civil War, and recruited Puerto Rican volunteers for the Brigades before joining them himself. He saw action in Europe in World War II, where he attained the rank of sergeant. In 1979, he helped found ALBA.

TAYLOR, JOSEPH "JOE" (1907–??), who was born in Georgia, worked as a machinist before becoming a section leader of Brigade scouts in Spain.

TISA, JOHN (1914–1991), who was born in Camden, New Jersey, left Rutgers to fight in Spain. After service as a military instructor during World War II, he became president of the Camden local of the Food, Tobacco, and Agricultural Workers Union. He was forced to relinquish his position after testifying before the House Committee on Un-American Activities.

VOGEL, SIDNEY "SID" (1904–1986), a surgeon and psychiatrist, was chief of the Casa Roja Hospital at Murcia. After participating in the army's North African and Italian campaigns, he practiced psychiatry in New York.

WAITZMAN, SAMUEL (1911–1982), who was born in New York and attended CCNY, worked as a journalist before going to Spain, where he saw action on the Ebro front. A member of the army's Medical Corps, he earned a Bronze Star in World War II. He was later active in the National Maritime Union.

WALLACH, DAVID HYMAN "HY" (1914–1999), a native of Poland, was a shipping clerk before he went to Spain, where he became a POW in 1938. During World War II, he was with the 15th Army Air Corps in North Africa and Italy.

WARREN, ALVIN (aka COHEN, 1913–1997), who was born in Brooklyn, was a truck and taxi driver and a CIO organizer before going to Spain to work in transport. A corporal in the 29th Infantry, he landed at Normandy as a demolitions expert. He was later a founder of an anti–Vietnam War group, the Veterans for Peace.

WEINBERG, GERALD "JERRY" (ca. 1914–1943), a Brooklyn native, won a Distinguished Flying Cross for his role during bombing raids on the Ploesti, Rumania, oil fields. He was killed in action over Germany in October 1943.

WEISSMAN, IRVING "IRV" (1913–1998), a factory worker and teacher from New York, served with the Mackenzie-Papineau Battalion in Spain and with an anti-aircraft unit in the European theater. He remained politically active after the war.

WHITE, DAVID McKELVY (1901–1945), the son of an Ohio governor, was a lecturer at Brooklyn College before going to Spain, where he was wounded at Brunete. After returning home, he became national chairman of the Friends of the Abraham Lincoln Brigade.

WOLFF, MILTON "MILT" (1915–), the last commander of the Lincoln Brigade, was attached to British Special Services and the U.S. Office of Strategic Services in 1941 and 1942, before joining the infantry, where he was posted to the China-Burma-India theater. He rejoined the OSS in 1944, operating as a paratrooper behind enemy lines in Italy.

WOLMAN, EUGENE (1913–1937), a Los Angeles native, was killed at Brunete.

YATES, JAMES (1906–1993) was born in Mississippi and was a railroad waiter before serving in transport in Spain. During World War II, he was a member of the Signal Corps. He wrote about his life in *From Mississippi to Madrid* (1986).

BIBLIOGRAPHY

PRIMARY SOURCES: LETTERS, MEMOIRS, AND AUTOBIOGRAPHIES

Bessie, Alvah, ed. *The Heart of Spain: Anthology of Fiction, Nonfiction, and Poetry*. New York: Veterans of the Abraham Lincoln Brigade, 1952.

Cane, Lawrence. *Fighting Fascism in Europe: The World War Two Letters of an American Veteran of the Spanish Civil War*. David E. Cane, Judith Barrett Litoff, and David C. Smith, eds. New York: Fordham University Press, 2003.

Dollard, John. *Fear in Battle*. New Haven, Conn.: Institute of Human Relations, Yale, 1943.

Felsen, Milt. *The Anti-Warrior: A Memoir*. Iowa City: University of Iowa Press, 1989.

Fisher, Harry. *Comrades: Tales of a Brigadista in the Spanish Civil War*. Lincoln: University of Nebraska Press, 1998.

Gates, John. *The Story of an American Communist*. New York: Nelson, 1958.

Hughes, Langston. *I Wonder as I Wander*. New York: Holt, Rinehart, and Winston, 1956.

Nelson, Cary, and Jefferson Hendricks, eds. *Madrid 1937: Letters of the Abraham Lincoln Brigade from the Spanish Civil War*. London: Routledge, 1996.

Tisa, John. *Recalling the Good Fight: An Autobiography of the Spanish Civil War*. South Hadley, Mass.: Bergin & Garvey Publishers, 1985.

Watt, George. *The Comet Connection: Escape from Hitler's Europe*. Lexington: University of Kentucky Press, 1990.

Yates, James. *Mississippi to Madrid: Memoir of a Black American in the Abraham Lincoln Brigade*. Seattle: Open Hand Publishing, 1989.

SECONDARY SOURCES

Books

Carroll, Peter N. *The Odyssey of the Abraham Lincoln Brigade: Americans in the Spanish Civil War*. Stanford, Calif.: Stanford University Press, 1994.

Carter, Allene G., and Robert L. Allen. *Honoring Sergeant Carter: Redeeming a Black World War II Hero's Legacy*. New York: Amistad, 2003.

Colodny, Robert Garland. *The Struggle for Madrid: The Central Epic of the Spanish Conflict, 1936–1937*. New York: Paine-Whitman, 1958.

De Seversky, Alexander P. *Victory through Air Power*. New York: Simon and Schuster, 1942.

Klehr, Harvey, John Earl Haynes, and Fridrikh Igorevich Firsov. *The Secret World of American Communism*. New Haven, Conn.: Yale University Press, 1995.

Landis, Arthur H. *The Abraham Lincoln Brigade*. New York: Citadel Press, 1967.

Rise, Eric. *The Martinsville Seven: Race, Rape, and Capital Punishment*. Charlottesville: University of Virginia Press, 1995.

Rosenstone, Robert A. *Crusade of the Left: The Lincoln Battalion in the Spanish Civil War*. New York: Pegasus, 1969.

Werner, Max. *The Great Offensive: The Strategy of Coalition Warfare*. New York: Viking, 1942.

Articles

Carroll, Peter. "Premature Anti-fascists Again." *The Vounteers* 25 (December 2003): 5–8.

Kelley, Robin D. G. "This Ain't Ethiopia but It'll Do." *"This Ain't Ethiopia but It'll Do":*
African Americans in the Spanish Civil War. Danny Duncan Collum and Victor A. Berch,
eds. New York: G. K. Hall, 1992. 5–57.
Prago, Albert. "Jews in the International Brigades." *Jewish Currents* (February, 1979):
15–21.

Novels

Bessie, Alvah. *Bread and a Stone.* New York: Modern Age Books, 1941.
Seghers, Anna. *The Seventh Cross.* Boston: Little, Brown, 1942.

INDEX

Aalto, William, 6, 49, 114n22, 164, 223n3, 265
Abraham Lincoln Battalion, xiin1, 23
Abraham Lincoln Brigade Archives (ALBA), xi, 266, 270, 271, 272
The Adakian, 7
Adamic, Louis, 245, 263n35
AFL-CIO, 141. *See also* CIO
Africa, 125, 172, 173, 268
African American veterans/volunteers, xi, xii, 2, 116–21, 269; support for, in United States, 136; treatment of, in Spain, 13–14, 26–28. *See also* Jim Crow; Prejudice; U.S. Army
Air Force, 53, 55, 125, 163
Airplane Factories (Hughes), 33
Alabama (AL), 58, 73, 91, 99, 124, 125
Albacete Auto Park, 271
Albacete, Spain, 18, 23, 95
Alderson, WV, 256, 257
Aleutian Islands, 7, 268
Alexander, Frank, 121
Algiers, 167
Almeria, Spain, 17
Altman, David, 92–94, 152, 197–98, 223n21, 223n22, 265
Amarillo, TX, 83
America First Committee, 114n27
America Firsters, 88
American-Chinese relationships, 194
American Civil Liberties Union, 230, 250, 253, 261
American Committee for Spanish Democracy/Freedom, 228, 235
American Export Airlines, 86, 87
American Federation of Labor, 263n33
American Legion post, New Haven, 43
American Medical Bureau, xiin1, 268
American Revolution, 161
American Youth Congress, 86
Anglin, B.H., 87
Anti-Communist campaign, 228; VALB as victims of, 226, 228–31, 230
Anti-Defamation League, 103
Anti-Semitism, 147

Anzio, Italy, 180, 270
Aragon front, 8, 26, 267
Arc de Triomphe, 221
Argeles, France Camp, 35
Arizona (AZ), 124, 125, 128, 133, 135, 232, 233, 262n17
Arkansas (AR), 90, 241
Arlington National Cemetery, 261
Armored Force Replacement Training Center, 49
Army Nurse Corps, 42, 188, 265, 269
Army Times, 99
Ashland, KY, 257
Assam, India, 200
Associated Actors and Artistes of America, 263n32
Asturias, Spain, 17, 185
Atlanta, GA, 41n29, 96
Atomic bomb: in Japan, 238
Auslander, Jackob, 255–57, 256
Australia, 190, 191, 197, 265
Australian Information Bureau, 91
Austria, 21, 40n28, 56, 86, 209

Badoglio, Pietro, 176, 223n13
Baird, G.H., 30
Balkans, 21, 162
Barcelona, Spain, 34, 86, 141, 157, 266
Barron, Joe, 39
Barrows, Ted, 219, 220
Barsky, Edward, 228–29, 248, 255–57
Batea, Spain, 30, 41n44
Battle of the Bulge, 120, 250–51, 266, 269
Beale, Ellis, 25–26, 265
Bedford Stuyvesant, Brooklyn, NY, 1
Belgium, 154, 206, 209, 218, 220
Belgrade, 205
Bell, Hilda, 190–91, 265
Bensonhurst, Brooklyn, NY, 80
Berg, Nils, 177–78
Bergman, Ingrid, 263n42
Bergonzoli, Annibale, 83, 114n25
Berkeley, CA, 148, 245
Berlin, 15, 55, 198, 204, 212, 214, 224n31

ABOUT THE EDITORS

PETER N. CARROLL is the author of *The Odyssey of the Abraham Lincoln Brigade: Americans in the Spanish Civil War* (Stanford, 1994). He is Chair of the Board of Governors of the Abraham Lincoln Brigade Archives (ALBA) and cocurator of two traveling exhibitions: *Shouts from the Wall: Posters of the Spanish Civil War* (with Cary Nelson) and *They Still Draw Pictures: Children's Art in Wartime from the Spanish Civil War to Kosovo* (with Anthony L. Geist). He has written many other books and teaches history at Stanford University.

MICHAEL NASH is the Director of New York University's Tamiment Library, a special collection documenting the history of labor and radical politics that administers the Abraham Lincoln Brigade Archives. He is the author of *Conflict and Accommodation: Coal Miners, Steel Workers, and Socialism, 1890–1920*, as well as numerous articles relating to American labor, social, and business history.

MELVIN SMALL is Distinguished Professor of History at Wayne State University and chair of the university's Abraham Lincoln Brigade Scholarship Fund. A member of the board of the Brigade archives, he is the author or editor of numerous books on American foreign relations, the most recent of which are *Antiwarriors: The Vietnam War and the Battle for America's Hearts and Minds* (2002) and *At the Water's Edge: American Politics and the Vietnam War* (2005).